D1262034

101 ACTION MOVIES
YOU MUST SEE BEFORE YOU DIE

GENERAL EDITOR
STEVEN JAY SCHNEIDER

BARRON'S

A Quint**essence** Book

First edition for the United States and Canada
published in 2010 by Barron's Educational Series, Inc.

ISBN-13: 978-0-7641-6350-0
ISBN-10: 0-7641-6350-7
QSS.ACTI

Library of Congress Number: 2010928094

All inquiries should be addressed to:
Barron's Educational Series, Inc.
250 Wireless Boulevard
Hauppauge, NY 11788
www.barronseduc.com

This book was designed and produced by:
Quint**essence**
226 City Road
London EC1V 2TT
www.1001beforeyoudie.com

Project Editor	Helena Baser
Editor	James Harrison
Designer	Nick Withers
Editorial Director	Jane Laing
Publisher	Tristan de Lancey

Color reproduction in Singapore by Pica Digital Pte Ltd.
Printed in China by 1010 Printing International Ltd.
9 8 7 6 5 4 3 2 1

CONTENTS

INTRODUCTION Steven Jay Schneider, General Editor

At their core, movies are made to entertain. They are the ultimate form of escapism, and no genre allows its audience to escape into a world of excitement more than the action movie. Defined by fast-paced action, large set pieces, high-speed chases, and mind-blowing special effects, the action movie has become the studio system's golden ticket. Action movies are one of the oldest genres in cinematic history, as evidenced by Edwin S. Porter's famed short, *The Great Train Robbery* (1903). In the early 1920s, swashbucklers such as Douglas Fairbanks Sr., rose to stardom with movies such as *The Mark of Zorro* (1920). Then, in the 1960s, audiences were introduced to cinema's best-known action hero when they first met Ian Fleming's James Bond in *Dr. No* (1962). With their elaborate chase sequences, exciting fight scenes, and state-of-the-art special effects, the Bond movies set a new standard in action filmmaking. While action movies became more and more popular, it wasn't until Steven Spielberg's *Jaws* (1975) that the world was introduced to the first true action "blockbuster." Capitalizing on the huge success of the genre, the studios released one action movie after another, making the 1980s and 1990s the "action era," and turning modestly successful actors, such as Sylvester Stallone, Bruce Willis, and Arnold Schwarzenegger, into archetypal action heroes, with movies such as *First Blood* (1982), *The Terminator* (1984), and *Die Hard* (1988). The success of the genre has justified the massive budgets of such movies, enabling pioneering filmmakers, such as James Cameron, to develop groundbreaking visual and special effects and bringing to life worlds that previously existed only in our dreams.

Steven J. Schneider

Hollywood, U.S.A.

EDISON FILMS

PATENTED AND COPYRIGHTED.

Replete with Thrilling and Exciting Incidents in Fourteen Scenes.

THE GREAT TRAIN ROBBERY

Was shown to enthusiastic houses during Xmas week in New York at the following theatres:

Hurtig & Seamon's
Circle Theatre
Proctor's 125th St.

SEND FOR FULLY ILLUSTRATED AND DESCRIPTIVE PAMPHLET.

Keith's 14th St.
Harlem Opera House
Tony Pastor's
Eden Musee
Huber's Museum
Orpheum, Brooklyn
Comedy Theatre
Orpheum Music Hall

LENGTH, 740 FEET.
PRICE, $111.
CODE WORD,
VACUNABAN.

Edison Exhibition Kinetoscope, $115.00.   Edison Universal Kinetoscope, $75.00.

MAIN OFFICE and FACTORY, Orange, N. J.

EDISON MANUFACTURING CO., NEW YORK OFFICE: 83 Chambers St.

OFFICE FOR UNITED KINGDOM: 52 Gray's Inn Road, Holborn, London, W.C., England.
EUROPEAN OFFICE: 32 Rempart Saint Georges, Antwerp, Belg

SELLING AGENTS:

THE KINETOGRAPH CO. .... 41 E. 21st St., New York
KLEINE OPTICAL CO. .... 52 State St., Chicago, Ill
PETER BACIGALUPI .... 933 Market St., San Francisco, Cal.

THE ORIGINAL AND ONLY

THE GREAT TRAIN ROBBERY 1903 (U.S.)

Director Edwin Porter **Producer** Thomas Edison Production Company
Screenplay Edwin Porter from a story by Scott Marble **Cinematography** Blair
Smith **Cast** A.C. Abadie, Gilbert M. "Broncho Billy" Anderson, Justus D. Barnes,
Mary Snow, George Barnes, Walter Cameron

Frequently credited as "the first narrative film" (as well as "the
first Western" and "the first heist film"), Edwin Porter's *The Great
Train Robbery* remains one of the most influential motion
pictures ever produced. Released over a century ago, the
impact of this eleven-minute one-reel production can be felt to
this day in the works of contemporary filmmakers like Martin
Scorsese, George P. Cosmatos, and Ridley Scott, who directly
reference Porter's classic in *Goodfellas* (1990), *Tombstone* (1993),
and *American Gangster* (2007), respectively.

A milestone of early cinema, *The Great Train Robbery*
continues a tradition that began with Auguste and Louis
Lumière's seminal *The Arrival of a Train at La Ciotat Station* (1895),
the first film to unite two of the industrial revolution's most
enduring technologies by using a motion camera to capture
the grandeur of the locomotive, arguably the period's most
vital means of transport. Likewise, *The Great Train Robbery*'s
plot is the result of a creative amalgamation, deriving its
premise through a combination of newspaper accounts of
actual railway thefts, and motifs familiar to readers of Western-
themed dime store novels.

◄
**The film that
showed it was
possible to edit
or "cut" between
events happening
at the same time
but in different
places without
disturbing the
continuity.**

Exceedingly violent even by today's standards, with several on-screen deaths and nearly every male character wielding a firearm, *The Great Train Robbery* is notable for both its cinematic innovations and its application of genre conventions. Comprised of fourteen shots, multiple setups, and a variety of framings that range from extreme long shots to close-ups, Edwin Porter's film is a landmark in the evolution of film

"ALMOST ALL [MOVIE] DEVELOPMENT SINCE PORTER'S DISCOVERY SPRING FROM THE PRINCIPLE OF EDITING." *G. SADOUL*

grammar. Porter's use of crosscutting to depict simultaneous actions transpiring in different locations is particularly noteworthy. This mode of continuity editing, also used in his *Life of an American Fireman* (1903), increased the tension audiences felt toward the events projected before their eyes.

Additionally, taking a cue from Thomas Edison's *Annabelle the Dancer* (1884) and the Lumière Brothers' *Serpentine Dance* (1896), several artists experimented with adding color to Porter's images by hand-painting portions of *The Great Train Robbery*, most notably the dresses of the young girl who discovers the bound telegraph operator and the women frolicking in the dance hall, the flash and smoke of the discharging weapons, and the attire of the deceased robber who, in what has become the film's signature (and most imitated) scene, reappears to fire his pistol dispassionately at the viewer. **JMcR**

► Porter's movie included several innovations, including filming the action from unusual angles and the use of the "pan," which is moving the camera in a sweeping shot to follow the escaping bandits.

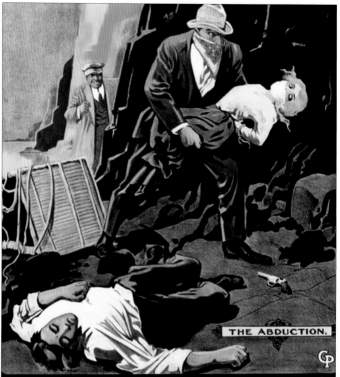

THE ABDUCTION.

THE ECLECTIC FILM COMPANY'S
GREAT $ 25.000 PRIZE PHOTO PLAY
THE PERILS
OF
PAULINE
6 TH EPISODE IN 2 PARTS
COPYRIGHTED 1914 ECLECTIC FILM CO.

THE PERILS OF PAULINE 1914 (U.S.)

Directors Louis J. Gasnier, Donald MacKenzie **Producer** Pathé
Screenplay Basil Dickey, Charles W. Goddard, Bertram Millhauser, George
B. Seitz **Cinematography** Arthur C. Miller **Cast** Pearl White, Crane Wilbur,
Paul Panzer, Edward José, Francis Carlyle

The film that gave birth to the term "cliffhanger," *The Perils of
Pauline* was a tale told in twenty "chapters," new twenty-minute
episodes appearing in movie theaters at two-week intervals.

The plot was not overly taxing. Young, feisty, and posh,
Pauline (Pearl White) is left a huge inheritance by a wealthy
uncle, with the stipulation that she may only claim the fortune
on her wedding day. Pauline has other ideas, pursuing instead
a series of exciting adventures to provide material for her own
dream—to become a famous author. The inheritance is left in
the care of her uncle's secretary, the dastardly Koerner (Paul
Panzer), who fiendishly plots her demise so he can pocket the
loot for himself. The show would invariably end with Pauline
facing dramatic imminent doom, a perpetual damsel in distress,
typically about to be squashed by a train, chopped up,
marooned in a hot-air balloon, or left hanging from the edge of
a cliff. The audience, gripping the edge of their seats, was left
with only one possible choice . . . return to the theater in two
weeks in eager anticipation of the next episode. Then Pauline
would make her miraculous escape before finding herself
caught up yet again in another tricky tangle.

◀

In 2008, *The
Perils of Pauline*
was selected for
preservation
by the Library
of Congress as
being "culturally,
historically, or
aesthetically
significant."

The Perils of Pauline was a massive and significant success of early cinema, making heroine Pearl White the first real cinematic leading lady. Released months before the first bullets of World War I were fired, the series is noteworthy as a template for the creation of suspense that remains at the heart of the modern action film. *The Perils of Pauline* also impresses modern sensibilities with its portrayal of a feisty young woman taking

"THERE IS NO ACTING IN A SERIAL. YOU SIMPLY RACE THROUGH THE REELS." *PEARL WHITE*

control of her own destiny, acting with an unflinching focus on her own desires and dreams. Such proactiveness would have been truly radical in the early twentieth century.

It is doubtful that anyone alive today can truthfully claim to have seen *The Perils of Pauline* in its entirety. Like an estimated ninety percent of *all* silent movies, eleven of the original twenty episodes have been long lost from the vaults: all that survives is a nine-chapter edit created in 1916 for European theaters—less than half of the epic 420 minutes of the original.

▶
Pauline's regular death-defying stunts were performed by the actress Pearl White herself, often resulting in serious injury.

So why were the pioneers of cinema so profligate with their efforts? It's true that there was little knowledge of the chemical frailty of the nitrate film stock used then. But, in truth, films at this time were considered to have little commercial value after they'd been shown, and without careful preservation the prints would quickly begin to decompose. **TB**

SAFETY LAST! 1923 (U.S.)

Director Fred C. Newmeyer, Sam Taylor **Producer** Hal Roach
Screenplay Hal Roach, Sam Taylor, Tim Whelan, H.M. Walker, Jean C. Havez,
Harold Lloyd **Cinematography** Walter Lundin **Cast** Harold Lloyd,
Mildred Davis, Bill Strother, Noah Young, Westcott Clarke

The fame of Charlie Chaplin, Bustor Keaton, and Laurel and
Hardy has tended to obscure the other shining lights of silent
comedy. Harold Lloyd was one of the most physically daring
and inventive comic actors of his age. *Safety Last!* is undoubtedly
Lloyd's comic masterpiece, part of a tradition of highly physical
silent comedy that Lloyd took to gymnastic new extremes,
making him the king of daredevil action-comedy. Listed simply
as "The Boy" and sporting the straw-boater hat and horn-
rimmed spectacles that would forever characterize him, in
Safety Last! Lloyd created his enduring on-screen persona: a
naive country boy who, despite his own lack of guile and the
best efforts of others, manages to make good in the city.

The film charts The Boy's progress as he leaves his country
home to seek his fortune in the city, planning to send for his
fiancée once he has established himself. After finding a lowly
job at the luxurious De Vore Department Store, he writes to tell
her how well he is doing. When his fiancée pays an unexpected
visit, mayhem ensues as The Boy attempts to both carry out his
low-rent sales job and fool her into believing that he is, in fact,
the store's manager. Seeking to maintain this charade, he

◄
**Fending off the
frightening female
shoppers is just
one of the tasks
lowly store clerk
Harold Lloyd—
the "optimistic
everyman"— has
to contend with
in this comedy
of thrills.**

attempts to assuage his boss's growing anger at his increasingly erratic behavior by accepting the challenge of devising a publicity stunt that will attract more clients to the store. But when he plans a madcap scheme involving his roommate pretending to be a human-fly who will scale a small portion of the store's frontage, things quickly go awry when a cop, who remembers the roommate from an earlier incident, turns up

"IN THE ONE IN WHICH I'M HANGING ON A CLOCK . . . WE DID THE FINAL SCENES OF THAT CLIMB FIRST." LLOYD

and attempts to chase him off. The Boy starts to scale the building—a twelve-story skyscraper—planning to swap with his friend on a higher floor once he has shaken off the law. What follows is a bravura piece of physical theater as Lloyd is forced further and further up the side of the department store by various obstacles that present themselves to him, before finally—perilously—he ends up dangling off the minute hand of the department store's clock face.

► **Lloyd's real-time defying stunt remains one of the most devil-may-care pieces of physical theater of early cinematic history.**

Such was the success of the "boy next door" formula that Lloyd used the character several more times in films such as *Girl Shy* (1924), *The Freshman* (1925)—his most successful film—*For Heaven's Sake* (1926), and *The Kid Brother* (1927). Lloyd made many films, particularly in the silent era, but it was *Safety Last!* that would cement his place among the pantheons of silent cinema's most iconic and daring comedy performers. **RH**

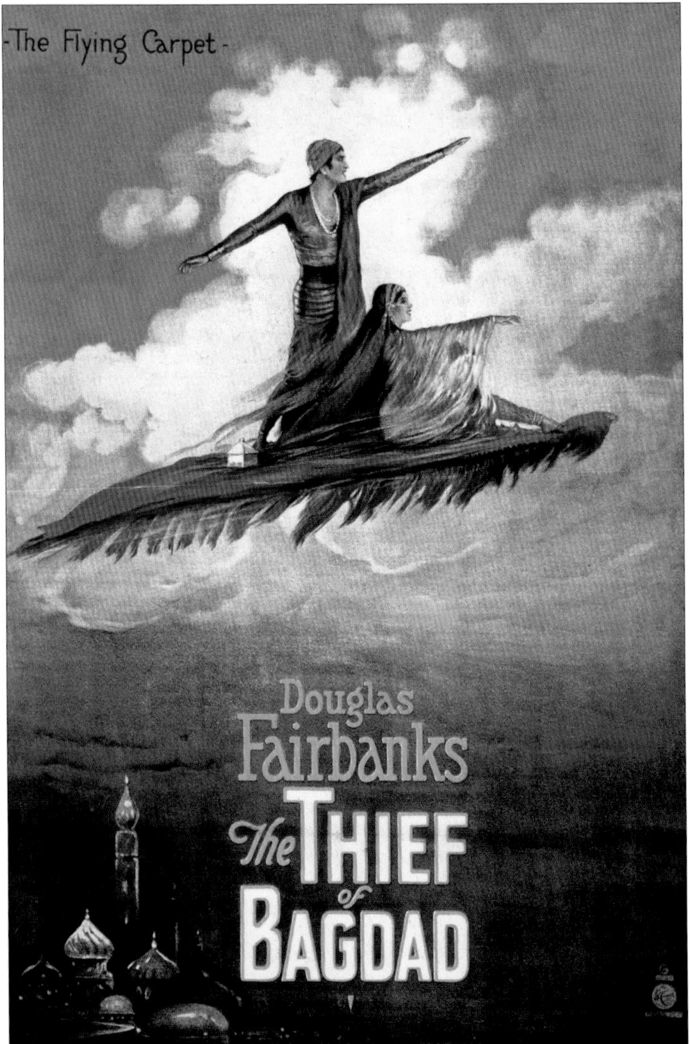
-The Flying Carpet-
Douglas
Fairbanks
The THIEF
of
BAGDAD

THE THIEF OF BAGDAD 1924 (U.S.)

Director Raoul Walsh **Producer** Douglas Fairbanks **Screenplay** Achmed Abdullah, Douglas Fairbanks **Cinematography** Arthur Edeson **Music** Carl Davies (1984)
Cast Douglas Fairbanks, Snitz Edwards, Charles Belcher, Julianne Johnston, Sojin, Anna May Wong, Brandon Hurst, Tote Du Crow, Noble Johnson

The undoubted star of *The Thief of Bagdad* is Douglas Fairbanks, who was one of the most important screen actors of the 1920s. In this Arabian Nights tale of fantasy and adventure, which presents extensive oriental sets and distinct moments of screen magic, it is Fairbanks's masculinity and exceptional physical ability that have been viewed as the film's primary attractions. His athleticism and positive, boundless energy saw him promoted as an ideal of American masculinity and earned him various labels within the media of the time such as "Mr. Pep" and "Mr. Electricity."

Fairbanks had previously appeared in action roles as the lead in *The Mark of Zorro* (1920) and *Robin Hood* (1922), and as D'Artagnan in *The Three Musketeers* (1921). His boyish enthusiasm for leaping into his next adventure made his silent spectaculars of the 1920s broad crowd-pleasers, but their central appeal appeared to be with children and boys in particular, who were said to have imitated Fairbanks's acrobatic stunts beyond the cinema. His healthy, playful spirit and outdoor youthful pursuits have been seen as connecting with the character-building of boys in the nascent boy-scouts movement of 1910.

◄

In addition to performing his own stunts, Fairbanks also helped with many of the dazzling set designs and exquisite costumes.

The Thief of Bagdad was the pinnacle of Fairbanks's screen career, which, by 1924, had become firmly associated with dashing heroes in historical adventure films. As Ahmed the Thief, Fairbanks vies with royal suitors from Persia and India, as well as the devious Prince of the Mongols, for the hand of the Caliph of Bagdad's daughter, The Princess (Johnston). Challenged by the Caliph to find the rarest of treasures, Ahmed

"EVERY WEEK WE HAD COSTUME AND PERIOD, COMEDY, TRAGEDY, MELODRAMA. THEY WERE ALL DIFFERENT." *FAIRBANKS*

travels far on exotic adventures to such places as the Valley of the Monsters and the Cavern of Enchanted Trees, where he encounters a prehistoric bird and a giant living statue. In the film's final spectacle, Ahmed approaches the high walls of the fortress city of Bagdad alone, and appears exposed. With the aid of magic, though, he quickly conjures an immense army that continues to multiply in puffs of smoke across the desert.

With the aid of a magic cloak, Ahmed makes himself invisible, and once again he has the freedom of the city, a vast set across which he had earlier climbed and leapt upon its balconies, stairs, and turrets. Designed by William Cameron Menzies, the set creates a seemingly limitless playground for Fairbanks, whose performance is also supported by the film's effects and the trick photography of a flying carpet and a magic rope. Fairbanks also had a hand in the production's striking design. **IC**

▶
Fairbanks was at his best with less rather than more garments so he could show off his naked muscular torso as an essential part of his performance of heroic masculinity.

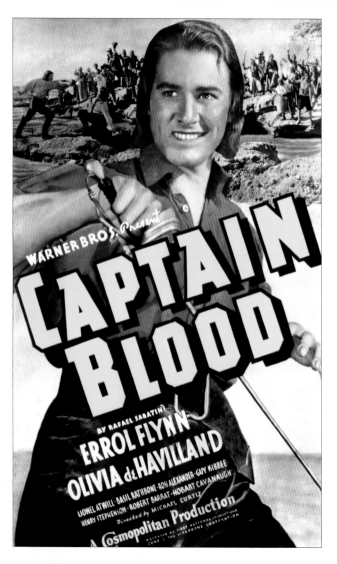

CAPTAIN BLOOD 1935 (U.S.)

Director Michael Curtiz **Producer** Harry Joe Brown, Gordon Hollingshead
Screenplay Casey Robinson **Cinematography** Ernest Haller, Hal Mohr
Music Erich Wolfgang Korngold **Cast** Errol Flynn, Olivia de Havilland,
Lionel Atwill, Basil Rathbone, Ross Alexander, Guy Kibbee

Captain Blood stands as an important moment in cinema
history for being the first adventure movie of the talkie era, and
thus paving the way for what proved to be a profitable trend. It
also marks the first starring role for Errol Flynn, as well as the
beginning of his fruitful collaboration with young actress Olivia
de Havilland and director Michael Curtiz—the flamboyant
Adventures of Robin Hood (1938) being probably the most
famous film that came out of their partnership.

    Captain Blood tells the story of Irish doctor Peter Blood who,
in the late seventeenth century, is unfairly convicted of treason
toward King James. His death penalty is commuted and, along
with real rebels, he is deported to Port Royal, Jamaica, to be sold
as a slave. When a Spanish ship attacks the town, he manages
to escape aboard the vessel and begins to scour the Caribbean
Sea with his comrades under the name of Captain Blood.

    Initially, *Captain Blood* delivers fewer thrills than expected, as
for nearly forty-five minutes we follow the ordeals of its
powerless protagonist. This shouldn't be considered a flaw,
however; this part of the film, which benefits from bold
photographic choices and brilliant camera work, provides some

◄

**The first costume
adventure "talkie"
and one that also
hinted at Flynn's
character being
the one with a real
but still relatively
tame eroticism—
something that
later costume
adventure pictures
didn't sometimes
hesitate to stress.**

solid and complex background for Blood's motivations; it also enables Flynn to demonstrate his growing talents not only as a sportsman but as an actor as well. In fact, a serious tone, interrupted with some moments of comic relief, dominates throughout. Through various characters, sometimes monstrous, sometimes ridiculous, the film even looks to titillate the antityranny feelings of the American spectators by mocking the British monarchy.

"I'VE MADE SIX OR SEVEN GOOD FILMS—THE OTHERS, NOT SO GOOD." ERROL FLYNN

Director Michael Curtiz had to use scale models as well as numerous shots taken from the 1923 adaptation of Rafael Sabatini's historical novel by David Smith—a not infrequent cheating that is accomplished here quite cleverly and seamlessly. *Captain Blood* nevertheless contains all the staples of the swashbuckling genre: plenty of daring swordplay, a montage sequence condensing several acts of heroic piracy, a lengthy sea battle that ends with the last-chance boarding of another ship, scenes of merry drinking sessions on the famous Tortuga Island, and the like.

► **Flynn indulges in classic swordplay against another ferocious pirate chief, colorfully interpreted by Basil Rathbone, one of Hollywood's famous bad guys of the 1930s.**

In tune with its political bias, *Captain Blood* also introduces the theme of fraternity among the buccaneers and links it with the notion of loyalty between a leader and his men. That said, the audience would have also been mainly impressed by the new glamorous couple to hit the big screen. **FL**

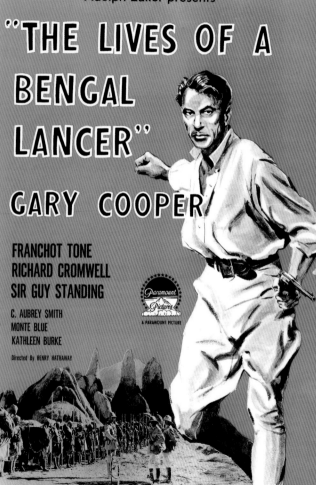

THE LIVES OF A BENGAL LANCER

1935 (U.S.)

Director Henry Hathaway **Producer** Louis D. Lighton **Screenplay** Waldemar Young, John L. Balderston, Achmed Abdullah **Cinematography** Charles Lang, Ernest Schoedsack **Music** Milan Roder **Cast** Gary Cooper, Franchot Tone, Richard Cromwell, Sir Guy Standing, Douglass Dumbrille, Kathleen Burke

---

History may always remember Henry Hathaway as a great director of Westerns—and why shouldn't it when he boasts *How The West Was Won* (1962), *The Sons of Katie Elder* (1965), and *True Grit* (1969) on his resume?—but it is a much earlier non-Western action flick that was really praiseworthy.

Originally based on Francis Yeats-Brown's novel, it took four years and many, many tweaks and changes before this finally made it to the big screen. In fact, all that really remains from the original story is the title and some of the locations; a whole team of writers, principally Grover Jones and William Slavens McNutt, and studio bosses saw to that. Happily, what emerged is one of the finest action films of its time.

The plot is a fairly simple one: The 41st Bengal Lancers, led by Colonel Tom Stone (Sir Guy Standing), are stationed in Northwest India, where some of the locals are proving unruly. And as if that isn't enough of an interruption to afternoon tea, his lieutenant, Alan McGregor (Gary Cooper), is assigned two new officers and has to prepare them for the battle ahead. These new men, of course, come with their own set of problems

◄

Hathaway had to battle for his choice of leading man. Cooper had been around a while but was not yet a major player. In a time when the studio boss's word was law, Hathaway bravely rebuked all other suggestions.

and issues. One, Lt. John Forsyth (Franchot Tone), is a sarcastic thrill seeker; the other, Lt. Donald Stone (Richard Cromwell), is not just slightly immature but is the son of the Colonel to boot —he has much to prove to his rather less than paternal father and initially doesn't seem to possess the character to do it.

Amid the sand dunes, the group gradually learns to work together, but then Donald is captured by the enemies and dear

"YOU DON'T LIKE POETRY?" LT. FORSYTHE
"HOW SHOULD I KNOW? I DON'T READ ANY." LT. MCGREGOR

old dad argues that trying to retrieve him would be foolish. Our heroes disagree, defy the boss, and mount a rescue anyway. What follows is a brilliant mix of wall-to-wall action and some eye-watering torture scenes at the hands of the ruthless Mohammed Khan (Douglass Dumbrille). Dumbrille also gets to deliver the most famous line of this movie, the often (mis) quoted, "We have ways of making men talk." Hathaway was also a stickler for detail and was not content with the lavish sets built in California for this big budget film, so he also incorporated specially shot documentary footage from India.

B-Movie genres fall in and out of fashion, but it is unlikely that we'll ever see the return of the British Imperialism action film. Still, if you see this for a movie of its time, you're assured a roller coaster ride of thrills, spills, and suspense, with a generous dose of humor thrown in for good measure. **RP**

▶
Cooper all robed up: the costumes were painstakingly researched and were so accurate that they were reused in Cecil B. DeMillle's epic *The Crusades* (1935).

THE ADVENTURES OF ROBIN HOOD
1938 (U.S.)

Director Michael Curtiz **Producer** Henry Blanke, Hal B. Wallis, Jack L. Warner **Screenplay** Norman Reilly Raine, Seton I Miller **Cinematography** Tony Gaudio, Sal Polito **Music** Erich Wolfgang Korngold **Cast** Errol Flynn, Olivia de Havilland, Basil Rathbone, Claude Rains, Melville Cooper, Patric Knowles, Eugene Pallette, Alan Hale

After popular King Richard the Lionheart (Ian Hunter) is taken captive and held for ransom while returning from the Crusades, his avaricious brother, Prince John (Claude Rains), claims power and control of the English Treasury. John, who cravenly covets his brother's throne, increases taxes on the pretext of raising Richard's ransom, but is really intent on exploiting the Saxon peasantry in an attempt to consolidate his own hold on power. Meanwhile, Robin (Errol Flynn), the Earl of Locksley, becomes an outlaw when he opposes John's growing tyranny and is forced into hiding in Sherwood Forest, where he adopts the title Robin Hood.

What follows is a classic swashbuckling romp, as Robin robs from the rich to give to the poor, wins the affections of King Richard's beautiful ward, the Lady Marian (Olivia de Havilland), infuriates John's ambition, and ensures that the devious Sir Guy of Gisbourne (Basil Rathbone) becomes his sworn enemy. Ultimately, Robin helps to restore Richard to his rightful place, and is pardoned by the king and free to marry the Lady Marian. Flynn's Robin Hood, which has for many film fans become the

◄
At nearly $2 million, this was Warner Bros.' most expensive film at the time of its release. It was filmed in three-strip Technicolor —one of the first of Warner Bros.' films to be shot in this way.

cinematic incarnation of the legendary English outlaw, is at once dazzlingly handsome, suave, charming, rakish, gregarious, and just a teensy bit flamboyant. He is ably supported by a stellar cast, which includes Olivia de Havilland as a feisty Maid Marian, Claude Rains in fine form as the malevolent Prince John, and Basil Rathbone as a waspish Guy of Gisbourne. Many of the film's scenes have now become set reference points for any

"THERE WAS A DEFINITE ON-SCREEN CHEMISTRY BETWEEN ERROL [FLYNN] AND ME." OLIVIA DE HAVILLAND

adaptation of the Hood legend: arrows thudding into nearby tree trunks as part of the outlaws very own instant-messaging system, corpulent nobles being held up in Sherwood Forest and relieved of their riches, an archery contest set as a trap to catch the outlaw, and outlandish moments of bravura as Robin trades witticisms with the devious Guy of Gisbourne before heroically defeating him.

▶
Errol Flynn's lighthearted but compelling Robin Hood has become *the* classic adventure film. It quickly replaced Douglas Fairbanks's earlier version in the public's affections.

Deftly directed by Michael Curtiz (who would go on to direct the equally iconic *Casablanca* in 1942), *The Adventures of Robin Hood* has proved popular ever since its premiere in 1938. It is re-released regularly on DVD and has become a staple of daytime TV movies. In fact, so great was the success of the film that Flynn's name was to be forever linked with Robin Hood in the public consciousness. Although much of the plot is pure escapist hokum, it remains, for many, *the* Robin Hood film. **RH**

THE MARK OF ZORRO 1940 (U.S.)

Director Rouben Mamoulian **Producer** Darryl F. Zanuck **Screenplay** John Taintor Foote (adapted by Garrett Fort and Bess Meredyth from the story by Johnston McCulley) **Cinematography** Arthur C. Miller **Music** Alfred Newman **Cast** Tyrone Power, Basil Rathbone, George Regas, Linda Darnell, Gale Sondergaard

By 1940, with film output reaching an unprecedented high, producers were not averse to glancing over their shoulders to plunder the archives of the silent era for "new" ideas. Based on the Johnston McCulley novel *The Curse of Capistrano*, *The Mark of Zorro* was a remake of a very popular 1920s swashbuckler featuring Hollywood's first great action hero, Douglas Fairbanks. Twenty years later, producer Darryl F. Zanuck made a bold choice in casting 20th Century Fox's top romantic lead, heartthrob Tyrone Power, as the swaggering sword-wielding star.

The story is set in Southern California during the 1820s, when foppish dandy, Don Diego Viega (Tyrone Power), the son of a wealthy ranchero, returns from a military academy in Madrid, only to find the region under the rule of villainous Governor Quintero (George Regas). Outraged at the new ruler's iron-fisted maltreatment of the peasants, Don Diego vows vengeance. For, unknown to his family, he is no longer the useless coxcomb of his youth but an expert swordsman and master caballero: in the dark of night he transforms into the mysterious Zorro (the "fox"), a masked, Robin-Hood-style defender of the poor. And just so the cruel Quintero knows who he is up against, Zorro

◄

Tyrone Power donned the new cape as action-adventure hero in this remake of a 1920s original starring the swaggering swashbuckler Douglas Fairbanks.

always leaves a calling card—taking his sword and slashing the letter "Z" at the scene of each new exploit. Of course there's not only an abundance of fast and flashy fencing, there's also the obligatory love interest, as Don Diego flirts outrageously with the governor's wife while romancing her beautiful niece.

The Mark of Zorro is enjoyable Hollywood-period hooey with lavish sets, an overly dramatized script, and a healthy smattering

"POWER WAS THE MOST AGILE MAN WITH A SWORD I'VE EVER FACED BEFORE A CAMERA." BASIL RATHBONE

of hammy acting. But it also features what is perhaps cinema's greatest dueling sequence—the climactic face-off between Zorro and Captain Pasquale (Basil Rathbone).

Now fondly remembered for his many appearances as Sherlock Holmes during the 1940s, Rathbone was an expert classical fencer in his own right, whose thrust and parry graced many an epic of the time. Moviegoers, however, were thrilled to discover that Power was also able to handle his blade with considerable aplomb. A breathtaking cocktail of ornate finesse and aggressive bluster, at times the duel is almost balletic in its elegance. Rathbone was deeply impressed with Power, and noted, when comparing him to the star with whom he had sparred two years earlier in *The Adventures of Robin Hood* (1938): "Tyrone could have fenced Errol Flynn into a cocked hat." From then on he was cast almost exclusively as an action hero. **TB**

► Tyrone Power's days as a light romantic lead ended with this film—he died tragically, at only forty-four, while filming a dueling scene for the biblical epic *Solomon and Sheba* in September 1958.

Lana Turner

as Lady de Winter
...wicked as she is lovely!

Gene Kelly

as D'Artagnan
...dashing soldier, audacious lover!

June Allyson

as Constance
...entangled in a web of intrigue!

Van Heflin

as Athos
...a roistering, daredevil adventurer!

Angela Lansbury

as Queen Anne
...for her, men gave their lives!

Frank Morgan
Vincent Price
Keenan Wynn
John Sutton
Gig Young

Screen Play by Robert Ardrey
Directed by GEORGE SIDNEY
Produced by PANDRO S. BERMAN

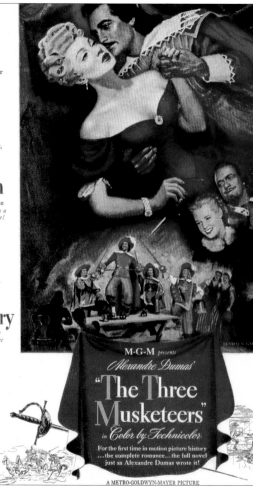

M-G-M *presents*

Alexandre Dumas'

"The Three Musketeers"

in Color by Technicolor

For the first time in motion picture history
...the complete romance...the full novel
just as Alexandre Dumas wrote it!

A METRO-GOLDWYN-MAYER PICTURE

THE THREE MUSKETEERS 1948 (U.S.)

Director George Sidney **Producer** Pandro S. Berman **Screenplay** Robert Ardrey (from the novel by Alexandre Dumas, pére) **Cinematography** Robert H. Planck **Music** Herbert Stothart **Cast** Gene Kelly, Van Heflin, Lana Turner, June Allyson, Vincent Price, Angela Lansbury, Vincent Price, Gig Young

The Three Musketeers is a wonderful action flick from Hollywood's golden age. Many remakes would follow, but this one remains the best. Set in mid-seventeenth century France, the multistranded—sometimes convoluted—plot revolves around precious jewels given by King Louis XIII to his wife, Queen Anne. Carelessly, she gives them to her illicit lover, the Duke of Buckingham—who also happens to be the Prime Minister of England. On discovering her indiscretion, the king's nefarious adviser, Richelieu, sees an opportunity to persuade the king to declare war on England. Meanwhile, young country lad D'Artagnon makes his way to Paris to join the king's musketeers. During an unexpectedly eventful journey, he fights alongside three other musketeers—Athos, Porthos, and Aramis—when they are attacked by soldiers loyal to Richelieu. They accept D'Artagnon among their ranks, and the four of them are dispatched to England to retrieve the jewels before King Louis finds out the sordid truth.

It's no surprise to find Hollywood playing fast and loose with the classics, and *The Three Musketeers* is certainly no exception. Among the many dramatic liberties taken is the

◄

Lana Turner, by now typecast as Hollywood's leading *femme fatale*, gives a smoldering performance straight out of *The Postman Always Rings Twice* (1946).

removal of all references to the Catholic Church, whose top man, the wily Cardinal Richelieu, is effectively the story's principal bad guy—here, he's even stripped of his title. But none of this matters much, and the film still manages to retain the "spirit" of Dumas's writing.

What really sets *The Three Musketeers* apart from other adventure films of the period is a plot that doesn't assume the

> ## "TO DIE AMONG FRIENDS. CAN A MAN ASK MORE? . . . IT'S ALL FOR ONE, D'ARTAGNAN, AND ONE FOR ALL." ATHOS

viewer has the attention span of a goldfish, as well as the sheer quality of the cast. Gene Kelly launches himself gung ho into the role of D'Artagnon, the naive country bumpkin seeking the glamor of a life serving King Louis. Even without his usual breathtaking song and dance routines—and allowing that, aged thirty-six, he was hardly the dreaming youth described by Dumas—the on-screen charisma that made Kelly one of Hollywood's most memorable stars is abundant in every scene. His swordplay may lack the finesse of more established cinematic swashbucklers, but his bravado and dazzling athleticism more than compensate.

▶

Gene Kelly choreographed the action scenes in as much detail as his most celebrated dance routines. This was a superstar at the top of his game.

By contrast, Van Heflin, one of Hollywood's sturdiest character actors (as Alan Ladd's costar in *Shane* in 1953), puts in a suitably dark turn as Athos, the high-minded, hard-drinking musketeer who harbors in his past a troubling secret. **TB**

THE WAGES OF FEAR 1953 (FRANCE • ITALY)

Director Henri-Georges Clouzot **Producer** Raymond Borderie, Henri-Georges Clouzot **Screenplay** Henri-Georges Clouzot, Jérôme Géronimi **Cinematography** Armand Thirard **Music** Geroges Auric **Cast** Yves Montand, Folco Lulli, Peter van Eyck, Charles Vanel, William Tubbs

Having previously directed the scathing social critique *Le Corbeau* (1943) and the tense police procedural *Quai des Orfevres* (1947), Henri-Georges Clouzot was neither a stranger to controversy nor a novice at creating tightly plotted and highly suspenseful narratives when he created his masterpiece, *The Wages of Fear*. Working at the peak of his skills as a filmmaker, Clouzot manipulates audience emotions and expectations with an almost surgical precision; consequently, over fifty years removed from its initial screenings, *The Wages of Fear* remains one of the most nerve-racking works of cinema ever created. What makes the film so successful is an amalgamation of its relatively straightforward plot, its focus on four disparate characters faced with increasingly dangerous obstacles and personal demons, and its condemnation of colonialist and capitalist enterprises that places profits before people, ultimately viewing human beings as disposable objects.

   The Wages of Fear begins in the arid desert town of Las Piedras, a dusty South American pueblo where children torture insects for fun and the local cantina provides the unfortunate populace with the alcohol and social interaction necessary to

◀

The movie was winner of the Grand Prix at the 1953 Cannes Film Festival. Remade as *Sorcerer* by director William Friedkin in 1977, Henri-Georges Clouzot's original remains the superior version.

make life bearable. Dominating the lives of the population of Las Piedras is the Southern Oil Company, an American corporation notorious for its social and ecological exploitation. When one of the company's oil fields catches fire, the film's four main protagonists—Mario (Yves Montand), Luigi (Folco Lulli), Bimba (Peter van Eyck), and Jo (Charles Vanel)—are hired at a price of $2,000 each to drive two trucks loaded with

"THOSE BUMS DON'T HAVE A UNION. . . IF THEY BLOW UP, NOBODY'LL COME AROUND FOR ANY CONTRIBUTION." BILL

nitroglycerine. These barrels filled with the highly unstable explosive will (according to the Southern Oil Company) prove integral to extinguishing the blaze and "capping" the open wells.

From the moment the four main characters embark on their potentially suicidal mission, the film becomes an edge-of-your-seat affair in which every pitted road, sharp swerve, and—in one particularly gut-wrenching sequence—a rickety series of boards forming a so-called "bridge" across a deep gorge could prove disastrous. One of the most action-filled narratives in the history of cinema, *The Wages of Fear* incessantly tests the nerves of both the characters and the audience, and when an explosive turn of events unexpectedly changes the film's trajectory, the suspense is ratcheted up several more notches. *The Wages of Fear* remains one of the unassailable benchmarks in the action film genre. **JMcR**

► **Hunky Yves Montand, as Mario, in fine form as one of the four deliverymen with a payload of potential death.**

NORTH BY NORTHWEST 1959 (U.S.)

Director Alfred Hitchcock **Producer** Herbert Coleman **Screenplay** Ernest Lehman **Cinematography** Robert Burks **Music** Bernard Herrmann
Cast Cary Grant, Eva Marie Saint, James Mason, Martin Landau, Edward Platt, Jessie Royce Landis, Philip Ober, Leo G. Carroll, Josephine Hutchinson

Fast-paced espionage thriller *North by Northwest* is, along with *Psycho* (1960), British director Alfred Hitchcock's most iconic film. It also contains some of the most memorable scenes of the action-adventure genre ever.

From the start, the plot proceeds at breakneck speed. No sooner is mild-mannered ad-man Roger Thornhill (perfectly pitched by Cary Grant) mistaken for an undercover agent and kidnapped from a business meeting by the heavies of criminal-cum-spy Phillip Vandamm (James Mason), than he embarks on a frantic search to find the spy he was mistaken for, the elusive George Kaplin. The fact that Kaplin does not actually exist and is an invention of the secret services is of little importance, as the police, the secret services, and Vandamm's henchmen pursue Thornhill across the United States.

Saul Bass's innovative title designs, the stylish, witty script by Ernest Lehman, and the pulsating score by regular Hitchcock contributor Bernard Herrmann lend *North by Northwest* a sense of urgency and crazed fun that is strongly underpinned by the director's own careful yet zesty direction. *North by Northwest* contains some of Hitchcock's most memorable scenes, as

◄

Nominated for three Oscars (Art Direction, Editing, and Screenplay), *North by Northwest* reaffirmed what everyone already knew: Alfred Hitchcock was the master of suspense.

Thornhill is attacked by a crop-spraying biplane in a cornfield and, in the thrilling finale, fights for his life on the nose of George Washington atop Mount Rushmore. No one is who they appear to be, and in this respect the film is archetypically Hitchcockian, standing as a masterpiece in the director's illustrious oeuvre. Trademark Hitchcockian themes of mistaken identity, deception, double crossing, and the all-important presence of a "MacGuffin"

"I DON'T LIKE THE WAY TEDDY ROOSEVELT IS LOOKING AT ME."

ROGER THORNHILL

(the director's famous term for a plot item that serves only to drive the action) combine to create a mélange of intriguing spy drama and gloriously fun action-thriller. The British director stated on more than one occasion that he wanted the film to be much more lighthearted than his previous works, and despite its Cold War undertones, the real success of *North by Northwest* is that it manages not to take itself too seriously. Grant's befuddled everyman Roger Thornhill is terrific fun, infused with a sense of playful tongue-in-cheek humor typical of Hitchcock. Never was Grant more at ease or more effortlessly debonair. Eva Marie Saint, a surprise choice at the time as the female double agent (in the film at Hitchcock's insistence after the studio wanted to use Syd Charisse), brings intelligent charm to her role, matching Grant's whimsical one-liners with her own steely personification of a conflicted double agent. **RH**

▶
The fourth and final collaboration with Hitchcock for Cary Grant, after *Suspicion* (1941), *Notorious* (1946), and *To Catch a Thief* (1955), it is undoubtedly one of his quirkier performances.

JAMES BOND

his new incredible women!

his new incredible enemies!

his new incredible adventures!

IS BACK!

HARRY SALTZMAN and ALBERT R. BROCCOLI

IAN FLEMING'S

FROM RUSSIA WITH LOVE

SEAN CONNERY AS JAMES BOND

PEDRO ARMENDARIZ · LOTTE LENYA · ROBERT SHAW · BERNARD LEE M · DANIELA BIANCHI

RICHARD MAIBAUM · JOHANNA HARWOOD · LIONEL BART · JOHN BARRY

HARRY SALTZMAN and ALBERT R. BROCCOLI · TERENCE YOUNG

TECHNICOLOR UNITED ARTISTS

FROM RUSSIA WITH LOVE 1963 (U.K.)

Director Terence Young **Producer** Harry Saltzman, Albert R. Broccoli
Screenplay Richard Maibaum (based on Ian Fleming's novel)
Cinematography Ted Moore **Music** John Barry **Cast** Sean Connery, Lotte Lenya,
Pedro Amandáriz, Robert Shaw, Bernard Lee, Daniela Bianchi

Hailed by many, including its star, Sean Connery, as the greatest
Bond film ever, *From Russia With Love* will come as something of
a surprise to twenty-first-century Bond fans, brought up on the
thrill-a-minute action of today's Bond.

In this, the second of the Bond movies, international crime
syndicate SPECTRE is plotting to hot up the Cold War by getting
its hands on a Soviet decoding machine. To accomplish this, it
plans to lure James Bond to Istanbul to obtain the decoder
from a Soviet girl who will pass it over in return for being
permitted to defect to the West. Once Bond has snatched the
decoder, a S.P.E.C.T.R.E. assassin will kill him in revenge for
Bond's killing Dr. No (in his first celluloid outing).

After a tense opening nighttime fight sequence in which
Bond appears to die, but which turns out to be a S.P.E.C.T.R.E.
exercise, the movie proceeds at a leisurely pace. The plot is
outlined in S.P.E.C.T.R.E.'s lair; Bond rouses himself from a liaison
with a beautiful blonde to report for duty and makes his way to
Istanbul. The action follows Ian Fleming's novel closely,
developing the characters and giving a sense of Cold War
paranoia, but leaving a modern audience glancing at their

◄
**The title song was
written by Lionel
"Oliver!" Bart and
sung by Matt
Monro.**

watches, wondering when the action is going to start. When the action sequences do finally start, they are pure Bond quality, although simpler than today's Bond.

The last half hour of the film is action packed, culminating in a gruesome fight in a railway carriage with Red Grant (Robert Shaw), the S.P.E.C.T.R.E. assassin, stalking him—a scene considered so violent at the time that it was cut from TV versions of the

"HORRIBLE, HORRIBLE WOMAN."

TATIANA ROMANOVA

"YES, SHE HAD HER KICKS." *JAMES BOND*

movie. The icing on the cake for Bond fans is the final helicopter chase and a boat chase, complete with plenty of explosions.

Many of the elements that were to become staples of the Bond series are here: Bond's briefcase is the first of Q's gadgets to save Bond from certain death; there are jokey touches, like the Russian spy escaping through a window set in the mouth of an actress in a giant film poster; the knife in Rosa Klebb's (Lotte Lenya's) shoes preempts Odd-Job's hat and Jaws's teeth. Later in the Bond series, these elements took over the movies, burying the story under gimmicks and jokes, but in *From Russia With Love* these elements are just one small part of a movie that is ultimately incohesive and not wholly satisfying. But Connery is right about one thing. This Bond is true to Fleming: elegant, sardonic, the essence of cool, but much colder and more ruthless than in later films. **CW**

► A taut and totally convincing helicopter chase climaxes this Bond movie—later to become a regular feature of many Bond movies.

JAMES BOND IS BACK IN ACTION!

EVERYTHING HE TOUCHES

TURNS TO EXCITEMENT!

ALBERT R. BROCCOLI
and HARRY SALTZMAN
present

SEAN CONNERY
as
AGENT **007**
in
IAN FLEMING'S

GOLDFINGER

STARRING
GERT FROBE as GOLDFINGER **HONOR BLACKMAN** as PUSSY GALORE
ALSO STARRING
SHIRLEY EATON SCREENPLAY BY RICHARD MAIBAUM and PAUL DEHN PRODUCED BY HARRY SALTZMAN and ALBERT R. BROCCOLI DIRECTED BY GUY HAMILTON
TECHNICOLOR® RELEASED THRU **UNITED ARTISTS** Exciting original motion picture soundtrack album available on United Artists Records.

GOLDFINGER 1964 (U.K.)

Director Guy Hamilton **Producer** Harry Saltzman, Albert R. Broccoli
Screenplay Richard Maibaum (from the story by Ian Fleming)
Cinematography Ted Moore **Music** John Barry **Cast** Sean Connery,
Honor Blackman, Gert Fröbe, Shirley Eaton, Harold Sakata

Welcome to a world of espionage, where sharply suited secret agents wage war on unspeakably evil, if terribly civilized, supervillains. The type who would rather dispatch their foes with a martini, a detailed explanation of their intentions, and an exotic laser-driven death-beam than an efficient bullet in the back. And judging by the longevity of the Bond franchise, we can't get enough of it.

British secret agent 007 ("The name's Bond . . . James Bond . . .") is back in action, this time charged with bringing to justice Auric Goldfinger, an evil, gold-obsessed villain who plans to nuke Fort Knox. As usual, the plot could fit on a postage stamp: Bond pursues villain, is captured, escapes, continues his pursuit . . . and so it goes, along the way bedding a bevy of beauties and disposing of baddies with the latest in cutting-edge weaponry. But that hardly matters, for it's *how* Bond goes about his business that keeps us watching.

Once again, Sean Connery delivers the goods, and it's not hard to see why. With his easy charm and sophistication, he's still our favorite incarnation of Bond after nearly fifty years. The eponymous foe is played with crazed zeal by veteran German

◄
Saltzman, Broccoli, Hamilton, and Connery are at the top of their game—not forgetting Shirley Eaton's iconic motion-picture moment covered fatally in gold.

actor Gert Fröbe: whether his curious phrasing could be attributed to speaking no English at all—he learned and recited his lines phonetically—we can't say, but it certainly ups the derangement factor.

Of course, no discussion of *Goldfinger* could take place without mention of the ever-present "Bond Girls"—beauties usually in the employ of the enemy, who after a plush hotel

"MY NAME IS PUSSY GALORE."
PUSSY GALORE "I MUST BE DREAMING."

JAMES BOND

room encounter with our hero would invariably defect. This time we are acquainted with the riské monikered Pussy Galore! Played by Avenger girl Honor Blackman, Pussy is an action girl employed by *Goldfinger* as a pilot. In what must rate as one of the most audacious displays of machismo (in a non-X-rated film, at least), Pussy, clearly lesbian (it's implied in the film, but quite explicit in the novel), nonetheless succumbs to Bond's irresistible manly charms. Thus Bond quite turns Pussy straight in all possible senses.

The Bond films were clearly never wholly serious affairs, but *Goldfinger* ups the camp by several notches. For the first time, the gadgetry so closely associated with Bond really starts to take center stage, perhaps the most iconic being his Aston Martin DB5. From *Goldfinger* onward, Bond's four-wheel fun would be every bit as sexy as his exploits between the sheets. **TB**

► Bond (Connery): "Do you expect me to talk?" Goldfinger (Fröbe): "No, Mr. Bond, I expect you to die!" A classic riposte from villain to hero in the third, and best—at least among the early collection—of James Bond movies.

LOO7 UP!

LOO7 DOWN!

LOO7 OUT!

HERE COMES THE BIGGEST BOND OF ALL!

ALBERT R. BROCCOLI and HARRY SALTZMAN present

SEAN CONNERY

IAN FLEMING'S "THUNDERBALL"

CLAUDINE AUGER · ADOLFO CELI · LUCIANA PALUZZI   Produced by KEVIN McCLORY Directed by TERENCE YOUNG Screenplay by RICHARD MAIBAUM and JOHN HOPKINS

Based on an original story by KEVIN McCLORY, JACK WHITTINGHAM and IAN FLEMING PANAVISION° TECHNICOLOR° Released thru UNITED ARTISTS

THUNDERBALL 1965 (U.K.)

Director Terence Young **Producer** Kevin McClory, Harry Saltzman
Screenplay Richard Maibaum, John Hopkins, Kevin McClory, Ian Fleming
Cinematography Ted Moore **Music** John Barry **Cast** Sean Connery, Lois Maxwell, Adolfo Celi, Bernard Lee, Desmond Llewelyn, Claudine Auger

By the time the fourth outing for Fleming's superspy hit the big screens, the public was well used to Sean Connery's suave but dynamic charmer equally capable of disarming both bomb and bombshell. But added excitement was in store in 007's latest adventure—the biggest, most lavish, most expensive, and longest at that time was not only the first to be filmed in Cinemascope, but also had the first ever (thrillingly impressive) underwater action sequences.

Originally meant to be the first in the Bond series, *Thunderball* became a casualty to the courts as cowriter Kevin McClory sued Fleming for the rights—and lost. And, as if that wasn't trouble enough for the producers, they had also decided to tackle the tricky problem of filming underwater, which was pretty much unheard of in Hollywood at the time. In fact, almost a quarter of the action takes place beneath the surf.

Lamar Boren, one of the world's most experienced underwater cameramen, was crucial to its success by putting together and overseeing a crew capable of capturing these sequences. The results were mind-blowing—Bond finds himself pitted against not just knife-wielding henchmen, but

◄

With a catchy title song by Tom Jones, frantic-paced underwater action scenes, and a tense chase in the middle of New Orleans' Mardi Gras (no room for that on the poster), *Thunderball* was stuffed with goodies.

sharks, subaqua scooters, and spearguns. Happily, he doesn't let his location dampen his ardor either and manages a little watery romance (with pouting French ingenue Claudine Auger as Domino) into the bargain.

And if you think Connery is brilliant at portraying fear when he comes up against those sharks, it's probably because, at one point, the actor actually got into the pool with the sharks

"MY DEAR GIRL, DON'T FLATTER YOURSELF. WHAT I DID . . . WAS FOR QUEEN AND COUNTRY." JAMES BOND

himself, unarmed and unprotected (but only once). Nevertheless, that fear is palpably real in his features. Plotwise, it's business as usual. 007 is charged with tracking down two atomic warheads that have been pinched by the dastardly S.P.E.C.T.R.E. organization, which is holding the world to ransom for £100 million ($150 million) worth of diamonds. His quest takes him to the Bahamas, where he meets and defeats the barrel-chested, mad, ruthless villain, Emile Largo (Adolfo Celi, having a ball while sporting a suitably sinister eye patch).

It received mixed reviews from critics, with some complaining the series was too repetitive. However, commercially speaking *Thunderball* was a big-time smash, with one cinema in New York playing it twenty-four hours a day to accommodate demand. It also picked up an Oscar for Special Visual Effects, and many fans still rate it as the best of the series. **RP**

► The movie features one of the series' classic precredits action sequences in which our hero bravely escapes an assassination attempt by strapping on a supercool rocket pack.

COME DRINK WITH ME 1966 (HONG KONG)

Director King Hu Hu Jinquan **Producer** Run Run Shaw **Screenplay** King Hu Hu Jinquan, Yang Erh **Cinematography** Tadashi Nishimoto **Music** Lan Ping Chow **Choreography** Ying Chieh Han **Cast** Yueh Hua, Cheng Pei Pei, Chen Honglie, Li Yunzhong, Yang Zhinging

Hu's visual masterpiece has been credited with single-handedly reviving the art of the Asian action flick. The uniquely Chinese *wuxia* movies (magical swordfight stories usually based on a popular novel) had suffered by being rather soulless and bloodless affairs up to this point.

Enter Hu, who'd studied under the Shaw brothers, the then-masters of Chinese action, but who also brought a genuine love of Chinese history and a clinical eye for detail, particularly in the areas of costume and design, to the mix.

This impressive directorial debut, set during the Ming Dynasty, sees mysterious swordswoman Golden Swallow (Cheng Pei Pei) on a quest to rescue her brother, a young official who has been kidnapped by the ruthless Five Tiger Gang. He's being held in a corrupt Buddhist temple, so posing as a knight and with the aid of a beggar and leader of a gang of bedraggled kids, she mounts an assualt on the enemy. Luckily for her, the beggar turns out to be none other than Drunken Cat (Yueh Hua), a Kung Fu master who is currently traveling incognito while he tries to avenge the death of his teacher. Even more luckily, it turns out that the same gang is

◄ Beijing-born Hu brought a fresh, poetic outlook and a charm into *Da zui xia* (its Chinese title) that breathed new life into the floundering dinosaur of Chinese *wuxia* flicks.

responsible for this crime, too. Let battle commence! Fans of the genre will notice some of what would become Hu's future trademarks, including the heroine in drag, combat in confined spaces, and percussion and cues from the Peking Opera, as well as the ever-present, gravity-defying swordfights that owe as much to dance as to brute force. For those who caught and loved Ang Lee's *Crouching Tiger, Hidden Dragon* (2000) but

> ## "THE AUDIENCE IS THE CAMERA. I DON'T WANT THE AUDIENCE TO SIT AND WATCH, I WANT IT TO MOVE." HU

thought that it was something brand new and original, this will be a revelation. That joint Chinese–Taiwanese–U.S–U.K. smash owes an enormous amount to *Come Drink With Me* and Hu's other features. Indeed, Lee even cast our brave heroine Cheng Pei Pei as the villainous Jade Fox in *Crouching Tiger*.

Hu's diligence and perfectionism were second to none (he insisted his crew worked to very specific storyboards and detailed sketches that he had made) but came at a high price—his on-set arguments with his producer, who wasn't used to working at such a pace, were legendary, and soon after the release of this movie, Hu left the Shaw brothers and branched out on his own.

Hu directed another ten movies, including such classics as *Dragon Gate Inn* (1966) and *A Touch of Zen* (1969) but his career never reached the dizzying heights reached here. **RP**

▶

Golden Swallow (Cheng) displays her master swordswomen skills in this choreographed fight scene.

"Our Man Flint"
makes love in 47 languages!
He's a Karate Champion, Brain
Surgeon, Swordsman and
Nuclear Physicist...
He's the top Master Spy
of all time, with his
Cigarette Lighter containing
82 Death-Dealing Devices,
his 2 Man-Eating Dogs,
his 4 Luscious Playmates
and his Love Nest—
Built—For—5.......

OUR
MAN
FLINT

20th Century-Fox
presents

JAMES COBURN · LEE J. COBB · GILA GOLAN · EDWARD MULHARE

PRODUCED BY SAUL DAVID   DIRECTED BY DANIEL MANN   SCREENPLAY BY HAL FIMBERG AND BEN STARR   CINEMASCOPE COLOR BY DE LUXE

OUR MAN FLINT 1966 (U.S.)

Director Daniel Mann **Producer** Saul David **Screenplay** Hal Fimberg, Ben Starr
Cinematography Daniel L. Fapp **Music** Jerry Goldsmith **Cast** James Coburn,
Lee J. Cobb, Gila Golan, Edward Mulhare, Benson Fong, Shelby Grant, Sigrid Valdis,
Gianna Serra, Michael St. Clare, Rhys Williams, Russ Conway

The James Bond series had been an unexpected hit in the
United States. A cocktail of action and glamor presented with
an air of gentle self-mocking British diffidence appealed to a
wide audience. Strange, perhaps, that 20th Century Fox would
deem something as preposterous as a Bond movie in need of
parody. Enter, then, Derek Flint, millionaire American spy, lady's
man, master of martial arts, philosopher, and . . . also . . . ballet
instructor. Taking its cues from the popular TV spy show *The
Man From U.N.C.L.E.*, *Our Man Flint* plays like a loose compilation
of the first three Bond movies but takes every typical Bond
scenario and expands it to the breaking point, traversing
successfully both action and comedy movie genres.

Retired spy Derek Flint (James Coburn) is lured back into the
field to deal with the threat of Galaxy (a clear parody of Bond's
archenemies, S.P.E.C.T.R.E.). A worldwide organization led by a
trio of mad scientists, Galaxy holds the world to ransom using a
climate-control apparatus to initiate earthquakes, volcanic
eruptions, and other natural disasters. Flint only takes the job
after Galaxy launches a preemptive assassination attempt on
him while he's dining at a restaurant with his four (count 'em)

◀
Our Man Flint was
a sufficiently sized
hit to spawn a
sequel. But
although 1967's *In
Like Flint* featured
the same cast, the
joke was becoming
threadbare and
ready to be laid
to rest.

beautiful live-in "playmates." The would-be assassin is a musician who fires a poisoned dart from the strings of her harp. Thereafter, Flint sets off on a wild globe-trotting adventure with no lesser objective than to save the world.

The action scenes in *Our Man Flint* dazzle, as our hero accesses an array of technical wizardry that would send 007 a deep shade of green, including a neat little cigarette lighter

> ## "THIS [GADGET LIGHTER] HAS 82 DIFFERENT FUNCTIONS—83 IF YOU WANT TO LIGHT A CIGAR." *DEREK FLINT*

that has eighty-three separate uses: pistol, two-way radio (communicating across the globe in a pre-satellite age), blow-torch, tear gas bomb, and dart gun, to name but a few. And, outdoing Bond and his Aston Martin, we also witness the first filmed appearance of the Lear Jet. Amusingly, Bond is alluded to on more than one occasion, once as we meet a sharply dressed British agent calling himself "0008," another as he dismisses a Bond briefcase gadget as "crude."

▶
Coburn's movie has a hint of the U.S. hippie/ counterculture about it that films such as *Head* (1968) and *Psych-out* (1968) later reveled in.

What makes *Our Man Flint* so likable is the central performance of James Coburn. The star's prior career had comprised almost entirely Westerns and GI flicks. He was accustomed to playing hard-nosed wiseguys, but few of his fans would have predicted such a natural comic lightness. Coburn was clearly having the time of his life here, and this shines through every scene. **TB**

ON HER MAJESTY'S SECRET SERVICE
1969 (U.K.)

Director Peter R. Hunt **Producer** Albert R. Broccoli **Screenplay** Richard Maibaum, Simon Raven **Cinematography** Michael Reed **Music** John Barry **Cast** George Lazenby, Diana Rigg, Telly Savalas, Gabriele Ferzetti, Isle Steppat, Angela Scoular, Lois Maxwell, Catherine Schell, George Baker, Bernard Lee, Desmond Llewelyn

---

Although commercially successful upon its release in 1969, *On Her Majesty's Secret Service* has become one of the most underrated entries in one of the longest running and most financially successful franchises in contemporary cinema.

Following Sean Connery's decision to leave the James Bond franchise after the completion of 1967's *You Only Live Twice*, the series' stalwart producer, Albert R. Broccoli, initially offered the role to U.K.-born actor Timothy Dalton, who would assume the superspy's mantel eighteen years later in *The Living Daylights*. After considering a number of actors, including Roger Moore and John Richardson, Broccoli offered the role to George Lazenby, an Australian actor who was quickly signed to a seven-picture contract. However, in what may be among the worst career moves in film history, Lazenby opted out after only one appearance because of his conviction that, given the changing sociocultural landscape of the late 1960s and early 1970s, the days of audiences longing to view the exploits of tuxedo-sporting secret agents were numbered. Lazenby's performance, however, was more than adequate. The combination of rugged

◄

Lazenby's performance laid the groundwork for the deliberately violent, if emotionally volatile, edge that Daniel Craig would eventually bring to the role in 2006's *Casino Royale*.

physicality and surprising sensitivity (from the former Big Fry chocolates commercials man) that he brought to the role offered a striking variation to Sean Connery's iconic portrayal.

On Her Majesty's Secret Service once again pits James Bond against master criminal Ernst Stavro Blofeld (in this outing played by Telly Savalas). Ensconced within his heavily fortified laboratory high in the Swiss mountains, Blofeld plans to use his

"THERE'S NO HURRY, YOU SEE. WE HAVE ALL THE TIME IN THE WORLD." *BOND'S LAST WORDS*

ten beautiful and brainwashed "angels of death" to unleash an agriculturally devastating toxin across the globe. Along the way, the bed-hopping Bond meets his match in, and subsequently loses his heart to, Tracy Draco (Diana Rigg), the daughter of a powerful mafioso.

► In his lone performance as cinema's most recognizable spy, George Lazenby (playing opposite Diana Rigg) left a lasting impression upon the franchise: James Bond as tragic hero.

Director Peter R. Hunt and editor John Glenn choreographed the motion picture's dizzying action sequences in a rapid-fire montage style, decades ahead of Paul Greengrass's similarly frenetic representations of high-speed chases in *The Bourne Supremacy* (2004). But what truly sets this Bond adventure apart from the series' previous and subsequent offerings is the producer and director's bold decision and enormous risk to end the film on a tragic note, to the strains of Louis Armstrong's mournful rendition of "We Have All the Time in the World." **JMcR**

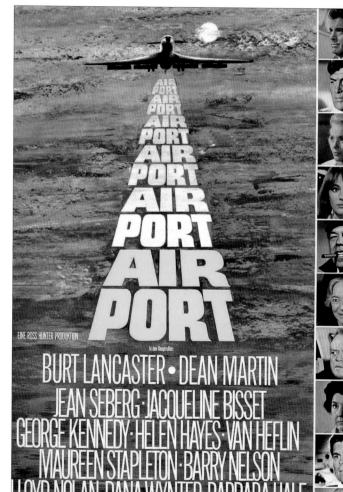

AIR PORT

EINE ROSS HUNTER-PRODUKTION

In den Hauptrollen:

BURT LANCASTER • DEAN MARTIN
JEAN SEBERG • JACQUELINE BISSET
GEORGE KENNEDY • HELEN HAYES • VAN HEFLIN
MAUREEN STAPLETON • BARRY NELSON
LLOYD NOLAN • DANA WYNTER • BARBARA HALE

Komposition und Orchesterführung: ALFRED NEWMAN · Nach dem Bestseller-Roman von ARTHUR HAILEY
Drehbuch und Regie: GEORGE SEATON · Produktion: ROSS HUNTER · TECHNICOLOR® · PANAVISION · EIN UNIVERSAL-FILM

AIRPORT 1970 (U.S.)

Director George Seaton **Producer** Ross Hunter, Jacque Mapes **Screenplay** George Seaton (from the best-selling novel by Arthur Hailey) **Cinematography** Ernest Laszlo **Music** Alfred Newman **Cast** Burt Lancaster, Dean Martin, Jean Seberg, Helen Hayes, Van Heflin, Jacqueline Bisset, George Kennedy, Maureen Stapleton

Airport represented a revival of the portmanteau novel (i.e., lots of interwoven stories with multiple characters), and when Arthur Hailey's best-selling book was brought to the screen, it duly heralded the resurgence of the portmanteau film. These all-star-cast, specific "disaster" movies, including the *Towering Inferno* (1974), became immensely popular in the 1970s, and *Airport* was the daddy of them all.

The movie's influence is still pervasive today: *Armageddon* (1998) and *The Day After Tomorrow* (2004), to name but two examples, both show traces of *Airport*. *Grand Hotel* in 1932 was the grand daddy and Les Keyser in his book, *Hollywood in the Seventies*, described this movie as "a Grand Hotel in the sky." The story line is pretty simple. As with all such pictures, a large life-changing event (mighty fire, crashing Zeppelin) inevitably affects the lives of many people in the center of the storm, or even on its fringes. Here, an unnamed midwestern U.S. hub airport is struggling to remain open despite the worst snowstorm in twenty-five years, with angry homeowners from a nearby housing plot hustling them and intransigent pilots refusing to obey noise abatement rules during the storm.

◀

Burt Lancaster heads a star-studded cast in what became a lucrative "disaster" movie series, but the actor reckoned that it was "the worst piece of junk ever made."

As usual, one man is trying to hold it all together. Burt Lancaster as Mel Bakersfield is the airport manager who must not only fight the weather and the homeowners but also his pilot, who is his playboy brother-in-law (Dean Martin as Captain Demerest), and his divorce-seeking wife, Cindy (Dana Wynter). Their characters are summed up by this exchange: "I suppose I'm like a lot of men. A bigamist. Married to both a woman and

"WHAT'S YOUR NAME, SIR?" QUONSETT "GUERRERO." GUERRERO "YOU LOOK MORE IRISH." "SO DID MY MOTHER."

a job." (Mel) "And I can't be number two wife any longer," (Cindy). Add to that the drama of a deranged man with a bomb, a plane stuck in the mud and blocking the main runway, a little old lady stowaway (Ada Quonsett played by Helen Hayes, who scooped the Best Actress Oscar for her role), and heavy airport commissioners breathing down your neck, and you have a recipe for a disaster movie. The recipe was retried with *Airport 1975* (1974), *Airport '77* (1977), and *The Concorde—Airport '79* (1979), all starring George Kennedy as Joe Patroni.

This was reckoned to be a very accurate depiction for its time of the day-to-day goings-on at a busy airport—with some extra high drama (well, it is Hollywood) thrown in to spice it up. At least, we hope it wasn't part of the accuracy—nevertheless, anyone who's seen the brilliant send-up of *Airport* that was portrayed in *Airplane!* (1980) will know what to expect. **MH**

▶

Dean Martin, as Capt. Vernon Demerest, made a mint out of this film, with ten percent of the gross yielding him an extra $7 million.

COLUMBIA PICTURES Presents

Sean Connery

in A ROBERT M. WEITMAN PRODUCTION

The Anderson Tapes

also starring

Dyan Cannon · Martin Balsam · Alan King

Screenplay by
FRANK R. PIERSON

Based on the best-selling novel by
LAWRENCE SANDERS

Music by
QUINCY JONES

Produced by
ROBERT M. WEITMAN

Directed by
SIDNEY LUMET

GP ALL AGES ADMITTED
Parental Guidance Suggested

71/212

THE ANDERSON TAPES 1971 (U.S.)

Director Sidney Lumet **Producer** George Justin, Robert Weitman
Screenplay Frank Pierson (from the novel by Lawrence Sanders)
Cinematography Arthur J. Ornitz **Music** Quincy Jones **Cast** Sean Connery,
Dyan Cannon, Martin Balsam, Alan King, Christopher Walken

While George Lazenby briefly took on the mantle of James
Bond, Sean Connery crossed to the other side of the law for this
enjoyable heist movie made with pal Sidney Lumet. The first
movie to really tackle the advancing march of technology, it's
awash with mics, cameras, TV screens, and bugging devices.
Connery has commented that it was an extraordinarily
prophetic picture being released, as it was just before the
Watergate scandal broke.

Connery plays likable rogue and safecracker Robert "Duke"
Anderson who, after serving ten years in prison, has finally been
released back into the community. But he remains completely
unrepentant as he leaves the prison and wastes no time in
plotting his next caper. After shacking up with his longtime
squeeze, Ingrid (Dyan Cannon), he decides that the apartment
building he is now living in, in a fashionable part of New York and
jammed full of wealthy tenants, is the perfect target. And he plans
to rob not just one or two of them but the whole lot. In one day.

As with all heist movies, it wouldn't really work without a
large injection of humor and a motley assortment of sidekicks,
each with their own special talent, drafted in to make sure that

◄
It's the ever-
present sense of
surveillance that
makes Lumet's
offering distinct
from previous
movies in this
genre.

such an ambitious plot goes off smoothly. So welcome Martin Balsam, fantastically camp as an antique dealer who assesses the value of the loot; stand-up comic Alan King playing brilliantly against type as the bankrolling mafia don; and Christopher Walken (in his first major movie role) as technology expert and Anderson's protégé, The Kid. The underlying theme is one of surveillance: the old-school thief trying to come to

"EVERYONE STEALS, THEREFORE EVERYONE HAS A RIGHT TO STEAL."

ROBERT "DUKE" ANDERSON

terms with the changes in technology since being banged up, along with the inability of agencies to work together, thus ultimately failing to prevent the crime. Duke is recorded at almost all his encounters with his band of merry men, but all by different people, and is never the target of the surveillance, so no one ever guesses what he's up to.

The movie was made on location in New York in a super swift six weeks and on a shoestring budget, and it's testament to Lumet's talent that he manages to pull off his own ambitious caper, complete with convoluted plot, modern technology, disguises, split-second timing, and awesome acrobatics, in such a short space of time. The original ending had Connery's cool crook escaping over state lines with the loot, but Columbia Pictures objected on moral grounds, saying that they couldn't be seen to endorse a picture showing that crime pays. **RP**

► **Anderson (Connery) doing what he does best—cracking a safe and heisting a precious hoard.**

DIAMONDS ARE FOREVER 1971 (U.S.)

Director Guy Hamilton **Producer** Harry Saltzman, Albert R. Broccoli
Screenplay Richard Maibaum, Tom Mankiewicz **Cinematography** Ted Moore
Music John Barry **Cast** Sean Connery, Jill St. John, Charles Gray, Lana Wood, Jimmy Dean, Desmond Llewelyn, Putter Smith, Bruce Glover, Bernard Lee, Lois Maxwell

Diamonds Are Forever preluded the spoof take on the international spy adopted by Roger Moore, although it offers its own mix of double entendre, absurd plot, and kitsch silliness that was popular in the 1970s. It followed *On Her Majesty's Secret Service,* which had disappointed at the box office, particularly in the United States, and George Lazenby's short-lived incarnation as James Bond was ill received. Producers Harry Saltzman and Albert R. Broccoli were keen to get Bond back on track, so they hired the winning team behind *Goldfinger:* director Guy Hamilton, production designer Ken Adam, and title song performer Shirley Bassey. Most importantly, Sean Connery was lured back by a then-exorbitant $1.25 million fee to play the British spy with the twinkly-eyed gravitas only he can provide. As the movie trailer declared: "He's back and we're back to what great movies are all about: outrageous, fun-making thrills."

Bond's archenemy, S.P.E.C.T.R.E. mastermind Ernst Stavro Blofeld, was also back, played as a supercilious crime boss by a sneering Charles Gray. Although Bond and the audience thought he was dead, the supervillain returns to hold the world to ransom with a diamond-powered satellite weapon.

Connery's image is central to the poster. Emphasizing his return as Bond was vital because Lazenby's outing as 007 had flopped at the U.S. box office.

The plot is secondary to the humorous one-liners, sheer style, and fast action that does provide the thrills it promises. Bond finds himself in a memorable, wonderfully choreographed car chase in a red Mustang that glides over parked cars and squeezes sideways down an alley on only two wheels. He even fights off two cartwheeling femme fatales in a scene that heralds more than a nod to martial arts movies. Admittedly, the

"ONE OF US SMELLS LIKE A TART'S HANDKERCHIEF. I'M AFRAID IT'S ME, SORRY ABOUT THAT OLD BOY." JAMES BOND

Bond babes Tiffany Case (Jill St. John) and Plenty O'Toole (Lana Wood) are perhaps some of the least memorable of the spy's female companions, and the scene when he drives across the Nevada desert in a Moon Buggy verges on ridiculous. But it is that very preposterous comedy epitomized by the gay hoodlums, Mr. Kidd (Putter Smith) and Mr. Wint (Bruce Glover), that make this movie such a joy to see.

While it may not have the realistic grit of some of the earlier 007 movies, it fulfills its promise to entertain. All the expected glamor is there, and the neon-lit streets and gambling halls of Las Vegas provide a suitable backdrop to a film that was a gamble for its producers. This is the last time Connery appears as Bond in a film produced by Saltzman and Broccoli, the reunification of this winning team is also its swan song, and that alone makes it a must-see movie. **CK**

▶
Gray plays Bond's nemesis, Blofeld, a chameleonlike villain known for his trademark Nehru suit. The criminal genius builds a laser satellite using stolen diamonds.

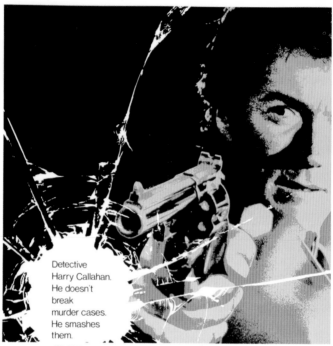

Detective
Harry Callahan.
He doesn't
break
murder cases.
He smashes
them.

Clint Eastwood
Dirty Harry

CLINT EASTWOOD in DIRTY HARRY A Malpaso Company Production Co-Starring HARRY GUARDINO · RENI SANTONI · ANDY ROBINSON · JOHN LARCH and JOHN VERNON as The Mayor · Executive Producer Robert Daley · Screenplay by Harry Julian Fink & R. M. Fink and Dean Riesner Story by Harry Julian Fink & R. M. Fink · Produced and Directed by Don Siegel · PANAVISION® · TECHNICOLOR® · Warner Bros., A Kinney Company

R

71/348

DIRTY HARRY 1971 (U.S.)

Director Don Siegel **Producer** Don Siegel **Screenplay** Harry Julian Fink,
Rita M. Fink, Dean Riesner **Cinematography** Bruce Surtees **Music** Lalo Schifrin
Cast Clint Eastwood, Andy Robinson, Harry Guardino, Reni Santoni, John Vernon,
John Larch, John Mitchum, Mae Mercer, Woodrow Parfrey, Josef Sommer

Dirty Harry marked the moment when Clint Eastwood finally left
behind his spaghetti Western stardom and became a fully
Americanized movie icon. His post-Italian, pre-*Dirty Harry* films
had contained interesting work, including *Coogan's Bluff* (1968),
which marked his first collaboration with director Don Siegel.
However, it was the cop thriller *Dirty Harry* that secured a screen
persona for its star that, in various inflections, would stand
Eastwood in good stead for a long time to come.

    The film's narrative is deceptively simple. A ruthless killer
known only as Scorpio attempts to extort money from the San
Francisco authorities. Maverick cop Harry Callahan (played by
Eastwood) eventually tracks down the miscreant and, in a
climactic shoot-out, kills him. As directed by Siegel, *Dirty Harry* is
not a whodunit—although we never know much about
Scorpio's background, his identity is not a mystery—but neither
is it to any great extent a police procedural. Harry stands largely
apart from his fellow police officers, and it is his self-motivated
actions, and the developing antagonism between him and
Scorpio, that provides most of the film's drama. Much like the
aforementioned *Coogan's Bluff*, *Dirty Harry* starts out as a

◄
**Despite its
emphasis on
violent action, the
film is also laden
with considerable
ambiguities in its
portrayal of Harry
as a figure without
a place in modern
society.**

modern-day Western, one in which the cowboy hero finds himself bewildered by modern urban life. The exhilarating early scene in which Harry takes on a gang of bank robbers, dispensing summary justice and delivering his famous "Did he fire six shots or only five" monologue, underlines an innate authority based more on Harry's charismatic individualism than on his police badge. However, this authority is increasingly challenged as the

> ## "YOU'VE GOT TO ASK YOURSELF ONE QUESTION: DO I FEEL LUCKY? WELL, DO YA, PUNK?" HARRY CALLAHAN

film progresses, not just by the legal restrictions on Harry's behavior, but also by the broader social milieu in which he is located. Harry turns out to be an intensely isolated figure, a hero without a context. Siegel slyly and sometimes not too subtly assigns a religious dimension to Harry's status (one scene has him standing under a sign that reads "Jesus Saves"), but this is always done ironically, as if this is a world that, unlike in the classic Western, really cannot be saved. After confronting Scorpio—and repeating his "Did he fire six shots" monologue, albeit with added bitterness—Harry throws away his police badge, and as the camera moves away from him, there is a sense of both his redundancy and his integrity. Some critics have accused *Dirty Harry* of being right-wing or even fascistic in its support for Harry's vigilante-like methods, which include—most notoriously—wounding and then torturing a suspect. **PH**

► Harry Callahan (Clint Eastwood) picked up his badge and resumed his activities for four sequels: *Magnum Force* (1973), *The Enforcer* (1976), *Sudden Impact* (1983), and *The Dead Pool* (1988)—albeit to decreasing effect.

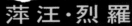

STARRING
LO LIEH
WANG PING
PRODUCER
RUN RUN SHAW
DIRECTOR
CHENG CHANG HO

KING BOXER
IN EASTMANCOLOR

A CHINESE PICTURE WITH ENGLISH SUBTITLES

FIVE FINGERS OF DEATH 1972 (HONG KONG)

Director Chang-hwa Jeong **Producer** Run Run Shaw **Screenplay** Yang Chiang **Cinematography** Yung-lang Wang **Music** Yung-Yu Chen **Cast** Lieh Lo, Ping Wang, Hsiung Chao, Chin-Feng Wang, Mien Fang, Feng Tien, James Nam, Shen Chan, Bolo Yeung, Wen Chung Ku, Lung Yu, Yukio Someno, Chi Chu Chin

In the early 1970s, if you saw only one Hong Kong martial arts film other than Bruce Lee's, chances are it was *Five Fingers of Death*. Made by the Shaw Brothers and picked up for distribution by Warners, it was the first Hong Kong film to play outside Chinatowns in the West. Reviewers patronized the film more often than they praised it, but it topped box office lists in Europe and the United States. For such an epochal film, *Five Fingers* has no pretensions to greatness. It adheres to several conventions already well established in the genre—rival schools, the "Iron Palm" technique, and antipathy toward Japan and its martial arts—and is a virtual remake of Wang Yu's *Chinese Boxer* (1970), also made by the Shaws.

Its story is simple—hero learns the "Iron Palm" technique (having his hands smashed proves a temporary obstacle), wins a major tournament, and avenges not one but two masters. The fights display neither the virtuoso skill of Bruce Lee nor the airborne poetry of *A Touch of Zen*, but they have a lurid, almost gothic, outlandishness that remains hard to resist: on two occasions, eyeballs fall casually from fingers that have just snatched them from some unfortunate's sockets. One image

◄
This was the film that launched the craze for kung fu movies in the United States.

in particular crystallizes the film's lasting appeal—as Lieh Lo channels his qi into his hands, they glow red, accompanied by a snatch of the theme from *A Man Called Ironside* (a musical theft quoted by Tarantino in 2003 in *Kill Bill*.)

Lo makes an engaging hero, but the film truly belongs to its villains. The best of these is the itinerant northern fighter Chen Lang, played with surly charisma by Gam Kei-chu, whose

> ## "THE STUDENTS HERE MUST BE ON THEIR TOES. YOU HAVE TO BE PREPARED FOR THE UNEXPECTED." SUN HSIN-PEI

forehead is shaved to administer his devastating trademark headbutt—in one delicious moment he uses it to shatter the sign above the hero's school. Initially menacing the hero, like Jack Palance trying to intimidate Alan Ladd in *Shane* (1953), defeat not only humbles Chen but seems to open his eyes to the cruelty of the villains who employ his skills. Movie critic Verina Glaessner, who had an eye for the Hong Kong genre, was so taken with him that she felt the film lost its appeal with his departure, gaining redemption through sacrifice.

It's perhaps easier to make a case for *Five Fingers'* cultural significance than to argue that it's a classic of the genre. It isn't groundbreaking in the way that *The Big Boss* (1971) or *The 36th Chamber of Shaolin* (1978) are. But for a film that was, above all, in the right place at the right time, it holds up amazingly well—formulaic filmmaking of the most enjoyable kind. **LH**

▶
Balletic action—a scene from the hero's school for the martial arts.

McQUEEN/MacGRAW

THE GETAWAY

STEVE McQUEEN/ALI MacGRAW IN "THE GETAWAY" A FIRST ARTISTS PRESENTATION · CO-STARRING **BEN JOHNSON · AL LETTIERI** AND **SALLY STRUTHERS** AS "FRAN" · SCREENPLAY BY WALTER HILL · FROM THE NOVEL BY JIM THOMPSON · MUSIC BY QUINCY JONES · A SOLAR/FOSTER-BROWER PRODUCTION · PRODUCED BY DAVID FOSTER AND MITCHELL BROWER · DIRECTED BY SAM PECKINPAH · FILMED IN TODD-AO 35 · TECHNICOLOR® · A NATIONAL GENERAL PICTURES RELEASE **PG** PARENTAL GUIDANCE SUGGESTED

THE GETAWAY 1972 (U.S.)

Director Sam Peckinpah **Producer** Mitchell Brower, David Foster,
Gordon T. Dawson **Screenplay** Walter Hill (from a novel by Jim Thompson)
Cinematography Lucien Ballard **Music** Quincey Jones **Cast** Steve McQueen,
Ali MacGraw, Ben Johnson, Sally Struthers, Slim Pickens

By the time Sam Peckinpah had begun making *The Getaway,* he
had gained a reputation as a director of films fascinated with
violence, disorder, gun battles, and slow-motion carnage. His
films *The Wild Bunch* (1969) and *Straw Dogs* (1971) were particularly
controversial, and while *The Getaway* was actually made as a
satire of bank heist movies, there was no hiding its brutality,
shoot-outs, explosions, and orchestrated action scenes. *The
Getaway* functions within the conventions of the action-
gangster film, but it also connects with the Western genre, with
which Peckinpah had become most associated. Parallels have
been seen with his first film, *The Deadly Companions* (1961), a
Western that dramatizes the falling out of partners.

The script for *The Getaway* was by action filmmaker Walter
Hill, and was based on the novel by Jim Thompson, a writer of
harrowing pulp fiction, whose book was refilmed by Roger
Donaldson in 1994. Donaldson's remake placed the then-real-
life couple Alec Baldwin and Kim Basinger in the lead roles.
Such casting can perhaps be traced back to Peckinpah's film,
which put Steve McQueen and Ali MacGraw in the lead roles of
the fractured couple, Doc and Carol McCoy, that off-screen saw

◄
**Peckinpah's
trademark gory
Western updated
for a road-gangster
thriller with two big
macs—McQueen
and MacGraw.**

them have an affair and marry in 1973. In the film, this modern-day Bonnie and Clyde are involved in a series of getaways from the law, and a corrupt businessman, Jack Benyon (Ben Johnson), and his henchmen. Also in pursuit is the tough Rudy Butler (Al Lettieri), who attempted to double-cross the McCoys following the bank robbery but was gunned down by Doc, only to be saved by his bulletproof vest. Mr. and Mrs. McCoy escape to El

"YOU KNOW I CAN SCREW EVERY PRISON OFFICIAL IN TEXAS IF I HAVE TO!" CAROL MCCOY

Paso, with refuge across the Mexican border being their goal. As with many other Peckinpah films, McCoy is a man who is operating out of his time. Leaving prison at the start of the film, he appears to be starting his retirement from robbing banks. Yet McCoy is a troubled hero, and as part of the film's satire of the bank heist genre it is revealed he has flaws. Doc and Carol clash repeatedly and are not effectively together as partners in crime. The garbage truck full of rubbish within which they take refuge during one getaway illustrates the distinct lack of glamor in this criminal lifestyle. Moreover, they are frequently compromised. During the bank robbery a guard is shot, Carol loses the luggage containing the loot at a train station when a conman tricks her by switching the keys to her locker, and Doc is recognized by a shopkeeper when his image is multiplied across TV sets in a shop. **IC**

► Doc McCoy (McQueen) blasts his way out of trouble cowboy-style—but with a pump-action shotgun—while his screen wife Carol (MacGraw) clutches the mobsters' loot.

THE POSEIDON ADVENTURE 1972 (U.S.)

Director Ronald Neame **Producer** Irwin Allen **Screenplay** Stirling Silliphant, Wendell Mayes (based on a novel by Paul Gallico) **Cinematography** Harold E. Stine **Music** John Williams **Cast** Gene Hackman, Ernest Borgnine, Stella Stevens, Red Buttons, Carol Lynley, Shelley Winters, Roddy McDowall

The box office success enjoyed by *The Poseidon Adventure* helped to kick-start a 1970s disaster movie cycle that included *Earthquake* (1974), *The Towering Inferno* (1974), and *Airport 1975* (1974). There had been films about major disasters before the 1970s, of course, but *The Poseidon Adventure* established a particular format that would resonate throughout later productions: a disaster connected with modern institutions, a starry cast, a small and socially diverse band of survivors reacting to events beyond their control, a perceived need for charismatic leadership, and an absolute ruthlessness in killing off characters. Seen together, these elements helped to give a sense of a world that was weak, vulnerable, and complacent, and that struggled to right itself in the disaster's aftermath.

A luxury liner is overturned by a giant tidal wave during New Years celebrations, and a group of ten survivors led by a no-nonsense priest (played by Gene Hackman) make their dangerous way through the upside-down ship to the engine room and eventual rescue. *The Poseidon Adventure*'s endorsement of positive action is underlined when all those who stay behind are drowned within a few seconds of the priest

◄

"Hell, Upside Down," screamed the marketing tagline for *The Poseidon Adventure*, and this is what the film duly provided. The visual effects earned a Special Achievement Award at the Oscars.

taking away his small band of believers. However, the self-reliance route is not without its pitfalls, and only six out of the original ten are still alive by the time the film concludes. Underlining the unforgiving toughness of the disaster movie experience, one partner from each of the happily married couples in the priest's group gets killed, and right at the end, the priest is forced to sacrifice himself to

> ## "... LET GOD KNOW THAT YOU HAVE THE GUTS AND THE WILL TO DO IT ALONE. YOURSELVES." *REV. SCOTT*

save the others, thus ensuring that the survivors' response to being rescued is not so much joy or relief as it is exhaustion.

► **The film's ideology is made clear shortly after the tidal wave has hit the ship. The survivors are given a choice: either act to save themselves under Gene Hackman's priest's leadership, or stay with the ship's purser and wait to be rescued.**

The Poseidon Adventure was produced by Irwin Allen—who would become firmly associated with the disaster movies for the rest of his career, most notably with *The Towering Inferno*—and directed by veteran British filmmaker Ronald Neame. It is worth seeing not just for its relentlessly downbeat quality but also for its extraordinarily claustrophobic atmosphere and its well-crafted moments of disturbing surrealism, as a familiar world is quite literally inverted and made strange. In terms of its narrative, at least, it is the most simple and pared-down of all the major 1970s disaster movies but remains a memorable experience. An inconsequential sequel, *Beyond the Poseidon Adventure* (1979), followed, and the original was "re-imagined," courtesy of C.G.I., as *Poseidon* in 2006. **PH.**

SLAUGHTER 1972 (U.S.)

Director Jack Starrett **Producer** Samuel Z. Arkoff, Monroe Sachson
Screenplay Mark Hanna, Don Williams **Cinematography** Rosalío Solano
Music Luchi De Jesus **Cast** Jim Brown, Rip Torn, Stella Stevens, Norman Alfe,
Don Gordon, Cameron Mitchell, Marlene Clarke, Robert Phillips, Marion Ashe

The simultaneous increase in gritty crime films and casting of black actors in leading roles in the late 1960s/early 1970s gave birth to the blaxploitation subgenre—action films featuring black heroes aimed at urban audiences—exploding across movie screens. Standing right alongside newfound stars like Richard Roundtree, Pam Grier, and Fred Williamson was real-life tough guy Jim Brown in *Slaughter*.

After the murder of his parents, Slaughter (Jim Brown) takes to the streets to get his revenge. His impulsive methods draw the attention of the U.S. government, and it quickly enlists the former Green Beret for a mission in South America. Slaughter is to find a super-computer utilized by Mafia kingpin Mario Felice (Norman Alfe). The assignment has special meaning for Slaughter, as his father had information about this group, and Felice's bigoted right-hand man Hoffo (Rip Torn) may have performed the killing.

As a blaxploitation film, the audience knows what to expect—smooth ladies' man, harsh dialogue, sultry women, funky score, and plenty of brawls. *Slaughter* sets itself apart, however, by removing the titular hero from the inner city and placing him in South America (the film was actually shot in

◄

Pump-action in a dinner jacket, macho N.F.L. fullback Jim Brown takes on the mafioso.

Mexico). The mafia plot echoes *The Godfather* (1972), and the scenario involving a super-computer with Slaughter showing up in a tuxedo to a casino produces an almost James Bond-esque feel. Of course, Slaughter lays down more cruel street-fighting punishment than Bond. The film wastes no time—within the first fifteen minutes Slaughter learns his parents were blown up, witnesses a friend being shot, shoots a mobster

"MAN, YOU'RE WEIRD, SLAUGHTER. I MEAN GODDAMMIT, YOU'RE JUST WEIRD." *HARRY*

in the head, smashes a plane with his car, roughs up a government agent, accepts a top secret assignment, and throws a naked woman out of his hotel room.

Key to the film's success is the lead performance from Jim Brown. Previously seen in supporting roles in action ensembles *The Dirty Dozen* (1967) and *Ice Station Zebra* (1968), Brown began establishing himself as a leading man in the late 1960s. With the explosion of the blaxploitation genre, a film like *Slaughter* on his resume seemed inevitable for the smooth-talking thespian. With his football physique, Brown creates a rugged authenticity to the role of a guy who hurls people off roofs and narrowly dodges speeding cars. The film proved to be a financial success with Brown returning for the action-packed sequel *Slaughter's Big Rip-Off* (1973). **WW**

► **Having played nine seasons of football for the Cleveland Browns, Brown brings a top level of athleticism that his contemporaries usually lacked.**

Their deadly mission: to crack the forbidden island of Han!

Enter The Dragon

The ultimate Martial Arts masterpiece! Lavishly filmed by Warner Bros. in Hong Kong and the China Sea!

ENTER THE DRAGON 1973 (HONG KONG • U.S.)

Director Robert Clouse **Producer** Paul M. Heller, Bruce Lee, Fred Weintraub,
Leonard Ho **Screenplay** Michael Allin **Cinematography** Gil Hubbs
Music Lalo Schifrin **Cast** Bruce Lee, John Saxon, Kien Shih, Ahna Capri, Angela Mao,
Jim Kelly, Robert Wall, Bolo Yeung, Betty Chung, Peter Archer

Enter the Dragon was the first Hollywood–Hong Kong
coproduction, the first English language kung fu film, the first
crossover vehicle for a Hong Kong star, and the final (complete)
film of one of action cinema's major icons.

If this indicates why the film is important, it also possibly
explains why it is prone to being either overrated ("the greatest
martial arts film ever made") or underrated (a dilution of Bruce
Lee for Western tastes). Tentative, compromised, and an
inevitably flawed mixture of styles and traditions, it nevertheless
remains a remarkable achievement. It may creak in places, but
Enter the Dragon includes some of the most iconic images in
action cinema—Lee wielding his nunchaku, to name just one.

If Ang Lee extended the audience for martial arts films in
2000 by making (in *Crouching Tiger, Hidden Dragon*) "*Sense and
Sensibility* with martial arts," *Enter the Dragon* did so with a
pulpier blend of James Bond, blaxploitation, and kung fu. This
formula doesn't come without some casualties—the film
inherits the colonial imagery of Bond (inscrutable one-handed
villain stroking white cat), and there's ongoing controversy
about Bruce Lee being saddled with two American costars

◄
**Warner Bros.
teamed up with
Lee's Hong Kong
production
company,
acknowledging
the man's already
immense on-screen
popularity in Asia.**

(exacerbated by John Saxon sharing equal billing with Lee). But Saxon and Jim Kelly are likable presences—this is perhaps the only Lee film that retains one's interest when the leading man is off-screen. Lee took charge of the fight sequences, none of which quite match his epic duel with Chuck Norris in the Colosseum in his previous film, *Way of the Dragon* (1972). His fight with Bob Wall's Oharra is brisk and economical, but

"WHAT'S YOUR STYLE?" PARSONS *"YOU CAN CALL IT THE ART OF FIGHTING WITHOUT FIGHTING."* LEE

testifies to Lee's breathtaking speed. Shaolin-monk-gone-bad Han proves a relatively ineffectual foe, either because of actor Shek Kin's advancing years or because of Lee's refusal to buy into the genre's tradition of formidable elderly fighters. While their fight in the hall of mirrors is fondly remembered, the film's most enduring action sequence is Lee's encounter with Han's guards in the island's underground caverns, whittling them down with pole, sticks, and nunchaku.

Enter the Dragon may not be the best example of Lee's on-screen persona, but it's unlikely to ever lose its place in the action canon. Bruce Lee's films may age around him—and Lee himself died before he could garner the accolades this action martial arts movie received on its release—but he remains vibrant and modern, and ultimately "charisma" is too small a word for his screen presence. **LH**

▶
One of several iconic moments in the movie: Lee is multiplied as he is reflected by mirrors, his glistening body bearing the wounds inflicted by Mr. Han's metallic claw.

FOXY BROWN 1974 (U.S.)

Director Jack Hill **Producer** Buzz Feitshans **Screenplay** Jack Hill
Cinematography Brick Marquard **Music** Willie Hutch **Cast** Pam Grier,
Antonio Fargas, Peter Brown, Terry Carter, Kathryn Loder, Harry Holcombe,
Sid Haig, Juanita Brown, Bob Minor, Fred Lemer

The wave of blaxploitation films, which stretched from the late 1960s to the mid-1970s, and which peaked around 1973, brought to the screen a group of iconic black leading actors that included Fred Williamson, Jim Kelly, Jim Brown, Pam Grier, and Tamara Dobson. Grier was the actress who came to represent blaxploitation, and *Foxy Brown* is one of her most recognizable roles. Grier effectively sealed her reputation the year before with the very successful *Coffy* (1973), produced by American International Pictures (AIP), and directed and scripted by Jack Hill. AIP hired Hill again to make *Foxy Brown* as a follow-up to *Coffy*, which as an exploitation action-gangster film foregrounded the subgenre's pulp elements of sex and violence. Such was the excessive nature of the film that eight minutes were cut from its British release.

Blaxploitation predominantly consists of black action films, with *Shaft* (1971), *Superfly* (1972), and *Truck Turner* (1973) as celebrated examples. Many of the films are grim, urban-set stories of organized crime, corruption, intimidation, revenge, drug dealing, and martial arts. In *Foxy Brown*, as in *Coffy*, Grier creates a trail of death and destruction as she seeks revenge for

◄
**Classic
blaxploitation.
The ever-watchable
Pam Grier is in
gun-toting revenge
mode, and every
white honky is
fair game.**

the loss of a loved one. Foxy's brother, Link (Antonio Fargas, who played Huggy Bear in *Starsky and Hutch*), reveals to drug dealers the secret narcotics agent identity of Foxy's boyfriend, who is subsequently killed. Independent and resourceful, Foxy works her way through to the heart of the gangsters' operations, which is headed by a drug queen, Katherine Wall (Kathryn Loder). En route, Brown expertly handles

"THE ONLY WAY TO HANDLE THOSE SMART-ASS HOODS IS WITH A BULLET IN THE GUT." *FOXY BROWN*

guns, cars, and a small airplane, which she drives through a gangster's ranch, using its propeller as a lethal weapon.

Grier's on-screen performance can be seen as an influence on 1980s tough broads as well as on Quentin Tarantino's *Jackie Brown* (1997) starring Pam Grier. In *Foxy Brown*, her almost comic-book action heroine effectively unites her femininity, sexuality, and physical dominance in a high-energy and single-minded character seeking retribution. She changes her identity to a prostitute in order to infiltrate the gang, hides her gun within her afro, and fights a bar full of karate-kicking lesbians. In the film's most extreme scene, Brown as the femme castrice literally castrates a leading gangster, Steve Elias (Peter Brown). He is the drug-queen's lover and as a final act of revenge, in which 1970s exploitation-action films appeared to delight, Brown presents her with the castrated part pickled in a jar. **IC**

▶
Grier is the precursor of the 1980s action heroine, and is followed by stars such as Cynthia Rothrock and Brigitte Neilsen.

THE TAKING OF PELHAM ONE TWO THREE 1974 (U.S.)

Director Joseph Sargent **Producer** Gabriel Katzka, Edgar J. Scherick
Screenplay Peter Stone **Cinematography** Owen Roizman **Music** David Shire
Cast Walter Matthau, Robert Shaw, Martin Balsam, Hector Elizondo, Earl Hindman,
Jerry Stiller, Julius Harris, James Broderick

New York City and crime—few simpler cinematic audience associations exist. Gene Hackman chased crooks through the NYC streets in *The French Connection* (1971) and Charles Bronson blasted Central Park muggers in *Death Wish* (1974). New York is crime and vice versa, according to Hollywood at least. And further helping to establish this connection is the action-thriller *The Taking of Pelham One Two Three* (1974).

Based on the novel by John Godey (pen name of Morton Freedgood), the film follows Zachary Garber (Walter Matthau), a lieutenant in the New York City Transportation Authority, whose routine day is interrupted when a group of armed men commandeer a subway car. The leader of the group (Robert Shaw), identified solely by his color-coded name Mr. Blue, relays a demand of $1 million dollars from the city in one hour before he starts killing hostages. From that point, it is a race as the city's political arm struggles to meet the demand while Garber tries to stave off the terrorist's impatience. Filled with nail-biting scenarios, the film is devoid of explosions and is instead filled

◄
Disaster-style movie meets terrorism head on. The formula worked well enough for two remakes: an ABC TV movie (1998) and a big budget, hi-tech, so-so update in 2009, directed by Tony Scott.

with brains and equally smart performances. Matthau brings a welcome everyman quality to the role, and Shaw is effectively chilly as the cold-blooded mercenary who is unflinching in his demands. The ensuing chess game between the two is completely enthralling. It is also a testament to the direction of Sargent that the adversarial relationship is so well formed, as the two leads spend ninety percent of the picture talking

> *"BE QUIET! NOW BE QUIET! NOTHING WILL HAPPEN AS LONG AS YOU OBEY MY ORDERS."* MR. BLUE

to each other via radio communication and have only one scene where the actors actually share the screen together.

Filmed at a time when New York City was in a political and economic shambles (thanks to an elevated crime rate and a political bureaucracy that had the city on the edge of bankruptcy), the city and its denizens are fantastic supporting characters. The film's screenplay highlights the city's fast pace and irascible reputation with characters as colorful as the Big Apple itself. Sharp dialogue allows everyone to get in a quip, including guys negotiating with armed criminals. There are also several well-placed jabs at inter-office squabbles and the political establishment.

Finally, in terms of influence, the designation of color-coded criminals resurfaced with a bang in the director Quentin Tarantino's debut *Reservoir Dogs* (1992). **WW**

▶

Robert Shaw is suitably sinister as the cold, calculating ex-mercenary bargaining with people's lives for a big payoff.

THUNDERBOLT AND LIGHTFOOT

1974 (U.S.)

Director Michael Cimino **Producer** Robert Daley **Screenplay** Michael Cimino
Cinematography Frank Stanley **Music** Dee Barton **Cast** Clint Eastwood,
Jeff Bridges, Geoffrey Lewis, Catherine Bach, Gary Busey, Jack Dodson, Gene
Elman, Bill McKineey, Erica Hagen, Buton Gilliam

Known for giving young directors a break, Clint Eastwood took
a gamble on the later legendary (but not for all the right
reasons) director Michael Cimino in this lighthearted action
film. Cimino, who would go on to win an Oscar for *The Deer
Hunter* (1978) and almost single-handedly ruin United Artists
and his own career with *Heaven's Gate* (1980), had impressed
Eastwood with the work he'd done on the rewrites for the
second Dirty Harry movie, *Magnum Force* (1973), a year earlier.
When he read his script for *Thunderbolt and Lightfoot*, he not only
wanted to be a part of it, but suggested that Cimino direct it, too.

Buddy movies live or die by the chemistry of the partnership
at the center of them; this one is perfectly judged and arguably
set the template for such odd couple pairings for years to come
(even between Clint and the orangutan in *Every Which Way But
Loose* four years later—albeit a slightly different buddy). Cimino
told Jeff Bridges that it was his job to make Eastwood laugh,
both on-screen and off. He did, and the result is a joy to behold.
While we still get the tough-guy Clint we all know and love,
there's a frivolity present that we're unused to seeing from him.

◀
**Noteworthy for
its laid-back
tone, prescient
for action-buddy
movies, and the
fact that all does
not end happily
(always a gamble)
for the "heroes."**

The plot is standard but amiable fare. After a failed attempt on preacher man Eastwood's life, our mismatched antiheroes are thrown together when Lightfoot (Bridges) runs over and kills the hitman. Speeding away in a stolen car, the two soon discover they have more in common than they thought. Eastwood is actually a retired bank robber by the name of Thunderbolt who is in hiding from the rest of the gang with whom he pulled a

"THUNDERBOLT AND LIGHTFOOT. THAT SOUNDS LIKE SOMETHING."

LIGHTFOOT

heist. Apparently it was a success, but no one can find the cash and he's getting the blame. Lightfoot is a small-time crook who dreams of bigger things and eventually persuades his new buddy to pull the same job again. They also decide to rope in the rest of the gang—yes, the ones that just moments ago were trying to kill them. Trouble inevitably ensues.

Set in Montana, Cimino makes the most of the landscape that surrounds him and produces the kind of movie you could never have made in a back lot in California. He also provides us with enough pokes at domesticity and a good helping of gags to keep things lighthearted, despite the obvious wrongdoings of our heroes and the violence and death they encounter on their quest. The supporting cast also gives good value, especially the dependable George Kennedy as the unhinged and excessively violent Red. **RP**

▶
"You ain't no country preacher, Preacher."
Thunderbolt (Eastwood) suffering in disguise in the Montana hills.

STEVE
McQUEEN

PAUL
NEWMAN

WILLIAM
HOLDEN

FAYE
DUNAWAY

IRWIN ALLEN's production of

THE TOWERING INFERNO

ONE
TINY SPARK
BECOMES
A NIGHT
OF BLAZING
SUSPENSE

The tallest
building
in the world
is on fire.
You are there
with 294
other guests.
There's no
way down.
There's no
way out.

The Fire Chief

The Architect

THE TOWERING INFERNO 1974 (U.S.)

Director Irwin Allen, John Guillermin **Producer** Irwin Allen, Sidney Marshall
Screenplay Stirling Silliphant **Cinematography** Fred J. Koenekamp **Cast** Paul
Newman, Steve McQueen, William Holden, Faye Dunaway, Fred Astaire, Susan Blakely,
Richard Chamberlain, Jennifer Jones, Robert Vaughn, Robert Wagner, O. J. Simpson

In celebration of creating the world's tallest building, the 138-floor Glass Tower, architect Doug Roberts (Paul Newman) and constructor James Duncan (William Holden) throw an extravagant soiree in the upper floors of the building. However, unbeknown to both, the building's wiring has been fitted on the cheap by Duncan's son-in-law Roger Simmons (Richard Chamberlain) leaving the building a potential death trap. As an array of well-heeled guests party the night away, a power outage sets light to some waste on the building's eighty-fifth floor. With everyone trapped above the rapidly rising flames, it falls to Roberts and the local fire chief, Michael O'Hallorhan (Steve McQueen), to avert disaster and devise a way to save everyone from the towering inferno that is fast enveloping the building. What follows is a template for disaster movies everywhere: as some of the famous names on show spectacularly bite the dust, others are spectacularly rescued, and the set spectacularly blows up on a regular basis.

Never had so many Hollywood stars faced quite so much peril at the same time. Boasting a cast of Hollywood luminaries, from then-massive stars McQueen and Newman, to faces from

◀
After much contractual negotiation, the credits were arranged diagonally in an attempt to negate any friction between the film's coleads, McQueen and Newman.

the industry's illustrious past such as Holden and Fred Astaire and newer players such as Robert Vaughn, Robert Wagner, and former American Football star O.J. Simpson. The scale of the film meant that it boasted a healthy $14 million budget and utilized two directors, veteran John Guillermin and producer-cum-director Irwin Allen, the latter of whom would focus upon co-coordinating the numerous high-octane scenes. The film

"FOR WHAT IT'S WORTH . . . THIS IS ONE BUILDING I FIGURED WOULD NEVER BURN." CHIEF O'HALLORHAN

is also notorious for co-lead McQueen's contractual wranglings, as he tried to ensure that his name would appear both above, and in slightly bigger letters than, Newman's. The result was a fudge.

As part of a glut of 1970s disaster movies that included such offerings as *Airport*, *The Poseidon Adventure*, *Earthquake*, *Airport 1975*, *Airport '77*, *The Cassandra Crossing*, and *Rollercoaster*, *The Towering Inferno* is undoubtedly the most iconic due to both the array of Hollywood talent on display and the scale of the movie's production. And, although the disaster genre would be later spoofed mercilessly with *Airplane!*, *The Towering Inferno* was a genuine genre high point, with a lavish cast, rollicking script, and utterly spectacular action-direction. It also leaves a stark message for the future: do not let greed get in the way of human safety. **RH**

► Paul Newman tries to evacuate the all-star cast from his blazing skyscraper in this epitome of the early 1970s disaster movie.

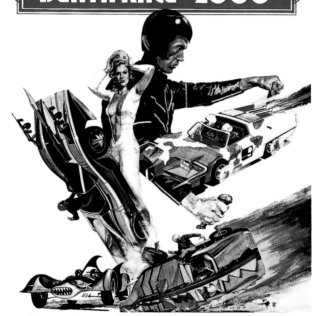

IN THE YEAR 2000 HIT AND RUN DRIVING IS NO LONGER A FELONY. IT'S THE NATIONAL SPORT!

DAVID CARRADINE
DEATH RACE 2000

DEATH RACE 2000
A CROSS COUNTRY ROAD WRECK

CO-STARRING **SIMONE GRIFFETH** • SYLVESTER STALLONE • LOUISA MORITZ • DON STEELE

SCREENPLAY BY ROBERT THOM and CHARLES B. GRIFFITH   ORIGINAL STORY BY IB MELCHIOR   PRODUCED BY ROGER CORMAN   DIRECTED BY PAUL BARTEL

METROCOLOR   **R** RESTRICTED

"DEATH RACE 2000"

DEATH RACE 2000 1975 (U.S.)

Director Paul Bartel **Producer** Roger Corman **Screenplay** Robert Thom, Charles Griffith **Cinematography** Tak Fujimoto **Music** Paul Chihara
Cast David Carradine, Simone Griffeth, Sylvester Stallone, Mary Woronov, Roberta Collins, Martin Kove, Louisa Moritz

As a prolific producer, king of the B-movies Roger Corman certainly knows how to please an audience, even if that sometimes means delivering superficially derivative films. Taking its cue from Norman Jewison's then-recent *Rollerball* (1975), *Death Race 2000* is based on a short story written by Ib Melchior, and is quite obviously set in a dystopian near future. David Carradine stars as Frankenstein, a driver who takes part in an annual transcontinental road race from New York to "New Los Angeles," while a group of rebels named The Army of the Resistance tries to abolish the competition by neutralizing all of the participants one by one with the help of an insider.

Made with a budget of approximately $300,000, *Death Race 2000* offers high-speed car races that may seem exciting but were clearly filmed at a reasonable speed and then accelerated during the editing process (using maybe the low-cost technique of frame-skipping). The vehicles themselves are customized and armed to look like chariots from ancient Rome; this resemblance to the often violent circus games is further enhanced by the killings of innocent passersby, which enables the players to earn points and are displayed with gory inserts. The film's attitude

◄

Self-destructive irony was just one of the explosive combinations in the films made by New World Pictures during the 1970s.

toward violence appears to be ambiguous, as it simultaneously criticizes its use by government that advocates the destruction of liberty for political purposes, and capitalizes on it in order to satisfy the expectations of some spectators.

Although there has been some debate regarding the modifications made by Corman himself after a public preview to increase the degree of violence offered by the film to the

"I WANTED A DARK . . . STRANGELOVIAN COMEDY THAT WOULD COMMENT ON INSTITUTIONALIZED VIOLENCE." ROGER CORMAN

detriment of its comedy elements, it should be noted that New World Pictures' productions were rarely straight (a lesson that Joe Dante, one of Corman's most talented employees, will remember), and *Death Race 2000* still remains interesting up to this day mainly for its satirical approach.

Paul Bartel, who began his career as a director with *The Secret Cinema* (1968), a seminal short film about a woman who suspects that her daily life is secretly filmed, doesn't miss a lot of targets: he pokes at the cynicism of politicians, journalists, and the media (and their necessary collusion with the institutions), the nature of heroism, fans and fan culture, the active support of religious authorities, and euthanasia, just to name a few. A cartoonish, tongue-in-cheek—some might say preposterous—sensibility prevails, notably through the over-the-top characterization of the competitors who look like wrestlers. **FL**

►

Sylvester Stallone is Carradine's archrival for driving supremacy and top movie billing. Both actors did much of their own driving for the movie.

ROLLERBALL

IN THE NOT TOO DISTANT FUTURE,
WARS WILL NO LONGER EXIST.
BUT THERE WILL BE ROLLERBALL.

JAMES CAAN in
A NORMAN JEWISON Film "ROLLERBALL"
starring JOHN HOUSEMAN · MAUD ADAMS · JOHN BECK · MOSES GUNN
PAMELA HENSLEY · BARBARA TRENTHAM and RALPH RICHARDSON
Screenplay by WILLIAM HARRISON · Music Conducted by ANDRE PREVIN
Associate Producer PATRICK PALMER · Produced and Directed by NORMAN JEWISON

ROLLERBALL 1975 (U.S.)

Director Norman Jewison **Producer** Norman Jewison **Screenplay** William
Harrison **Cinematography** Douglas Slocombe **Music** André Previn
Cast James Caan, John Houseman, Maud Adams, John Beck, Moses Gunn, Pamela
Hensley, Barbara Trentham, John Normington, Ralph Richardson, Shane Rimmer

Rollerball belongs to a cycle of 1970s American dystopian
dramas; other films of its type include *THX 1138* (1971), *Soylent
Green* (1973), and *Logan's Run* (1976). As a group, they project
forward into not-too-distant futures a range of contemporary
social and political anxieties. However, *Rollerball* remains the
most violent and opaque of the bunch.

Adapted by William Harrison from his own short story, and
directed by Norman Jewison (fresh from success in quite a
different genre with the musicals *Fiddler on the Roof* and *Jesus
Christ Superstar*), *Rollerball* is set in a world in which corporations
have replaced democratic governments and where the only
emotional outlet for a compliant population is a violent contact
sport called rollerball.

The film follows Jonathan, a champion rollerball player, as he
attempts to discover why the corporate authorities want him to
retire. Ultimately it is revealed that the game's social function is
to demonstrate the futility of individual action, and that
Jonathan's success and popularity is threatening this. The film
concludes with an especially brutal rollerball contest with the
odds stacked up against Jonathan.

◀

**An action movie
with pretensions to
art house quality,
to the extent that
Harrison has
compared the film
to the European
art house classic
*Last Year at
Marienbad* (1961).**

Rollerball focuses mainly on the social elite who lead comfortable but soulless existences, with a desire for violence lurking just beneath the surface. This is most obvious in their fascination with the rollerball game, but it manifests in other ways, especially in a scene in which a band of partygoers in evening dress torch a beautiful tall pine tree for no reason other than their own decadent delight.

"MISPLACE SOME DATA?" JONATHAN *"THE WHOLE OF THE THIRTEENTH CENTURY."* LIBRARIAN

Rollerball's action is confined to the rollerball scenes themselves, and the visualization of these is the film's greatest achievement. There are three increasingly violent game scenes, which are all filmed in a realist style that bestows an absolute believability on the game itself.

The paradox of a film that is both antiviolence and packed full of exciting combat scenes is not finally resolved, and the film's conclusion is suitably ambiguous. A victorious Jonathan is being cheered on by the crowds when the image suddenly freezes. The consequences of his victory—for himself, the game, and for society—are deliberately left unclear. It is a mark of *Rollerball*'s ambition and seriousness that it is prepared to offer such a provocatively open ending, but it is also a limitation, with the film apparently incapable of imagining any positive way forward for this bleak, oppressive world. **PH**

► *Rollerball*, as personified by Jonathan (James Caan), conveys brilliantly the sport's visceral excitement while at the same time seeks to edge us to a realization of its appalling elements.

A WHITE-HOT NIGHT OF HATE!

ASSAULT ON PRECINCT 13

THE GANG THAT SWORE A BLOOD OATH TO DESTROY PRECINCT 13... AND EVERY COP IN IT!

IRWIN YABLANS Presents a CKK PRODUCTION "ASSAULT ON PRECINCT 13"

Starring AUSTIN STOKER

DARWIN JOSTON · LAURIE ZIMMER · Executive Producer JOSEPH KAUFMAN

R RESTRICTED   Written and Directed by JOHN CARPENTER · PANAVISION˙ METROCOLOR˙ Distributed by

©Copyright 1976 CKK Corporation   Produced by J.S. KAPLAN

ASSAULT ON PRECINCT 13 1976 (U.S.)

Director John Carpenter **Producer** J.S. Kaplan **Screenplay** John Carpenter
Cinematography Douglas Knapp **Music** John Carpenter **Cast** Austin Stoker,
Darwin Joston, Laurie Zimmer, Martin West, Tony Burton, Charles Cyphers,
Nancy Kyes, Kim Richards, Peter Bruni, John J. Fox

Although its screenplay is said to be inspired by the bloody
Watts Riots of 1965, *Assault on Precinct 13* clearly doesn't strive to
consciously produce a social and/or political comment—
something its director John Carpenter would later do in films
such as *They Live* (1988). Central to his playful approach is the
transformation of contemporary material into some kind of
realist modern and (pseudo)urban Western picture that is
combined with various horror components, with the main
theme of the siege linking the two genres. It's quite notorious
that here Howard Hawks's *Rio Bravo* (1959) stands as the prime
example of the first genre, and George Romero's *Night of the
Living Dead* (1968) of the second (but film buffs will no doubt
spot other interloping references).

Much has been said about the supposed political view of
Assault. The whole story revolves around a small group of
people (policemen, secretaries, convicts) besieged inside a
soon-to-be abandoned police station by a street gang, after
one of its warlords has just been killed by a vengeful father and
six young members have been shot down by merciless officers.
Some critics stress that the depiction of the armed gang as a

◀

**Contrary to
contemporary
action films, the
narrative here
knows how to take
its time, but as
the story unfolds,
action rises
relentlessly to
a crescendo.**

horde of faceless assailants betrays a right-winged point of view. They represent the monstrous Other, like the Native Americans in the Westerns (the group is multiracial but mostly nonwhite), or the creatures that haunt the horror genre (they are unstoppable ghostly figures that move in the dark without making any sound). If certain details do indeed corroborate this interpretation, other elements of the film, such as the

"BASICALLY, THIS IS AN EXPLOITATION ACTION PICTURE MODELED AFTER RIO BRAVO." *JOHN CARPENTER*

dehumanization of the policemen during the initial shoot-out sequence, illustrate a more progressive stance. This profound ambiguity can be found in most of the pictures that Carpenter went on to do afterwards.

From a stylistic angle, it should be noted that this first professional feature film by John Carpenter manages to build up tension through what will soon become part of his trademark. A precise use of the Panavision widescreen aspect ratio is mixed with frequent dolly shots, whose slowness gives an eerie feeling (even to the sunny Los Angeles exteriors where much of the action takes place during the first sequences). The extreme simplicity and the repetitive aspects of the electronic score (composed by the director himself), as well as the crosscut editing that prepares the ground for the main confrontation(s), effectively convey a sense of dread. **FL**

▶

In *Assault*, pure efficiency seems to be the key word, both for the director and the characters—a lesson that the 2005 remake is not able to retain.

THE ANNUAL TRANS-AMERICAN OUTLAW ROAD RACE—
A CROSS COUNTRY DEMOLITION DERBY WITHOUT RULES!

SEE THE PILE-UP OF THE CENTURY!

DAVID CARRADINE is _____

CANNONBALL

CANNONBALL • A FILM BY PAUL BARTEL starring BILL McKINNEY • VERONICA HAMEL
BELINDA BALASKI • ARCHIE HAHN as Zippo   Produced by SAM GELFMAN • Directed by PAUL BARTEL
Screenplay by PAUL BARTEL and DONALD C. SIMPSON • Executive Producers RUN RUN SHAW and GUSTAVE BERNE   Metrocolor

A NEW WORLD PICTURES RELEASE   A Shaw Brothers Ltd. and Harbor Productions Inc. Presentation
of a Cross-Country Production

CANNONBALL 1976 (U.S.)

Director Paul Bartel **Producer** Samuel W. Gelfman, Run Run Shaw, Peter Cornberg, Gustave M. Berne **Screenplay** Paul Bartel, Don Simpson **Cinematography** Tak Fujimoto **Music** David A. Axelrod **Cast** David Carradine, Bill McKinney, Veronica Hamel, Robert Carradine, Gerrit Graham, Mary Woronov, Archie Hahn

Following the huge success of *Death Race 2000* (1975) the previous year, Roger Corman's New World Pictures again signed up director Paul Bartel for this high-octane car chase movie. It had some competition, although *Death Race* had had such an impact on audiences that it spawned a rash of copycats, the most notable being *The Gumball Rally* (1976), which arrived in cinemas at pretty much the same time but played things more for laughs.

While Bartel was again working with his *Death Race* star (David Carradine), he was never really happy helming the project. He had virtually no interest in cars and was very aware that another hit could easily pigeonhole him for life as an action director. To his credit, this lack of enthusiasm is barely noticeable. The entire cast and impressive crew—including legendary Chinese action producer Run Run Shaw and writer Don Simpson, who would go on to produce *Top Gun* (1986) and *Beverly Hills Cop* (1984)—throw themselves into the making of a hugely enjoyable and explosive flick.

The action centers on an illegal coast-to-coast road race that is held every year, "The Trans-America Grand Prix," in which

◄

Director Bartel and star Carradine teamed up again to repeat the success of *Death Race 2000*. Michael Avallone was responsible for novelizing this film and *The Cannonball Run* (1981).

anything with four wheels is invited to take part in a scramble from Santa Monica to the finish line in New York. The $100,000 prize money is tempting enough to drag our hero, Coy "Cannonball" Buckman (Carradine), a legendary racer, out of retirement even though just one speeding ticket could land him back in jail—something his smoking-hot girlfriend and parole officer Linda Maxwell (a pre-*Hill Street Blues* Veronica

"ONE SPEEDING TICKET AND YOU'RE BACK IN PRISON. THAT'S OUR FUTURE . . . I'M LEGALLY RESPONSIBLE . . ." *LINDA*

Hamel) is swift to point out. In the end, she's persuaded to come along for the ride . . . to keep him out of trouble, obviously.

The full-throttle action that follows never lets up for a second, as Buckman in his souped-up red Trans Am screams across the screen in a bid for victory. In hot pursuit is the obligatory lineup of oddball characters that provide the comic relief. But babes, car crashes, fights, explosions, and a fistful of gags aside, one of the best reasons for watching this is to play "spot the director cameo." Bartel is particularly good as a mobster with Cole Porter pretensions, who serenades Buckman's brother as his goons beat him to a pulp for unpaid gambling debts. And at least six others pop up, including Roger Corman, Joe Dante, and Martin Scorsese (who is seen sharing a bucket of chicken with an unknown Sylvester Stallone). It may not be one of cinema's most poetic creations, but if it's action you're after, *Cannonball* delivers. **RP**

▶
The climax is one of cinema's most over-the-top crash scenes, where at least twenty assorted cars and trucks explode into a giant fireball on the New Jersey turnpike.

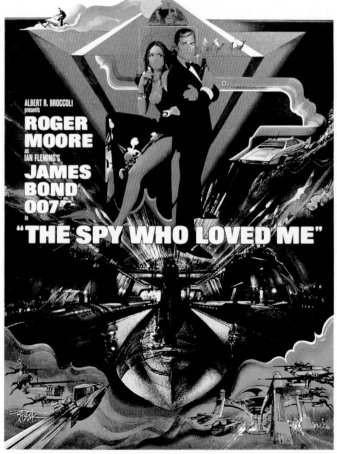

THE SPY WHO LOVED ME 1977 (U.K.)

Director Lewis Gilbert **Producer** Albert R. Broccoli **Screenplay** Christopher Wood, Richard Maibaum **Cinematography** Claude Renoir **Music** Marvin Hamlisch

Cast Roger Moore, Barbara Bach, Curt Jurgens, Richard Kiel, Caroline Munro, Walter Gozell, Bernard Lee, Lois Maxwell, Desmond Llewellyn

This was the debonair Roger Moore's third outing as James Bond, and the looming shadow of Sean Connery was at last receding into the mists. Moore is the most accurate representation of his creator; Ian Fleming may have fancied himself as an action hero in the Connery mold, but stories suggest his persona was similar to the one Moore developed. Although Fleming didn't have such a sense of fun, Moore is the 007 who always has a remarkably good time and doesn't take himself too seriously in the process.

The Spy Who Loved Me opens with one of the greatest precredit sequences of any movie. Sure, it was an established Bond tradition to throw in the kitchen sink to grab immediate attention; this drove the screenwriters, direction, cast, and crew to dizzying heights on each successive picture. Here was one they've never yet surpassed. Mountains, skis, the chase, Bond trapped into hurtling into a crevasse from which there can be no escape. He plunges into the abyss, to doom, until . . . a button pressed, and a Union Jack parachute floats him far from pursuit to safety on patriotic winds (remarkably, for the Austrian Alps). Cue audience applause and all-around smiles.

◄

This was the first Bond movie to feature an American doing the music, Marvin Hamlisch, who also cowrote the Oscar-nominated theme song "Nobody Does it Better" with Carole Bayer Sager (sung by Carly Simon).

Stromberg, the villain, played by the impressively rugged Curt Jurgens, perhaps lacks the magnificent, sonorous menace of predecessor Christopher Lee, or the fastidious precision of Michel Lonsdale, his successor, but he sets the plot (ridiculous hokum involving hijacked nuclear submarines from East and West as the Cold War thaws) and action in motion from his underwater lair to wonderful effect. And those action scenes

"STILL, YOU DID SAVE MY LIFE." JAMES BOND
"WE ALL MAKE MISTAKES, MR. BOND."

MAJOR ANYA AMASOVA

depend on one man: Jaws. Richard Kiel contrives to make the Alps look small. An unbelievably formidable opponent for 007, he is tackled with suave panache by Moore, ex-star of the TV shows *The Saint* and *The Persuaders*, who's no stranger to brawls. Their clashes are titanic: the producers swiftly re-engaged Jaws as the heavy in *Moonraker (1979)*.

As the leading girl, Barbara Bach (also known as Mrs. Ringo Starr) is a worthy adversary who metamorphoses without effort into a highly credible love interest. She receives more double entendres than any other Bond heroine—surely the highest of accolades that can be bestowed. In addition there's sultry Caroline Munro, imperious sultana of Lamb's Navy Rum advertising fame, to whet jaded appetites. And it's that mixture of happy pre-Aids sex and romance with staggering action that filmgoers remember. **MH**

► The Lotus Esprit S1 turbo sports car gives Bond's classic Aston Martin DB5 a good run for its money as the secret agent's most iconic car—especially with its sleek, submarine features.

To break the driver, the cop was willing to break the law.

THE DRIVER

A LAWRENCE GORDON PRODUCTION RYAN O'NEAL · BRUCE DERN · ISABELLE ADJANI in "THE DRIVER"
Co-Starring RONEE BLAKLEY · Associate Producer FRANK MARSHALL · Produced by LAWRENCE GORDON
Written and Directed by WALTER HILL · Music MICHAEL SMALL · A Twentieth Century-Fox /EMI Films Presentation

780004

"THE DRIVER"

THE DRIVER 1978 (U.S. • U.K.)

Director Walter Hill **Producer** Lawrence Gordon **Screenplay** Walter Hill
Cinematography Philip Lathrop **Music** Michael Small **Cast** Ryan O'Neal,
Bruce Dern, Isabelle Adjani, Ronee Blakley, Matt Clark, Felice Orlandi,
Joseph Walsh, Rudy Ramos, Frank Bruno, Denny Macko

In Walter Hill's second film as a director, a particularly talented
professional getaway driver (Ryan O'Neal) succeeds in escaping
the police after a robbery, but he crosses the path of a cop
(Bruce Dern) who becomes so obsessed with catching him that
he blackmails a bunch of trigger-happy hoodlums into hiring
him for a new "fake" heist. A cat-and-mouse game between the
two men then ensues.

   If such a story can't really be praised for its novelty, *The Driver*,
as a self-conscious, neo-noir film, nevertheless manages to
transcend its narrative material through a rather impressive
degree of stylization and abstraction. Both main characters are
plunged into a highly depersonalized environment: despite all
the money he makes, O'Neal lives in seedy hotels or rented
rooms that are devoid of personal touches; Dern doesn't seem
to have an office and works inside a gray van parked in seedy
alleys, when he is not bringing suspects into an empty bar in
order to interrogate them. A skillful use of Los Angeles—a city
that is more often than not reduced to wet and deserted
streets, claustrophobic parking lots, labyrinthine warehouses,
and tunnels—gives the movie a sense of pervasive desolation.

◄

**As befits the noir
genre instilled
by Walter Hill's
direction, Bruce
Dern and Ryan
O'Neal's characters
are defined mainly,
if not only, by
their actions.**

Such a lifeless quality is consistent with the fact that none of the characters are given names: all are merely designed by their function (The Driver, The Detective, and so forth), and this unusual bias illustrates their complete lack of social interaction or involvement, except on a purely professional basis. Even Isabelle Adjani's attractive character won't elicit any emotional response from O'Neal—nor will he really elicit one from her. As

> ## "I THINK THE DRIVER WAS THE PUREST SCRIPT THAT I EVER WROTE."
>
> *WALTER HILL*

it was the case with the German *Kammerspiel* films of the 1920s, this anonymity produces strong archetypes, but here it also expresses an existential angst.

Before it ends with a status quo or bleak lose-lose situation, *The Driver* offers more than a thrill. While the protracted high-speed car chases are all filmed without music (and virtually without any word), the emphasis on the screeching of tires and the sound of sirens give them a kind of realistic, almost organic feel. *The Driver* remains calm—even deadpan.

The spectator, however, has to shudder because of Hill's directorial choices: fast cuts, subjective shots, and the camera placed near the ground, for example. Sometimes he uses reflections on car windows to further suggest the isolation of a character whose life is entirely centered on and can be reduced to his driving abilities. **FL**

► The movie, with plenty of high-speed car chases, was originally written for Steve McQueen—he presumably would have brought along his superb *Bullitt* (1968) and *Le Mans* (1971) stunt driving skills.

DRUNKEN MASTER 1978 (HONG KONG)

Director Yuen Woo-Ping **Producer** Ng See-Yuen **Screenplay** Lung Hsiao,
Ng See-Yuen, Yuen Woo-Ping **Cinematography** Chang Hui **Music** Chou Fu Liang
Cast Jackie Chan, Siu Tien Yuen (as Su Hua Chi/Sam Seed), Jang Lee Hwang,
Hsia Hsu, Tien Lung Chen, Ging Man Fung, Linda Lin

Often hailed as the greatest classic kung fu film of all time,
Drunken Master is certainly one of the most influential and the
one cited by many a Jackie Chan fan as their favorite. Reuniting
the team of Chan and director Yuen Woo-Ping, who had found
success with *Snake in the Eagle's Shadow* (1978), the film displays
a tongue-in-cheek flair that would become the star's trademark.
Indeed, if there is one film in Chan's career where you can
pinpoint the transition from the old-fashioned to the new, it's
this one. Chan's performance displays his growing confidence
as an artist—both his physical genius and the comedic charm
and charisma that would eventually make him a global star are
all in evidence here. Basically, *Drunken Master* set the tone for
almost all his subsequent movies.

The plot is sketchy in all senses of the word. It's effectively
broken down into what amounts to little more than a series of
sketches. In effect, there's just not the room for a complicated
plot when a movie is seventy-five percent action. The stunning
fight scenes alone were deemed worth the price of an
admission ticket and stand up well even today, as do some of
Chan's death-defying stunts.

◄
**Yuen Woo-Ping
eventually
found fame in
Hollywood as the
choreographer
of the mind-
blowingly brilliant
fight scenes in *The
Matrix* (1999) and
*Crouching Tiger,
Hidden Dragon*
(2000).**

We begin with some entertaining scenes designed to introduce us to our star—the folk hero Wong Fei Hung (Chan) as a young man. Portrayed here as a rather impish and naive character, Wong gets himself embroiled in all types of trouble (cue some jaw-dropping fight scenes) with some unlikely opponents, including his teacher and the mother of a girl he fancies. After one too many of these kung fu action encounters,

"AN UNDISCIPLINED BOY MUST LEARN DRUNKEN FIST KUNG FU IN ORDER TO STOP AN ASSASSIN." SU HUA CHI / SAM SEED

his father decides to take matters into his own hands and sends his errant son away to be disciplined by the infamous drunken kung fu master, Su Hua Chi (Sam Seed), who is also notorious for torturing his students.

Much humor is to be found in the irreverent master-student relationship that develops between the two stars, as well as Wong's attempts to escape or cheat his way out of training before he inevitably buckles down and tries to master the Eight Drunken God Styles. Keep an eye out for the "five-hour water stance," where he is forced to squat over a wooden spike while balancing cups on his body. The skills he learns will eventually help him as he tries to save his father's life from some unscrupulous property developers.

A career milestone for Chan, and one of his personal favorites, the movie also showcases the talent of its director. **RP**

▶
This is 1970s chop-socky at its best. Here, Jackie Chan fends off his sadistic teacher.

THE FIVE DEADLY VENOMS
1978 (HONG KONG)

Director Cheh Chang **Producer** Mona Fong, Run Run Shaw
Screenplay Cheh Chang, Kuang Ni **Cinematography** Kung Mo To,
Hui-Chi Tsao **Music** Chen Yung-Yu **Cast** Sheng Chiang, Philip Kwok,
Chien Sun, Meng Lo, Feng Lu, Pai Wei, Meng Lo, Lung Wei Wang

A fantastic introduction to the Shaw Brothers catalog, this superb example of their kung fu movies is directed by the godfather of Hong Kong action, Cheh Chang. While best known for their martial arts movies, the Shaws were nothing if not prolific, and churned out literally hundreds of movies in their time, including some more modern crime and gangster-related epics as well as taking a trip (in all senses of the word) into the popular psychedelic freakout films of the day.

The plot of *The Five Deadly Venoms*, however, is not trippy, but a beautifully crafted tale about a young martial arts student, Yang Tieh (Sheng Chiang), who is summoned by the master of his school and head of the Poison Clan, to his death bed. He's charged with the task of tracking down the master's former students to make sure they have not gone to the dark side and are not bringing the school's reputation into disrepute.

This is no mean feat. Yang has to first figure out the identities of these mysterious warriors before deciding who is corrupt and who, if anyone, he can trust. It cracks along at a decent pace thanks largely to good direction.

◀

The Five Deadly Venoms is a story of heroism and mystery, which makes for a well-acted, directed, and choreographed drama that has certainly lasted the test of time, and one whose influence is still felt today.

Such a complicated story could have easily become confusing in the hands of a lesser talent. The neat trick in this film is that each of the protagonists, while all having trained under the same man, have each been schooled differently, so they have their own set of special skills (and weaknesses). A special mention needs to go to martial arts master Leung Ting for this, as he was the genius behind the development of each

> ## "ONCE AN EVIL DEED IS DONE, THEN IT NEVER ENDS . . . IT GOES ON AND IT GOES ON FOREVER." SCORPION

of these fight styles. And boy does that work pay off. They all have really cool names, too: Centipede (whose superfast punches are designed to break bones), Snake, Scorpion, Lizard (who can scale walls), and Toad. On reflection, Toad may not be a supercool name, but he is impervious to all attacks from blades and other projectiles, which kind of makes up for it.

The fight scenes are groundbreaking stuff, though they feature exactly the meticulously choreographed moves we've become accustomed to, particularly from Asian cinema, over the years. You'll also notice their influence in such modern classics as Tarantino's *Kill Bill* (2003). Here, though, the action is almost entirely made up of hand-to-hand combat, gymnastics, and some wire work (with the odd projectile literally thrown into the mix for Toad's benefit). And some of the sequences astonishingly last for several minutes without a cut. **RP**

► The movie offers five distinct styles of kung fu fighting, as our student-hero is charged with seeking out five other mysterious students who may have defected to the dark side.

YOU'LL BELIEVE A MAN CAN FLY.

ALEXANDER SALKIND presents MARLON BRANDO · GENE HACKMAN in a RICHARD DONNER FILM

SUPERMAN

STARRING   ALSO STARRING

CHRISTOPHER REEVE · NED BEATTY · JACKIE COOPER · GLENN FORD · TREVOR HOWARD · MARGOT KIDDER
VALERIE PERRINE · MARIA SCHELL · TERENCE STAMP · PHYLLIS THAXTER · SUSANNAH YORK

STORY BY MARIO PUZO · SCREENPLAY BY MARIO PUZO, DAVID NEWMAN, LESLIE NEWMAN and ROBERT BENTON
CREATIVE CONSULTANT TOM MANKIEWICZ · DIRECTOR OF PHOTOGRAPHY GEOFFREY UNSWORTH B.S.C.
PRODUCTION DESIGNER JOHN BARRY · MUSIC BY JOHN WILLIAMS · DIRECTED BY RICHARD DONNER
EXECUTIVE PRODUCER ILYA SALKIND · PRODUCED BY PIERRE SPENGLER · PANAVISION® TECHNICOLOR®
AN ALEXANDER AND ILYA SALKIND PRODUCTION
RELEASED BY WARNER BROS. Ⓦ A WARNER COMMUNICATIONS COMPANY   TM & © DC Comics Inc. 1978

RECORDED IN
 DOLBY STEREO   ORIGINAL SOUNDTRACK AVAILABLE ON WARNER BROS. RECORDS AND TAPES   PG PARENTAL GUIDANCE SUGGESTED
WARNER SUPERMAN BOOKS AT BOOKSTORES AND NEWSSTANDS

SUPERMAN 1978 (U.S.)

Director Richard Donner **Producer** Alexander Salkind **Screenplay** Mario Puzo, David Newman, Robert Benton **Cinematography** Geoffrey Unsworrth **Music** John Williams **Cast** Christopher Reeve, Gene Hackman, Margot Kidder, Marlon Brando, Ned Beatty, Jackie Cooper, Glenn Ford, Terence Stamp

Blockbuster action science-fiction films were a growing trend in the second half of the 1970s, and *Superman* became a live-action feature as a result. The impact of *Star Wars* (1977) and *Close Encounters of the Third Kind* (1977) inspired films such as *Battlestar Galactica* (1978), *The Black Hole* (1979), and *Buck Rogers in the 25th Century* (1979). Within this fantasy rush, the pilots for *Marvel's Spider-Man* and *The Incredible Hulk* TV series were both released at the cinema in 1978. D.C. Comics had their own superhero, *Superman*, who had not experienced a cinema outing in thirty years. His first and only previous live-action film was the 1948 *Superman*, a fifteen-part serial.

Huge hype and expectations surrounded the new version, with Marlon Brando's reported fee of an exorbitant $2.5 million, to play Jor-El, Superman's father, dominating the film's media prior to its release. Gene Hackman (Lex Luthor) and Margot Kidder (Lois Lane) expertly played key characters, but it was the then-almost-unknown Christopher Reeve who was so effective as Clark Kent/Superman. Likewise, John Williams's rousing theme tune, which rises as Superman is called into action, has become a popular signature for this comic book legend.

◄

Richard Donner, whose previous film was the horror blockbuster *The Omen* (1976), had a major budget of $40 million to make the action sequences and Superman's flying effects special.

The plot follows the basic D.C. Comic premise: Superman, from the advanced planet Krypton, is dispatched to earth by his parents, as a child, at the point that his own world is destroyed. On earth, his powers are superhuman, and later as an adult he works as both a reporter for the *Daily Planet* newspaper and as a superhero who saves the population from disastrous situations. Villain Lex Luthor seeks world domination and fires

"YOU HAVE GREAT POWERS, ONLY SOME OF WHICH YOU HAVE AS YET DISCOVERED." JOR-EL

two rockets at California's San Andreas fault, with the plan that there will be a new west coast of America. Weakened through exposure to Kryptonite, Superman recovers just in time to halt one of the rockets. The second rocket, however, strikes its target and causes a massive earthquake. This leaves Superman busy saving a bus full of school kids on the Golden Gate Bridge from falling into the harbor below, allowing a speeding train to keep on its tracks by lying down and presenting his steel-like body as part of the train line, and then creating a new barrier for a collapsed dam.

▶

Christopher Reeve's mesmerizing and totally believable performance as Superman/Clark Kent made him forever coupled with the motion-picture action superhero.

The action in *Superman* can be, literally, out of this world, creating excessive but highly memorable moments, as demonstrated at the film's end by Superman flying around the earth at great speed in order to reverse time and bring Lois back to life. **IC**

FOR YOUR EYES ONLY 1981 (U.K.)

Director John Glen **Producer** Albert R. Broccoli **Screenplay** Richard Maibaum, Michael G. Wilson (from a novella by Ian Fleming, unattributed) **Cinematography** Alan Hume **Music** Bill Conti **Cast** Roger Moore, Carole Bouquet, Topol, Lynn-Holly Johnson, Julian Glover, Cassandra Harris, Michel Gothard, Jill Bennett, Jack Hedley

Now in his fifth outing as Bond, Roger Moore had successfully made the role his own. The triumvirate of Bond films made between 1977 and 1981—*The Spy Who Loved Me* (1977), *Moonraker* (1979), and *For Your Eyes Only* (1981)—represent the peak of his acting powers: he knew exactly what was required for the part by then, and his debonair *sang-froid* and magnificent minimalism had not yet been touched by Time's inevitable ravages.

The film shows 007 leaving flowers at the grave of his late wife, Tracey Bond—Diana Rigg, killed at the climax of *On Her Majesty's Secret Service* (1969) on Blofeld's orders. *For Your Eyes Only* carries many echoes of this earlier Bond movie: the sleigh ride 007 takes with Melina (Carole Bouquet) deliberately evokes the final fatal journey of the happy honeymooners, when Tracey is assassinated. And where a precursor (George Lazenby) to a *Saint* (Moore's great TV role) met an *Avenger* (Rigg's) in 1969, so does a wiser Saint (still Moore) meet a young avenger (Bouquet describes herself as such, since she's tracking her parents' killers, a modern Greek version of the pursuing fates) in 1981.

◀

The poster caused some scandal when the model wearing the swimsuit was asked to put it on back to front for the photoshoot. It was considered too revealing by some censorship boards.

The MacGuffin that gets the plot going is the opening scene, where bad guy Kristatos (Julian Glover) steals the deadly A.T.A.C. system, planning to sell it to the Russians, giving them control over the West's nuclear submarines. Immediately, we're plunged into another classic opening sequence where Bond escapes from a pilotless helicopter, swirling high above the Thames and some famous London landmarks.

"FORGIVE ME, FATHER, FOR I HAVE SINNED." JAMES BOND "THAT'S PUTTING IT MILDLY, 007!" Q IN DISGUISE

Long-serving Bond franchise crewman John Glen (2nd unit director on *On Her Majesty's Secret Service* in 1969) helmed the picture and knew what 007 needed. He pulled the story back from the—albeit enjoyable and critically underrated—"space wars" excesses of *Moonraker*, and delivered a straight-ahead action-thriller: great chases, great "sensible" locations, and the perennial Bondian *leitmotif*—great music. French supermodel Carole Bouquet, fresh from her striking debut as the ice-cold seductress in Bunuel's *That Obscure Object Of Desire* (1977) is one of the most beautiful Bond girls, with a nice line in mercurial temperament. English stage thespian Julian Glover as Kristatos and Michel Gothard, deranged inquisitor from *The Devils* (1971), as Locque supply suitable villainy, and the likable Topol manages to make us forget *Fiddler On The Roof* as he assists 007 and Melina to the triumphant conclusion. **MH**

► Bond (Moore) and Havelock (Bouquet) in a classic underwater clinch after Kristatos (Glover) tries to drown them.

GEORGE A. ROMERO'S
KNIGHTRIDERS

The Games...
The Romance...
The Spirit...

Camelot is a
state of mind.

BORIS

UNITED FILM DISTRIBUTION CO. Presents A LAUREL™ PRODUCTION
"KNIGHTRIDERS"™ Starring ED HARRIS · GARY LAHTI · TOM SAVINI · AMY INGERSOLL
PATRICIA TALLMAN · CHRISTINE FORREST · co-starring: WARNER SHOOK · BROTHER BLUE
Produced By: **RICHARD P. RUBINSTEIN** · Written & Directed By: **GEORGE A. ROMERO**
Executive Producer: SALAH M. HASSANEIN · Associate Producer: DAVID E. VOGEL
Director of Photography: MICHAEL GORNICK · Production Design: CLETUS ANDERSON · Music By: DONALD RUBINSTEIN

KNIGHTRIDERS 1981 (U.S.)

Director George A. Romero **Producer** Richard P. Rubenstein **Screenplay** George A. Romero **Cinematography** Michael Gornick **Music** Donald Rubenstein
Cast Ed Harris, Tom Savini, Gary Lahti, Amy Ingersoll, Patricia Tallman, Brother Blue, Christine Forrest, Cynthia Adler, John Amlas, Don Berry

George A. Romero has made his name as a director of zombie films, but as a result his movie *Knightriders* has been unfairly neglected. This is a shame, as it is one of Romero's most personal films. Rejecting the gore and apocalyptic horror of earlier productions, Romero's *Knightriders* joins medievalism and the biker movie for a modern-day tale of a traveling troupe of biker-jousters who perform in tournaments and live by feudal rules. The knights of this modern-day Camelot attempt to live by chivalry, a romantic idealism, and the ethical codes of King Arthur, with commercialism and unrestrained business practices presenting the "dragon" that they must fight.

The troupe is lead by King Billy (Ed Harris) and his wife, Lady Linnet (Amy Ingersoll), and includes a Merlin (Brother Blue), a black doctor who shares Billy's philosophy and mystical views. A division within the troupe threatens its existence with Morgan, the Black Knight (played by cult special effects artist, Tom Savini), motivated more by his love of bikes and the possibilities of fame and fortune. When Morgan departs, others leave with him, but he later becomes disillusioned with the falsity of the parties, drinking, and easy sex. The remnants of

◄
Screenwriter
Stephen King
takes a boozy
cameo role—just
one of the many
odd, anachronistic
things about this
biker-hippie King
Arthur movie.

Billy's troupe continue to provide the same tournament package, but stunts fail and one spectator is almost killed. These knights in armor ride modified motorbikes with protective shields. Such is their centrality to the film, which features lengthy stunts, that the producers acquired around sixty motorbikes and hired the group, Stunts Unlimited, who had worked previously on films such as *Smokey and the Bandit*

"MAGIC AIN'T GOT NOTHING TO DO WITH ORGANS . . . MAGIC GOT TO DO WITH THE SOUL, MAN." MERLIN

(1977). Many elements of the medieval jousts are translated to *Knightriders* with men on bikes carrying lances, charging at each other and fighting with swords, maces, and flails.

Of the sixty bikes, few survived with many crashes occurring during filming. The real-life bike stunts of Evel Knievel had been popularized throughout the 1970s, with *Knightriders* emerging from a distinct bike culture that had been drawing crowds to demonstrations and challenges.

Films such as *Mad Max* (1978) and *Mad Max II* (1981) also foregrounded the action of men clashing in modified machines, with *Mad Max II* similarly presenting a vision of neo-medievalism. The road represents both freedom and the end, and as Billy rides out in the film's last reel, having lost his crown to Morgan but having attained his spiritual goal, a hurtling truck approaches. **IC**

► **Knights on horse power. This is an iconic biker film in the mold of *Easy Rider* (1969) and *Electra Glide in Blue* (1973).**

The creators of JAWS and STAR WARS now bring you the ultimate hero in the ultimate adventure.

HARRISON FORD · KAREN ALLEN · PAUL FREEMAN · RONALD LACEY · JOHN RHYS-DAVIES · DENHOLM ELLIOTT

JOHN WILLIAMS · GEORGE LUCAS · HOWARD KAZANJIAN

FRANK MARSHALL · STEVEN SPIELBERG · LAWRENCE KASDAN · GEORGE LUCAS · PHILIP KAUFMAN

RAIDERS OF THE LOST ARK 1981 (U.S.)

Director Steven Spielberg **Producer** George Lucas, Frank Marshall
Screenplay Lawrence Kasdan **Cinematography** Douglas Slocombe **Music** John
Williams **Cast** Harrison Ford, Karen Allen, Ronald Lacey, John Rhys-Davies, Denholm
Elliott, Alfred Molina, Wolf Kahler, William Hootkins, Anthony Higgins, Vic Tablian

Directed by Steven Spielberg and produced by George Lucas, *Raiders of the Lost Ark* was a marriage of two of the most commercially successful filmmakers of the time. Lucas had long held a wish to create a feature film that presented a modern and polished version of the action, adventure, and cliff-hanger thrills that were so much a part of the Saturday serials of the 1930s and 1940s. Such has been the success of *Raiders of the Lost Ark* that to date it has spawned three sequels, a TV series, many film imitations, and merchandise that includes a range of lego sets.

Central to the franchise is Indiana Jones (in the films played by Harrison Ford), a university professor, archaeologist, and adventurer with a trademark hat and whip, who is in the mold of the heroes of the serials and has a touch of James Bond in his character. The film's famous opening is a clever prologue that creates expectations as to the innovative and dare-devil nature of Jones's character and the extent of the film's action ambitions. Working his way through the underground passages and chambers of an ancient Peruvian temple, Jones manages to dodge various traps, poisoned darts,

◄

Inspired by the adventure serials of the 1930s, Spielberg updated them with an injected blend of James Bond style, witty dialogue, and spectacular action.

spiked walls, and a giant boulder, which is released after he steals a golden idol and rumbles inexorably after him.

Lucas appears interested in mythology and quest narratives, and the rest of the film, set in the late 1930s, pits Jones against Nazi soldiers and treasure seekers who are searching for the lost Ark of the Covenant, which Hitler believes will give him incredible power. Legend says the holder of the Ark will have

> ## "MARION, DON'T LOOK AT IT. SHUT YOUR EYES, MARION. DON'T LOOK AT IT, NO MATTER WHAT HAPPENS!" *INDIANA JONES*

the power of God. Setting much of the film in Cairo, with excavations, hidden temples, and relics with markings to be deciphered, the story is transformed into an exotic fantasy that is essentially one long race. Jones has to locate the Ark before the Nazis, and has to unlock and protect a series of clues and mysteries that aid its discovery.

Once the Ark is taken by the Nazis, the film becomes a chase, with Jones undergoing a series of physical tests in order to stop its transportation to Germany. A relentless action sequence begins with Jones forced to fight a fearsome German mechanic on a moving tank, and is followed with Jones riding a horse after a convoy of vehicles. This chase took two weeks to film, as it is crammed with stunts involving Jones who then clambers precariously over a series of vehicles while continuously fighting with the Nazis. **IC**

▶
Harrison Ford played "Indy" part Errol Flynn, part Humphrey Bogart to great effect. The film won five Academy Awards and was nominated for Best Picture.

The boys are back in town.
Nick Nolte is a cop. **Eddie Murphy** is a convict.

They couldn't have liked each other less...
They couldn't have needed each other more.
And the last place they ever expected to be
is on the same side.
Even for...

48 HRS.

PARAMOUNT PICTURES PRESENTS A LAWRENCE GORDON PRODUCTION · A WALTER HILL FILM · NICK NOLTE · EDDIE MURPHY · "48 HRS." · ANNETTE O'TOOLE · MUSIC BY JAMES HORNER
EXECUTIVE PRODUCER D. CONSTANTINE CONTE · WRITTEN BY ROGER SPOTTISWOODE AND WALTER HILL & LARRY GROSS AND STEVEN E. de SOUZA
PRODUCED BY LAWRENCE GORDON AND JOEL SILVER · DIRECTED BY WALTER HILL · DOLBY STEREO IN SELECTED THEATRES · A PARAMOUNT PICTURE

Copyright © MCMLXXXII by Paramount Pictures Corporation
All Rights Reserved

48 HRS. 1982 (U.S.)

Director Walter Hill **Producer** Joel Silver, Lawrence Gordon **Screenplay** Roger Spottiswoode, Walter Hill **Cinematography** Ric Waite **Music** James Horner **Cast** Nick Nolte, Eddie Murphy, Annette O'Toole, Frank McRae, James Remar, David Patrick Kelly, Brion James, James Keane, Sonny Landham

48 Hrs. is an amalgamation of genres—action, comedy, thriller, and police procedural—all resulting in an explosive cocktail of a film. It is one of the first—and remains one of the best—of the buddy-buddy action films that besieged cinemas in the 1980s. It is a credit to the film that Hollywood still tries to emulate the film's story line nearly thirty years after its release.

Jack Cates (Nick Nolte) is a gruff San Francisco cop tracking down two cop-killers. Following leads, Cates ends up talking to convict Reggie Hammond (Eddie Murphy), a former associate of the criminals. When Hammond offers to help locate the bad guys, Cates illicitly has Hammond released into his custody for forty-eight hours and hopes the allotted time will give the duo enough time to track down the killers.

The film's success lies in its fine balancing between the thrilling and the hilarious, never undermining one for the other. Director Walter Hill established himself with tough-guy films like *The Warriors* (1979) and *Southern Comfort* (1981), and his familiarity with the genre lends credibility to the film's action scenes—the shoot-outs are violent, the chases dynamic, and the suspense exhilarating. Leads Murphy and Nolte help

◄

Cop and criminal team up for a touch of macho bonding—if not outright buddy friendship—in this violent action film.

contribute to create the realistic tough-guy aesthetic. While it may seem like an odd coupling, the on-screen rapport between the two actors is vital to the film's success, as they go from trading racial barbs to respecting each other.

Already a star thanks to his work on the sketch comedy show *Saturday Night Live*, the twenty-one-year-old Murphy could have taken the easier route of goofy comedy for his film

"WE AIN'T PARTNERS, WE AIN'T BROTHERS, AND WE AIN'T FRIENDS!"

JACK CATES

debut. Instead, he chose an unquestionably more mature film that emphasized his versatility. Murphy, who was given license to improvise, shines in his film debut as the quick-witted Hammond with his shakedown of a redneck bar being the film's highlight ("There's a new sheriff in town"). The performance also earned him a Golden Globe nomination for New Star of the Year.

► Nick Nolte as the grouchy, disheveled, hacked-off cop is a perfect foil to Eddie Murphy's "lighten-up," wise-crackin', streetwise superfly.

The combination of action and comedy proved to be a success—the *New Yorker* likened it to a blending of *Dirty Harry*, *Butch Casssidy* and *French Connection*—as *48 Hrs.* became one of the top ten grossing films of 1982 at the U.S. box office and the highest ranking action film that year. This film, along with *Beverly Hills Cop* (1984), solidified Murphy as a genuine box office star. Director Hill reunited with leads Murphy and Nolte for the equally successful sequel, *Another 48 Hrs.* (1989). **WW**

STALLONE
This time he's fighting for his life.
FIRST BLOOD
MARIO KASSAR and ANDREW VAJNA Present
A TED KOTCHEFF Film
SYLVESTER STALLONE FIRST BLOOD RICHARD CRENNA
Starring BRIAN DENNEHY Music by JERRY GOLDSMITH Director of Photography ANDREW LASZLO Executive Producers MARIO KASSAR and ANDREW VAJNA
Co-Executive Producer HERB NANAS Produced by BUZZ FEITSHANS Screenplay by MICHAEL KOZOLL & WILLIAM SACKHEIM and SYLVESTER STALLONE
Based on the novel by DAVID MORRELL Directed by TED KOTCHEFF
R RESTRICTED
UNDER 17 REQUIRES ACCOMPANYING PARENT OR ADULT GUARDIAN
DOLBY STEREO
An ORION PICTURES Release

FIRST BLOOD 1982 (U.S.)

Director Ted Kotcheff **Producer** Buzz Feitshans **Screenplay** Michael Kozoll,
William Sackheim, Sylvester Stallone **Cinematography** Andrew Laszlo
Music Jerry Goldsmith **Cast** Sylvester Stallone, Brian Dennehy, Richard Crenna,
Bill McKinney, Jack Starrett

With the tagline "This time he's fighting for his life," *First Blood* is
a powerful action movie in addition to a thoughtful examination
of the postwar treatment of veterans. Based on the novel by
David Morell, the film draws a parallel between the fighting on
the battlefield and the struggles faced within the homeland.

Vietnam vet John Rambo (Sylvester Stallone) wages a
personal battle following his arrest by harassing small-town
sheriff Will Teasle (Brian Dennehy). Having flashbacks to his
time as a P.O.W., Rambo escapes the city jail and seeks refuge in
the woods. He is quickly the focus of a manhunt by National
Guardsmen, but no one knows Rambo's ability to thrive in this
warlike environment. With the troops overwhelmed by Rambo's
survival skills, help arrives in the form of Col. Trautman (Richard
Crenna), Rambo's former commanding officer and seemingly
his only ally in this clash.

While acknowledging the struggles of veterans, *First Blood*
works purely as an action vehicle, and headlining Stallone
shines. He was in peak physical condition for the physically
grueling shoot and did a majority of his own stunts. Continually
surviving impossible situations—hanging off a cliff, traversing a

◄

**With his bulging
muscles, ragged
bandana, and torn
T-shirt, Sylvester
Stallone trades
Rocky's satin shorts
for military fatigues
in the first of the
Rambo outings.**

rat-infested tunnel—Rambo is the embodiment of a solider who seems to only be comfortable in war. The film's middle section, where Rambo uses his survival skills to surreptitiously ensnare several soldiers, is the highlight.

The finale—where Rambo steals a truck and literally destroys the ironically named small town, Hope—is appropriately explosive. In addition to the on-screen turmoil, the normally

> ## "WHAT POSSESSED GOD . . . TO MAKE A MAN LIKE RAMBO?" TEASLE "GOD DIDN'T MAKE RAMBO. I MADE HIM." TRAUTMAN

reticent Rambo delivers a memorable monologue about the horrors he encountered during and after the Vietnam War.

A project kicked around Hollywood for nearly a decade, *First Blood* seemed destined to originate in the overblown action cinema of the 1980s. The initial reception was harsh, with critics taking aim at the film's level of violence. Yet the film's body count is surprisingly low: one. It wouldn't stay that way, however, as Stallone took creative control of the character. As with his *Rocky* series, Stallone took the complicated character and made him increasingly superhuman in the sequels, *Rambo: First Blood Part II* (1985), *Rambo III* (1988), and *Rambo* (2008). The character of John Rambo surpassed cinema itself and, despite Morell and Stallone's concern, became a world renowned symbol of U.S. heroism, culminating with President Ronald Reagan mentioning Rambo in a speech on U.S. foreign policy. **WW**

▶
Stallone delivers one of the finest acting performances of his career, especially at the finale with a stirring speech.

전세계가 인정한 소림사 무술!!
[동방불패], [황비홍], [용행천하]의 이연걸 주연

소림사

THE SHAOLIN TEMPLE

LI LIAN-JIE   DIN HAI   YUE HAI   YUE CHEN-WEI   JI CHUAN-HWA   HU CHIEN-CHIANG   ZHANG JIEN-HWU   HUANG KWANG-CHUAN
WRITTEN BY SIT HAU   LU SHAU-CHANG   PHOTOGRAPHER CHAU PAK-LING   MUSIC BY HUANG LI-PING
ACTION CHOREOGRAPHER PAN CHING-FU   HUANG CHANG-KHAI MA SIAN TA
EXECUTIVE PRODUCER LIU YET-YUEN   DIRECTED BY CHANG HSIN-YEN

THE SHAOLIN TEMPLE 1982 (CHINA)

Director Xinyan Zhang **Producer** Chung Yuen Motion Picture Company
Editor Xinyan Zhang **Cinematography** Lau Fung Lam, Chau Pak Ling
Choreography Pan Qingfu **Cast** Jet Li, Wang Jue, Sin Jian Kui, Ding Lan,
Liu Huai Liang, Yan Di Hua, Chun Hua Ji, Hu Jian Qiang

Back in the 1970s, when Nixon still had control of the White House, there was a softening in relations between the United States and China that resulted in a visit to Washington from the Chinese National Wushu Team (*wushu* being the generic term for martial arts). Their demonstrations, involving both classic weapons and hand-to-hand combat, entranced Western audiences and even had the President himself asking one of the team's stars if he'd consider being his personal bodyguard.

That star was Jet Li, and the answer was no. And we're very grateful for that, for if he had accepted we wouldn't have the majesty of his performance in *The Shaolin Temple* to savor. Just sixteen when production started, Jet Li, who had won more gold medals and accolades in his martial arts career than we care to count, is a revelation in this very traditional Chinese folktale, and displays some of the flashes of brilliance that would propel him to world fame as a movie star in years to come.

It's not big on plot; if you've seen one kung fu flick, you won't need to guess what happens. Boy's father is killed by ruthless overlord, boy seeks refuge in temple where he is schooled in the noble art of kung fu, and boy wreaks his revenge on his

◄
**Also known as
Shaolin Si, the
movie is beautiful
to look at.
Audiences used
to studio-made
kung fu movies
are treated to a
location-shot film
that shows rural
China in all
its glory.**

father's killer. Does this sound familar? It's not the story that makes these movies the massive draw they are, though, or the acting (which is just as well in this case because all the actors are athletes really, and their ability to portray a character with any degree of realism is not surprisingly limited). No, it's the action; on that score, it's the business. The dynamic martial arts scenes, of which there are many, are expertly choreographed

"I STEPPED INTO THE MARTIAL ARTS MOVIE MARKET WHEN I WAS ONLY 16. I THINK I HAVE PROVED MY ABILITY." *JET LI*

by Pan Qinfu who, having been a coach for the National Wushu Team, really knows what he's doing. There are no special effects, no arty moves, no stunt doubles, no cables, wires, cranes, or other "cheats" or effects—all you see on the screen is real. This is kung fu pared down to basics, with performances of such speed and grace they could only have come from a lifetime's study of the art—which of course is exactly what they are.

The only real downside is the few rather less than subtle propaganda elements thrown in by the Chinese government of the day. Thus, you see the Buddhist monks (the good guys) drinking, eating meat, and killing people. But, if you can get past that (and the sight of Jet Li eating dog), you're in for a treat, as Jet Li's debut feature shows perfectly why the early 1980s became a boom time for kung fu flicks. **RP**

► **The scenes shot around the Shaolin temple in Luoyang are particularly sumptuous.**

Let's Party!

SCHWARZENEGGER
COMMANDO

TWENTIETH CENTURY FOX PRESENTS A SILVER PICTURES PRODUCTION ARNOLD SCHWARZENEGGER "COMMANDO"
RAE DAWN CHONG MUSIC BY JAMES HORNER ASSOCIATE PRODUCERS JOSEPH LOEB III AND MATTHEW WEISMAN SCREENPLAY BY STEVEN E. DE SOUZA
STORY BY JOSEPH LOEB III & MATTHEW WEISMAN AND STEVEN E. DE SOUZA PRODUCED BY JOEL SILVER DIRECTED BY MARK L. LESTER

RESTRICTED
R
UNDER 17 REQUIRES ACCOMPANYING
PARENT OR ADULT GUARDIAN

DOLBY STEREO
IN SELECTED THEATRES

Copyright © 1985 Twentieth Century Fox

COMMANDO 1985 (U.S.)

Director Mark L. Lester **Producer** Joel Silver **Screenplay** Steven E. de Souza
Cinematography Matthew Leonetti **Music** James Horner **Cast** Arnold
Schwarzenegger, Rae Dawn Chong, Dan Hedaya, Vernon Wells, David Patrick Kelly,
Alyssa Milano, Bill Duke

The 1980s is generally known as an era of excess, and nowhere is this more apparent than in the action films coming out of Hollywood at the time. Overflowing with tough guys who bust jokes as quickly as heads, films like *Rambo: First Blood Part II* (1985), *Invasion U.S.A.* (1985), and *Death Wish 3* (1985) set new standards for on-screen mayhem. Standing atop these films, however, is the Arnold Schwarzenegger vehicle *Commando*.

Retired Army Special Forces Col. John Matrix (Schwarzenegger) finds himself waging an individual war campaign after his daughter, Jenny (Alyssa Milano), is kidnapped by Bennett (Vernon Wells), a psycho soldier from Matrix's past. Bennett is taking orders from exiled Latin American dictator Arius (Dan Hedaya), who wants his rival in the fictional country of Val Verde assassinated and feels kidnapping Jenny will secure Matrix's services. Matrix has other plans and, with the help of stewardess Cindy (Rae Dawn Chong), heads to Arius's island fortress to unleash a one-man war and save his daughter.

As with most Schwarzenegger vehicles from the 1980s, the film is essentially synonymous with his off-screen presence and penchant for the pithy one-liner. The trivial script offers little in

◄
This is a live-action boys' comic gone crazy, with the indestructible Schwarzenegger's bulging pecs and gleaming torso dominating even the skimpy dialogue.

terms of originality, except for new ways to kill someone, and therein one finds the appeal of *Commando*. Similar to the aforementioned *Rambo*, the film climaxes with the lone hero taking on an army. Schwarzenegger and Stallone—the genre's two biggest stars, known for their good-natured cinematic rivalry—seem intent on showing who can do the most damage humanly possible on-screen. Schwarzenegger wins the battle

"I EAT GREEN BERETS FOR BREAKFAST. AND RIGHT NOW, I'M VERY HUNGRY."

JOHN MATRIX

this year, thanks mostly to a final twenty-minute siege on the enemy camp that features him dispatching troops by gun, grenade, knife, machete, pitchfork, saw blade, and his bare hands. While never officially confirmed, this final confrontation pushes the film's total body count past eighty bodies at least.

Director Lester realizes the absurdity of a doting single father massacring to save his daughter and amps up the exploitation quotient fittingly. For action, viewers could not ask for anything more, as cars are crushed, buildings blown up, and nameless bad guys killed by the dozens. In addition, he secured a fine supporting cast for the villains, particularly Wells, previously seen as the Mowhawk punk in *The Road Warrior* (1982). With its nonstop action and Herculean feats, *Commando* is pure comic book. Where else can you see a film where the hero picks up a phone booth and throws it at someone, too? **WW**

▶

Arnie in total comic strip destruction mode does a lighthearted *Rambo* and ratchets up the body count to eighty (Rambo's was one!).

POLICE STORY

STARRING

JACKIE CHAN

HONG KONG LEGENDS

POLICE STORY 1985 (HONG KONG)

Director Jackie Chan **Producer** Raymond Chow, Leonard Ho **Screenplay** Edward Tang **Cinematography** Yiu-Tsou Cheung **Music** J. Peter Robinson (U.S. version) **Cast** Jackie Chan, Brigitte Lin, Maggie Cheung, Kwok-Hung Lam, Bill Tung, Yuen Chor, Charlie Cho, ChiWing Lau-Cho Yeun

Following his own disappointment with *The Protector* (1985), the movie supposed to make him popular in the United States, Hong-Kong-based Jackie Chan decided to take matters into his own hands and produced this no-holds-barred, pure action movie. It marks his move into the big blockbuster films he's known for, though in truth none of the subsequent offerings reach the crazy heights of the stunts pulled in this one.

Chan stars as an honest Hong Kong cop who is assigned to look after superhot informer Selina (Brigitte Lin) until she can testify against her former boss, the evil drug baron Cho. He's reluctant, she won't do as she's told, and his girlfriend (Maggie Cheung) is annoyed that he's spending so much time with another woman. Things go from bad to worse when Chan loses his witnesses, his girl walks out on him, and he's framed for the murder of a fellow officer.

The crime-thriller elements keep us intrigued, and there's plenty of Chan's trademark humor to keep things light, but it's the action we're here for. From the jaw-droppingly crazy opening sequence, which involves Chan hanging on to a speeding bus with just an umbrella, to the lengthy finale in a

◄

Jingcha Gusha (original title) combines chop-socky action with slapstick and stylish physical stunts shoehorned into a *Dirty Harry*-style story line.

shopping mall, the frenetic pace never lets up. Bear in mind that this is before the introduction of C.G.I., and Chan's achievements are all the more remarkable.

As well as starring and directing, Chan also choreographed the fight scenes and coordinated the stunts, asking a tremendous amount from his cast and crew. But it was nothing he wasn't prepared to do himself.

> ### *"LOOK, I DON'T NEED YOUR PROTECTION, SO GET LOST! . . . I HATE YOU. YA BIG JERK." SELINA TO KEVIN*

Performing most of his own stunts, he came very close to ending his career (and his life). The final stunt alone, which sees him jump the seven floors from the top to the bottom of a shopping mall with nothing but an electrical pole to slide down on to, left him with second-degree burns on his hands, a dislocated pelvis, and two suspected broken vertabrae. Another death-defying stunt saw him hospitalized when he stopped breathing, having crashed through a glass canopy.

► **Detective Chan Ka-Kui (Jackie Chan) makes his escape from a police station by threatening his uptight boss Superintendent Raymond Li (Lam Kwok-Hung).**

With a mixture of slapstick and danger not witnessed since the days of Buster Keaton, Chan embarks on some of the most dangerous stunts ever slapped on film. It's no wonder after this that he found it impossible to get insurance for his movies. Endlessly copied by filmmakers both in Hollywood and Asia, this is one of the most influential action flicks of all time—although things never got quite this crazy again, not even for Chan. **RP**

UP THERE
WITH THE BEST
OF THE BEST.
A DON SIMPSON/JERRY BRUCKHEIMER PRODUCTION
TOM CRUISE · KELLY McGILLIS
TOP GUN
PARAMOUNT PICTURES PRESENTS
A DON SIMPSON/JERRY BRUCKHEIMER PRODUCTION
A TONY SCOTT FILM TOM CRUISE TOP GUN
KELLY McGILLIS VAL KILMER ANTHONY EDWARDS
TOM SKERRITT MUSIC SCORE BY HAROLD FALTERMEYER
WRITTEN BY JIM CASH & JACK EPPS, JR.
PRODUCED BY DON SIMPSON AND JERRY BRUCKHEIMER
DIRECTED BY TONY SCOTT A PARAMOUNT PICTURE
PG

TOP GUN 1986 (U.S.)

Director Tony Scott **Producer** Don Simpson, Jerry Bruckheimer
Screenplay Jim Cash, Jack Epps, Jr. **Cinematography** Jeffrey L. Kimball
Music Harold Faltermeyer **Cast** Tom Cruise, Kelly McGillis, Val Kilmer,
Anthony Edwards, Tom Skerrit

Top Gun is pure, unadulterated popcorn with a hint of propaganda shoed in. It's slick, noisy, and shallow, from the fabulous, stirring opening credit sequence of dawn over a dusty airfield, with technicians rushing around readying the planes for takeoff, to the final scenes when our hero gets the girl and the job and proves not only that he's the best but also that he can be part of a winning team.

Maverick (Tom Cruise) is a U.S. Navy jet fighter pilot sent to train at the Navy's elite weapons school along with his best friend, Goose (Anthony Edwards), the Radar Intercept Officer who shares his cockpit. The ultimate accolade for any pilot on the course is to win the Top Gun trophy. Maverick's main rival in this competition is Iceman (Val Kilmer), who does everything by the book and is disgusted by Maverick's rule-breaking. When Goose dies in an accident, Maverick loses his nerve and thinks of quitting. But after some soul-searching, he comes back to the school and proves himself in action.

This was the breakthrough role that turned Tom Cruise from a cute teen with one hit to his name, *Risky Business* (1983), into a superstar. Maverick is supposed to be tough, sexy, and tortured,

◄
Macho action boys'n'toys movie or U.S. Navy air pilots' recruitment film? You decide.

and Cruise's characteristic expressionlessness serves this purpose well enough for most of the movie, though looking happy is clearly too much for him, as his smile has the air of a grin of agony. He's at his worst in a vapid and unbelievable romance with astrophysics instructor, Charlie (Kelly McGillis, who is equally wooden here). The only flashes of authentic emotion from Cruise's character are in the relationship between Maverick

"YOU DON'T HAVE TIME TO THINK UP THERE. IF YOU THINK, YOU'RE DEAD."

MAVERICK

and Goose, though this is largely due to the Goose character being well written as well as excellently handled by Edwards.

But you don't watch *Top Gun* for the plot or the characters. The planes are the stars of this movie. It was filmed at the Miramar Naval Air Station in California, the real "Top Gun" training school, using an entire squadron of Naval pilots, aircraft carriers, real F-14 Tomcat jets, and the converted F-5 Tigers the Navy regularly uses to simulate Russian MiG-28s. The cockpit close-ups of the actors had to be shot in mock-ups, but they integrate seamlessly with the film of actual flight. In return for their cooperation, the U.S. Navy stipulated that the movie must be in good taste and must benefit the service, and that the script must be authentic. While this certainly dumbed down the script and cleaned up the language, the Navy's input makes for spectacular, exhilarating, and truly genuine aerial footage. **CW**

► A movie that names its central character Maverick (Cruise) and makes him a rebel who breaks the rules but gets results was never going to be a movie that made great demands on an audience.

MEL GIBSON · DANNY GLOVER

Two cops.
Glover carries a weapon...
Gibson is one.
He's the only L.A. cop registered as a

LETHAL WEAPON

WARNER BROS. Presents MEL GIBSON · DANNY GLOVER
A SILVER PICTURES Production   A RICHARD DONNER Film "LETHAL WEAPON"
GARY BUSEY   Film Editor STUART BAIRD   Production Designer J. MICHAEL RIVA
Director of Photography STEPHEN GOLDBLATT   Music by MICHAEL KAMEN and ERIC CLAPTON
Written by SHANE BLACK   Produced by RICHARD DONNER and JOEL SILVER   Directed by RICHARD DONNER

LETHAL WEAPON 1987 (U.S.)

Director Richard Donner **Producer** Richard Donner, Joel Silver
Screenplay Shane Black **Cinematography** Stephen Goldblatt
Music Michael Kamen, Eric Clapton **Cast** Mel Gibson, Danny Glover,
Gary Busey, Tom Atkins, Darlene Love, Traci Wolfe, Jackie Swanson

This first film in the phenomenally successful *Lethal Weapon* series is fast, violent, stylish, and sporadically funny. Its three sequels souped up the comedy, but this first movie is darker and more intense. The core of the movie is the relationship between a couple of mismatched L.A. detectives. Roger Murtaugh (Danny Glover) is a respectable, by-the-book homicide cop with a loving family and nice home. "I'm too old for this shit," he murmurs repeatedly as things kick off. He's looking forward to retirement and he's got a lot to lose if things go wrong. Murtaugh's new partner, Martin Riggs (Mel Gibson), is the "lethal weapon" of the title—he's a loose cannon with a death wish because, unlike Murtaugh, he has nothing to lose. The death of his wife has left him suicidal, and although he can't gather the courage to do the deed himself, he throws himself into his work with the zeal of a guy not just prepared but desperate to die in action.

No prizes for guessing that the two opposites clash and then grow to respect and like each other. It may be a movie cliché, but the chemistry between the two leads is so perfect that it seems fresh and original here.

◀
Gibson oozes charm as the ex-Vietnam Vet with a death wish alongside his placid partner Glover, who seeks a quiet retirement but realizes it is slipping away as the violence escalates in style and brutality.

As events threaten Murtaugh's cozy middle-class life, he finds himself drawn closer to Riggs's gung ho mayhem. Meanwhile, exposure to the happiness of Murtaugh's family mellows Riggs, bringing him back from the edge.

The two cops uncover an international drug operation when investigating what appears to be a routine murder. But the villains aren't about to roll over and give up the game. Every

"ARE YOU REALLY CRAZY? OR AS GOOD AS YOU SAY YOU ARE?" MURTAUGH "CRAZY? YOU WANT TO SEE CRAZY?" RIGGS

witness meets a grisly end, and since Murtaugh and Riggs seem to know too much, they're next on the list. The plot doesn't have a lot of substance, but it makes sense and holds together in spite of the movie's frenetic pace. Shoot-outs, hostage-taking, torture, car chases, and explosions provide enough violent action to keep macho thrill-seekers happy, but since it's linked to the fate of strong, sympathetic characters, even the less action-oriented are likely to experience the adrenaline rush.

▶ *Lethal Weapon* **literally rides high on the chemistry and charisma of its two stars—making up an action-packed "odd couple."**

There are a few dodgy jokes ("What did the shepherd say to the sheep? Let's get the flock out of here," says Riggs, as they leave the scene of their torture), and a weirdly gratuitous final fight sequence (why does Riggs not simply arrest bad guy Joshua (Gary Busey) instead of engaging in a messy fist fight while other cops stand around watching?) And you've got to love those massive 1980s cell phones, too. **CW**

STARRING INTERNATIONAL MARTIAL ARTS SENSATION
JEAN CLAUDE VAN DAMME

The secret contest where the world's greatest warriors
fight in a battle to the death.

Based on a true story.

CANNON INTERNATIONAL PRESENTS
JEAN CLAUDE VAN DAMME IN A NEWT ARNOLD FILM BLOODSPORT
DONALD GIBB · LEAH AYRES · NORMAN BURTON · FOREST WHITAKER
AND BOLO YEUNG AS CHONG LI MUSIC BY PAUL HERTZOG EDITED BY CARL KRESS DIRECTOR OF PHOTOGRAPHY DAVID WORTH
STORY BY SHELDON LETTICH SCREENPLAY BY SHELDON LETTICH AND CHRISTOPHER COSBY & MEL FRIEDMAN
CANNON RELEASING CORPORATION PRODUCED BY MARK DiSALLE DIRECTED BY NEWT ARNOLD   R RESTRICTED

BLOODSPORT 1988 (U.S.)

Director Newt Arnold **Producer** Mark DiSalle, Yoram Globus, Menahem Golan **Screenplay** Christopher Cosby, Mel Friedman, Sheldon Lettich **Cinematography** David Worth **Music** Paul Hertzog **Cast** Jean-Claude Van Damme, Donald Gibb, Leah Ayres, Bolo Yeung, Roy Chiao, Norman Burton, Forest Whitaker

Bloodsport centers on Frank Dux (Jean-Claude Van Damme), a U.S. military officer and martial artist who found stabilization in his youth through the Ninjutsu training offered by Senzo Tanaka (Roy Chiao). Dux dismisses his orders and journeys to Hong Kong to participate in the Kumite, a secret, invitation only, full-contact fighting event featuring martial artists from all over the world. Dux's intention is to represent his style of martial arts to honor his master, whose own son died before competing in the Kumite. Inspired by a true story, the scenario featured in *Bloodsport* is fairly routine and highly embellished, but provides the perfect avenue to depict various forms of martial arts and the code of honor that accompanies them.

Early on, Tanaka explains to the parents of the wayward Dux that martial arts will provide the mental and physical discipline he needs. A grueling training sequence—which features Van Damme's trademark splits—shows the adult Dux overcoming his physical limitations by embracing the life philosophy offered to him. In addition, the film extols the fraternity and warrior spirit of the competitors in Dux's relationship with Ray Jackson (Donald Gibb), a fellow competitor whose beating from villain

◄

Bloodsport helped re-establish Hollywood's love affair with displaying martial arts on film and, like Bruce Lee before it, carries on the tradition of promoting the system's mental and physical aspects.

Chong Li (Bolo Yeung, who filled the same adversarial role in Bruce Lee's *Enter the Dragon* in 1973) fuels Dux's desire for revenge.

Naturally, the fighting is at the center of the film's significance. Filling up nearly an hour of the picture, the fight scenes are brutal, hard-hitting, and violent. On display are numerous contact fighting styles, including boxing, Jiu-Jitsu, judo, karate, kung fu, Muay Thai, and more. Most importantly, they are

"MARTIAL SCIENCE . . . BRINGS MIND, BODY, AND SPIRIT TOGETHER."

SENZO TANAKA

recognized as incredibly accurate by practitioners of these various disciplines. In addition, the film rejects Hollywood's practice of stunt trickery as Van Damme skillfully performs all of his own moves. The final showdown between Dux and Li is unabashedly primal, yet the fighting scenes take on an almost balletic quality, as Eastern-influenced music balances the slow motion capturing Van Damme's graceful moves (in addition to martial arts, Van Damme studied ballet).

Bloodsport emerged as a surprise hit at the box office. Van Damme—previously limited to villainous supporting roles—saw his career as an action leading man skyrocket following the film's release. This, in turn, led to an ensuing decade of theatrical releases for the Belgian actor, with increasing budgets and healthy box office returns. Watch out also for Forest Whitaker's cameo, which adds some piquancy to the proceedings. **WW**

▶
Frank Duk (Van Damme) and Chong Li (Yeung) tough it out at the secret international martial arts competition.

DIE HARD 1988 (U.S.)

Director John McTiernan **Producer** Lawrence Gordon, Joel Silver
Screenplay Jeb Stuart, Steven E. de Souza **Cinematography** Jan de Bont
Music Michael Kamen **Cast** Bruce Willis, Bonnie Bedelia, Alan Rickman, Reginald
VelJohnson, Paul Gleason, De'voreaux White, William Atherton, Hart Bochner

New York cop Detective John McClane is an ordinary guy who tries to do the right thing. Estranged from his wife, Holly Gennaro, he visits her in Los Angeles for Christmas. He goes to her firm's Christmas party held in a fancy suite in a skyscraper and fast finds himself a fish out of water among a bunch of sharp-suited executives. Soon he is in even deeper water when the party guests are taken hostage by some Eastern European terrorists, who are really just villains intent on stealing $640 million held in a vault in the building. McClane escapes capture and resolves to bring the hostages—and his wife—to safety. His first problem is that no one knows what is going on, and he has to somehow inform the police, even if that means dropping a corpse onto a patrol car. Such fast thinking is typical of McClane, a reluctant barefoot hero. He scrambles around the building, improvising with whatever comes to hand, whether that is a machine gun or duct tape, trying to outgun his adversaries.

Bruce Willis plays McClane in the role that shot him to stardom—until *Die Hard* he was best known for his comic role as a wisecracking detective in the TV series *Moonlighting*. Willis's

◄
The original poster did not feature Willis; producers thought his image might stop non-Willis fans from seeing the movie. It was changed when the film became a box office hit.

unmatched ability to deliver one-liners and his unlikely casting made him all the more credible as an ordinary guy who finds himself in an extraordinary situation. McClane wins the day by his wits, guts, bad-ass attitude, and cowboy swagger.

Director John McTiernan came to the movie with perfect credentials, having taken the helm of the sci-fi action-thriller *Predator* (1987), and his command of pyrotechnics and nifty

> ## "BUT WHAT DO YOU WANT WITH THE DETONATORS, HANS? I ALREADY USED ALL THE EXPLOSIVES. OR DID I?" McCLANE

camera work makes for some superb action sequences, resulting in a raft of explosions and death-defying leaps that never seem heavy-handed. He is enabled by a strong cast, notably Willis, Bonnie Bedelia as Gennaro, and Alan Rickman as the cruel but sophisticated bad guy Hans Gruber, and a script packed with snappy dialogue and black humor.

▶
A comic actor, Willis quickly rose to the challenge of being an action hero. He performed many of his own stunts, even jumping off a 25-foot ledge into an air bag, followed by a ball of flames.

At a time when action movies were prone to depicting superheroes, *Die Hard* returned to a classic story line of how a true hero is someone who wins the hard way. When the cops come on the scene to help out with a S.W.A.T. team, followed by the F.B.I., they look like arrogant dullards as the Machiavellian Gruber anticipates their every move. It is left to a maverick cop to fight the battle alone. *Die Hard* reinvigorated the action genre on its release, spawning a series of follow-ups; but none are quite as good as the original, which is, frankly, flawless. **CK**

BATMAN 1989 (U.S.)

Director Tim Burton **Producer** Peter Guber, Jon Peters **Screenplay** Sam Hamm, Warren Skaaren **Cinematography** Roger Pratt **Music** Danny Elfman
Cast Michael Keaton, Jack Nicholson, Kim Basinger, Robert Wuhl, Jack Palance, Pat Hingle, Michael Gough, Jerry Hall, Tracey Walter

The character of The Batman first appeared in comic books in 1939. The stories of the "caped crusader" were written in the style of the detective "pulps" of the time and described a cruel Batman waging a relentless war on crime. During the 1950s Batman took on an increasingly lightweight tone, culminating in his 1960s small-screen debut—a beloved TV institution and a benchmark in kitsch. The Batman legacy was upturned in print with a pair of groundbreaking "one-shot" graphic novels: Frank Miller's *Batman: The Dark Knight Returns* (1986) and Alan Moore's *Batman: The Killing Joke* (1988). Both sold beyond the traditional comic book market and helped give gravitas to the idea of the graphic novel as a serious art form.

Acquiring the film rights to Batman, Warner Bros. chose as director a young Tim Burton, fresh from his low-budget debut success with *Pee-wee's Big Adventure* (1985). Burton was excited by the dark tone of Moore's book and vowed that there would be nothing "camp" about his film. The project was eventually given the green light after the massive (and unexpected) success of Burton's sophomore outing, the supernatural comedy *Beetlejuice* (1988); controversially, he chose his lead,

◄
Batman would become one of the biggest box office hits of all time. Its success established Burton as a major Hollywood player.

Michael Keaton, to take on the role of Batman. Setting the scene, *Batman* opens with young Bruce Wayne walking down an alleyway in Gotham City with his wealthy parents when they are mugged and murdered. The boy's life is shaped then and there—he will devote himself to avenging their deaths and ridding Gotham of all criminals. Fast-forwarding twenty or so years, we find Bruce Wayne the city's wealthiest and most

"IT'S A FIGHT BETWEEN TWO DISFIGURED PEOPLE, A COMPLETE DUEL OF FREAKS." *TIM BURTON*

eligible bachelor. But hidden away in the bowels of his mighty mansion is an armory of the most incredible technology—remember he is no superhuman himself—that enables him to transform into Batman.

The viewer also learns about Batman's most infamous foe. One of Gotham's biggest underworld figures, Jack Napier is foiled during a robbery, and after a struggle with Batman drops into a vat of acid. Cosmetic surgery leaves him with the appearance of a grotesque clown. Completely insane, he rechristens himself "The Joker" and wreaks his revenge by waging chemical warfare on Gotham City. Delving beneath the plotline, we can see that, although enemies, Batman and The Joker share much in common. Their lives are both given compulsion by a single, life-changing incident—we understand that and maybe even sympathize. **TB**

► Jack Nicholson's audacious portrayal of The Joker (here seen on-screen)—not so much scene-stealing as grand theft cinema—has to be seen to be believed.

A JOHN WOO FILM
"the best hong kong film ever"
hotdog magazine
THE KILLER
CHOW YUN FAT

THE KILLER 1989 (HONG KONG)

Director John Woo **Producer** Hark Tsui **Screenplay** John Woo
Cinematography Peter Pau, Wing-Hung Wong **Music** Lowell Lo (Lowe)
Cast Chow Yun-Fat, Danny Lee, Sally Yeh, Kong Shu, Kenneth Tsang,
Fui-On Shing, Wing-Cho Yip

Set against Hong Kong's postmodern cityscape of glittering skyscrapers and pulsing neon nightlife, *The Killer*, John Woo's twentieth feature film, cemented his reputation as one of world cinema's premier action film directors and further propelled Chow Yun-Fat into the upper echelon of Hong Kong motion picture megastars. It was the actor and director's third consecutive cinematic pairing, following the phenomenal *A Better Tomorrow* (1986) and *A Better Tomorrow II* (1987).

While clearly influenced by largely "Western" genres like the police procedurals and gangster films, as well as narrative conceits informed by both film noir and "new wave" sensibilities, Woo's film deployed elements that not only reflected the cinematic artistry of East-Asian cinema in general (e.g., the rogue assassin living by a code of honor) and Hong Kong action film in particular (e.g., the exaggerated hyperkineticism of martial arts pictures), but did so with a visual panache to which directors like Quentin Tarantino and the Wachowski brothers pay homage. Through rhythmic editing, intense close-ups, and dramatic slow-motion scenes, John Woo transformed what could have been merely a reiteration of Sam Pekinpah-esque epic shoot-

◄
The Killer's blend of "Western" and "Eastern" film motifs reflected the complex social mélange of a British colonial metropolis still deeply informed by national traditions and less than a decade away from its historic return to mainland China.

outs into a kind of gunpowder poetry, a highly stylized and deftly choreographed "ballet of bullets" that transformed blood-soaked brutality into a seductive dance of death.

Perhaps one of the most important aspects of *The Killer*'s initial appeal and eventual influence upon the visual landscape of action films around the globe emerges not so much from its innovative representations of acrobatic gun play, but rather

"I ALWAYS LEAVE ONE BULLET, EITHER FOR MYSELF OR FOR MY ENEMY."

JEFFREY CHOW

from John Woo's reluctance to reduce his characters into the simplistic categories of "good" and "evil" that marked the ethical parameters of far too many Hollywood productions. Jeffrey, the film's titular assassin, no longer wishes to take lives, acknowledging that "everybody has the right to live." What's more, he selflessly dedicates himself to protecting the beautiful Jennie (Sally Yeh), whose eyesight he inadvertently damages in one of the film's opening battles. Facing off against him is Police Inspector Li Ying (Danny Lee), who slowly transforms from a jaded, renegade cop who views the death of innocent bystanders as mere collateral damage to a more caring person. Ultimately partnering with Jeffrey against the forces of organized crime, Li even goes as far as having Jeffrey promise that should he die in their campaign, Jeffrey will do everything in his power to make sure that Jennie receives his corneas. **JMcR**

► **Steeped in overt symbolism and heavy doses of melodrama, *The Killer* challenges viewers' preconceptions by positing Li and Jeffrey as equally flawed human souls in search of redemption.**

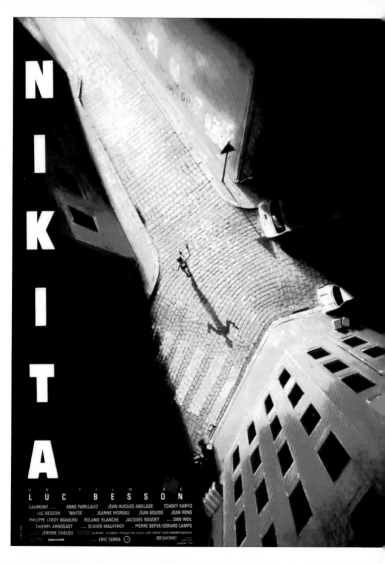

LA FEMME NIKITA 1990 (FRANCE • ITALY)

Director Luc Besson **Producer** Claude Besson, Luc Besson, Mario Cecchi Gori, Vittorio Cecchi Gori, Patrice Ledoux **Screenplay** Luc Besson **Cinematography** Thierry Arbogast **Music** Eric Serra **Cast** Anne Parillaud, Marc Duret, Jean Reno, Tchéky Karyo, Jeanne Moreau, John-Hughes Anglade

Punkish wastrel and drug addict Nikita (Anne Parillaud, director Luc Besson's wife) appears to be heading for a life behind bars (or perhaps worse) after she shoots a policeman in the face following her bungled attempt to rob a pharmacy with two friends. After being taken into custody and given a lethal injection that she is assured will kill her, Nikita instead wakes up to find that she has been saved from death for another, far more sinister purpose. Facing clinical French secret service agent Bob (Tchéky Karyo) in an austere interrogation room, she is offered the opportunity to train as a government assassin but is told that "Nikita" can no longer exist. Given that the alternative seems to be death, Nikita accepts a new identity, effectively burying her past. What follows is a tough regimen designed to make her both an efficient and deadly killing machine and a plausible but anonymous member of polite society.

The transition from punky street fighter—during her martial arts training she defeats an instructor by biting him on the ear and then kicking him in the genitals—to *femme fatale* over the course of three years transforms the once-rebellious Nikita. After a memorable "test" of her new skills—while having dinner

◄
The poster sets the scene for this stylish, moody thriller—as does the ambient music with Eric Serra's atmospheric, keyboard-laden soundtrack.

with the coldly businesslike Bob to celebrate her birthday, she is given a gun and simply told that she must kill the man next to her—Nikita proves a talented and adept killer. Her redemption, it seems, will be in paying back society for her previous ills by helping the government eliminate enemies of the state. But Nikita is conflicted, and Parillaud brilliantly brings out the duality in her character: she is at once torn between

"THERE ARE TWO THINGS THAT ARE INFINITE: FEMININITY AND MEANS TO TAKE ADVANTAGE OF IT." AMANDE

her role as a calculating and controlled government contract killer and her love for Marco (John-Hughes Anglade), the boyfriend she meets in the local supermarket who knows nothing of her real profession.

Key to the movie's success is Besson's urgent direction, with the plot moving along at a rapid, action-packed pace. Equally important is an underlying sense of loss and sadness that lends an oddly existential, reflective atmosphere to the film.

La Femme Nikita spawned a Hong Kong remake, *Black Cat* (1991), and John Badham's *The Assassin* (1993), starring Bridget Fonda, but both films failed to capture the ominous, dark mood underlying Besson's work and lacked the hard edge of the original. More successful was the Canadian-produced TV series, *La Femme Nikita*, which ran for five seasons from 1997 through to 2001. **RH**

▶
Parillaud's female lead is nothing like the muscle-bound, testosterone-charged heroes so frequently found in action-thrillers. Nikita is a reluctant assassin but no less effective for being a woman.

THE HUNT IS ON.
The director of "Die Hard" takes you beyond the realm of danger into the very heart of suspense.
From the thrilling #1 bestseller comes the electrifying motion picture.
JOIN THE HUNT.
SEAN CONNERY
THE HUNT FOR RED OCTOBER
ALEC BALDWIN

THE HUNT FOR RED OCTOBER
1990 (U.S.)

Director John McTiernan **Producer** Mace Neufeld **Screenplay** Larry Ferguson, Donald Stewart **Cinematography** Jan de Bont **Music** Basil Poledouris **Cast** Sean Connery, Alec Baldwin, Scott Glenn, Sam Neill, James Earl Jones, Tim Curry, Joss Ackland, Courtney B. Vance, Larry Ferguson

Set during the Cold War, *The Hunt for Red October* draws on the paranoia of the time in a film where the intentions of one man have both the United States and Soviet Union on the alert. That man is Captain First Class Marko Ramius, played by a craggy-faced, bearded Sean Connery.

A legend in the Soviet submarine corps, Ramius is the commanding officer of the Red October, the most deadly submarine ever built thanks to its revolutionary stealth propulsion system, which allows it to go undetected. It has the ability to launch a couple of hundred warheads at Washington, D.C. before anyone would even know it was there. When the U.S. government realizes that the submarine is off the east coast of the United States, it is understandably worried. It supposes that Ramius has had a mental breakdown and intends to launch an attack on the United States. But one fresh-faced young C.I.A. analyst, Jack Ryan (played by Alec Baldwin) has another hypothesis. Ryan suggests that Ramius is attempting to defect, and he is given the chance to prove his theory when he is sent into the field to attempt to liaise with the wayward

◄
The movie has a twinge of authenticity due in part to the U.S. Navy's cooperation on the production, as some of the extras were serving submariners.

captain and his vessel before either the Soviet or U.S. fleets can destroy it. Given that the action takes place on board a submarine and all the strictures that entails—and that when the film was made, special effects were nowhere near as sophisticated as modern-day computer-generated imagery can provide—it is surprising how effective *The Hunt for Red October* is in providing exciting entertainment. The murky

"I'M NOT AN AGENT, I JUST WRITE BOOKS FOR THE C.I.A."

JACK RYAN

underwater scenes are menacing and the confines of the submerged vessels heighten the claustrophobic sense of tension. This is not least due to the attention to detail and realism of the environment depicted.

The assured helmsmanship of *Predator* (1987) and *Die Hard* (1988) director John McTiernan plays its part and he creates a suspenseful film that is intelligent in pace and stylish to look at, much aided by the epic composition of Basil Poledouris for the soundtrack, which adds a sense of grandeur to the movie. Based on the best-selling novel by Tom Clancy, *The Hunt for Red October* has a superb plot that works well on the screen, posing questions about human nature and the wisdom of the escalation of nuclear missiles. Connery plays the captain as a credible figure: a man of grit with a conscience who is questioning what his role in life should be. **CK**

▶
Baldwin's Ryan is a thoughtful man literally at sea, who realizes that he is expendable but is still prepared to risk his life because of his faith in humanity's innate goodness.

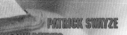

POINT BREAK 1991 (U.S.)

Director Kathryn Bigelow **Producer** James Cameron, Peter Abrams, Robert L. Levy **Screenplay** W. Peter Iliff, Rick King **Cinematography** Donald Peterman **Music** Mark Isham **Cast** Patrick Swayze, Keanu Reeves, Matt Taylor, Mary Busey, Lori Petty, John C. McGinley, James LeGros

Hardly a major success on release, *Point Break* has emerged as a much-loved action oddity, the wild enthusiasm of its fan base leaving other moviegoers perhaps somewhat baffled. Sometimes described in lazy "so-bad-that-it's-good" terms, *Point Break* is actually not a particularly poorly made film, but it certainly is a preposterous one.

Young Keanu Reeves plays Johnny Utah (a heroic name if ever one existed!), an athletic, young, rookie F.B.I. agent and former college football star. His job is to investigate a band of bank robbers known as the Ex-Presidents. Covering their faces during robberies rather than going with the traditional stocking over the head, they wear fancy dress masks depicting former U.S. Presidents Johnson, Nixon, Carter, and Reagan. Pursuing the idea that the gang is, in fact, a bunch of surfer bums, Agent Utah uses his evident athleticism to infiltrate the surfing community. In doing so, he develops a complex and close friendship with philosophy-spouting Bodhi (Patrick Swayze) and his surf buddies, as well as a growing attraction to their adrenaline-charged lifestyle—including gorgeous surf chick Tyler (Lori Petty.) But Agent Utah is soon hit by an awful truth—

◄
Although seemingly a star vehicle for Keanu Reeves, it is Patrick Swayze's memorable surfer dude who receives the praise. Reeves would subsequently become one of the biggest—if least convincing—action heroes at the box office.

Bodhi and his fellow adrenaline-junkie dudes *are* the Ex-Presidents. Will he be able to put the finger on his friends?

A clever mix of exhilarating surfing footage and traditionally gripping macho action movie fare, *Point Break* proceeds to chart Utah's two-year pursuit of Bodhi as they spar in all manner of exotic and unlikely scenarios. The movie's defining action moment takes place in the air, as Bodhi, evading capture, leaps

"YOU CROSSED THE LINE. PEOPLE TRUSTED YOU AND THEY DIED. YOU GOTTA GO DOWN." *JOHNNY UTAH*

from a plane using the last remaining parachute. Refusing to admit defeat, Utah leaps out of the plane chuteless, catches up with Bodhi, and grabs on to his parachute. *Point Break* is noteworthy for the beauty and authenticity of its surfing scenes. Prior to filming, the stars trained on the Hawaiian island of Kauai with world-class professional surfer Dennis Jarvis. The filming of the surfing sequences proved to be challenging for both actors: Swayze in particular refused to use a stunt double for any of his scenes and ended up cracking four of his ribs. Even more surprising, he also insisted on doing the major skydiving scenes himself—that really *was* him jumping out of the plane uttering memorably, "Adios, amigo!" Swayze ended up making fifty-five jumps. On first release, *Point Break* received very mixed reviews, but even the film's worst detractors couldn't deny that it was a sumptuous visual feast. **TB**

► The movie's defining moment is truly breathtaking stuff as Swayze and Reeves battle it out in freefall— possibly prompting *Time* magazine's Richard Corliss sideswipe: "Looks ten; Brains three."

TERMINATOR 2: JUDGMENT DAY
1991 (U.S.)

Director James Cameron **Producer** James Cameron, B. J. Rack **Screenplay** James Cameron, William Wisher Jr. **Cinematography** Adam Greenburg **Music** Brad Fiedel **Cast** Arnold Scharwzenegger, Linda Hamilton, Edward Furlong, Robert Patrick, Earl Boen, Joe Morton, S. Epatha Merkerson

The 1980s action film was dominated by hypermasculine action heroes such as Sylvester Stallone, Dolph Lundgren, and Arnold Schwarzenegger. The characters they played were often relentless killing machines—powerful, monosyllabic in speech, and devoid of emotion. Of these figures, Schwarzenegger in the role of the Terminator, a cyborg from the future, perhaps best came to represent this development of the action film.

The Terminator (1984), directed by a young James Cameron, was a low-budget cult hit, which Cameron returned to seven years later with a much bigger budget, greater effects, and bolder concepts. In the sequel, Schwarzenegger's T-800 cyborg is surpassed and challenged by the newer T-1000 (played totally creepily by Robert Patrick), a cyborg of liquid metal that can transform itself into a frightening variety of shapes and objects. Both have been sent from a future with the single aim of either protecting a teenage boy (the T-800's mission) or destroying him (the T-1000's mission). Early in the film, the T-1000 demonstrates its power by literally walking through metal bars and then emerging from a checker board floor, within which it

◄

In a film fearful of a technology-controlled future, it is the computer-generated effects that make the action scenes so astonishing.

had lain hidden. This trickster can grow lethal metal knives on the end of its arms, or completely adopt the identity of a discarded human, effortlessly adjusting its metallic form into a perfect copy. Significantly, whereas the threat from Schwarzenegger's action figure is represented in his immense size, towering presence, and bulging biceps, Patrick's T-1000 presents power in being sleek, lithe, and able to blend in with

> ## "MY CPU IS A . . . LEARNING COMPUTER. BUT SKYNET PRE-SETS . . . TO READ-ONLY WHEN WE'RE SENT OUT ALONE." T-800

his environment. Against these cyborgs, there is the action heroine of Sarah Connor (Linda Hamilton). She is a mother who is protective of her teenage son, John Connor (Edward Furlong), a future leader of great importance, and who has an obsessive mission to save humankind from an envisioned subjugation to machines in a post-apocalyptic world. Her commitment is total, even when locked up in a state hospital at the start of the film. Focused on fighting the future that she knows will come, she is shown using parts of her cell as an improvised gym to build up her strength.

▶
Linda Hamilton as Sarah Connor gives a truly gutsy performance in which she is so driven that at points she acquires an almost dehumanized and mechanized compulsion.

Advancements in special effects, something that Cameron followed, allowed the action scenes in *Terminator 2* to be extraordinary screen spectacles. Extreme stunts, such as a motorbike that is driven from a tower block into a flying helicopter, are real high adrenaline moments. **IC**

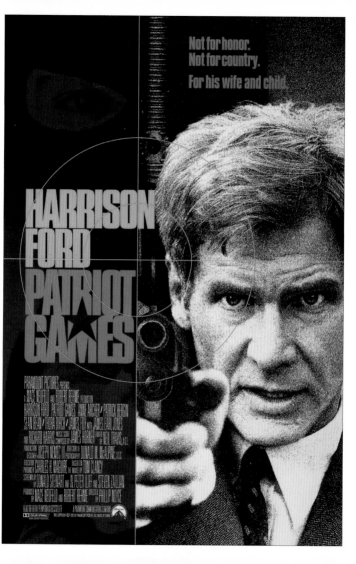

PATRIOT GAMES 1992 (U.S.)

Director Phillip Noyce **Producer** Mace Neufeld, Robert G. Rehme
Screenplay W. Peter Iliff, Donald E. Stewart, Steven Zaillian **Cinematography**
Donald M. McAlpine **Music** James Horner **Cast** Harrison Ford, Patrick Bergin, Sean
Bean, Anne Archer, James Fox, Samuel L. Jackson, Richard Harris, James Earl Jones

Australian director Phillip Noyce came to Hollywood's attention
with the thriller *Dead Calm* (1989), which helped make Nicole
Kidman into a star. He brings the same elegant mastery of
storytelling to this adaptation of Tom Clancy's best-selling
novel featuring Harrison Ford as Jack Ryan, a former consultant
to the C.I.A. The stakes were high in making *Patriot Games*, since
it followed on from the box office hit *The Hunt for Red October*
(1990), which also features Ryan as its hero. Yet a strong cast led
by Ford with support from Samuel L. Jackson, James Earl Jones,
and James Fox as the good guys, Lieutenant Commander
Robby Jackson, Admiral Jim Greer, and Lord William Holmes, as
well as Sean Bean, Patrick Bergin, and Anne Archer as the
baddies, Sean Miller, Kevin O'Donnell, and Polly Walker , helped
make it a comparable success that led to a sequel starring Ford
as Ryan, *Clear and Present Danger* (1994).

◄
**Retired C.I.A. agent
Jack Ryan on his
second outing
hunting down
despicable baddies,
courtesy of a clean-
cut, clean shaven
Harrison Ford.**

Ford is one of the best action stars of his generation, and he
brings his mix of intelligence, gravitas, and chutzpah to his role
as the reluctant hero, Ryan, in *Patriot Games*. The film begins
with Ryan no longer working for the C.I.A., but enjoying life as a
college professor and family man on a trip to London with his

wife and daughter. There he witnesses the attempted kidnapping of Holmes by members of an Irish terrorist splinter group led by Miller. An incensed Ryan shoots Miller's accomplice brother, captures Miller, and is awarded a knighthood for his bravery. When Miller escapes from prison, he decides to avenge his brother's death and hunt down Ryan and his family. To protect his wife and daughter from the deranged Miller, Ryan

"I'M AFTER THE MAN WHO WANTED TO KILL MY FAMILY. I AM TELLING YOU I WANT BACK IN!" JACK RYAN

believes his only choice is to return to work for the C.I.A. The film follows Miller's journey that takes him to the United States via Africa and eventually to Ryan's own home in what makes for a suspenseful climax to the film.

The action includes a notable speedboat chase, but Noyce is intelligent in his handling of any violence, choosing to focus on the battle of wills between Ryan and Miller. He also handles his subject matter delicately. *Patriot Games* touches on the troubles in Northern Ireland but sidesteps a partisan view because Miller is depicted as a terrorist gone rogue in pursuit of a vendetta. However, a scene with Ryan and Richard Harris as Irish-American I.R.A. supporter Paddy O'Neil illustrates the complexity of the situation and what happens when men are trained to live by the bullet. The plot is intricate, but at its heart this is a movie about revenge and one man's mission to save his family. **CK**

▶

Action man Ryan (Ford) foiling a kidnapping by members of an Irish terrorist splinter group led by Miller (Bean).

STEVEN SEAGAL

In 1992 a battleship's been
sabotaged by nuclear pirates out to steal its warheads.
Now, surrounded by terrorists, a lone man stands with a deadly plan of attack.

UNDER SIEGE

WARNER BROS. PRESENTS

IN ASSOCIATION WITH REGENCY ENTERPRISES, LE STUDIO CANAL +, AND ALCOR FILMS AN ARNON MILCHAN PRODUCTION AN ANDREW DAVIS FILM STEVEN SEAGAL TOMMY LEE JONES UNDER SIEGE GARY BUSEY
MUSIC ROBERT A. FERRETTI A.C.E. PRODUCTION BILL KENNEY DIRECTOR FRANK TIDY B.S.C. MUSIC GARY CHANG CO-PRODUCER JACK B. BERNSTEIN AND PETER MACGREGOR-SCOTT STORY J.F. LAWTON SCREENPLAY GARY GOLDMAN & J.F. LAWTON
PRODUCED ARNON MILCHAN, STEVEN SEAGAL AND STEVEN REUTHER DIRECTED ANDREW DAVIS

UNDER SIEGE 1992 (FRANCE • U.S.)

Director Andrew Davis **Producer** Arnon Milchan, Steve Reuther, Steven Seagal, Joel Chernoff **Screenplay** J. F. Lawton **Cinematography** Frank Tidy **Music** Gary Chang **Cast** Steven Seagal, Tommy Lee Jones, Gary Busey, Erika Eleniak, Colm Meaney, Patrick O'Neal, Hiram Bullock, Andy Romano

Of all the martial arts-trained action heroes, Steven Seagal is at once the most affable and the easiest to parody. His softly spoken, overearnest characters and latter-career tendency to focus somewhat zealously on environmental themes has often seen him ridiculed as too high-minded and lacking the credibility—and acting skills—to be taken seriously. If Seagal has a masterpiece, it is undoubtedly *Under Siege*, an efficiently crafted and—above all else—fun naval actioner.

Playing Casey Ryback, an insubordinate, lowly cook on board the U.S.S. *Missouri*, Seagal is locked in a meat cooler by rent-a-villain Gary Busey's Commander Krill. Krill has dastardly plans for the soon-to-be-decommissioned U.S. Navy ship involving a hijack by international terrorists. They kill the ship's captain (Patrick O'Neal) and lock the crew in the bowels of the ship. Foolishly, they forget about Ryback—who also happens to be a highly decorated ex-Navy SEAL. The cook promptly foils an attempt on his life and causes havoc for their carefully laid plans. The plot is essentially a load of old hokum involving the sale of the ship's nuclear missiles overseen by both Gary Busey's officer-turned-bad and Tommy Lee Jones's rogue ex-C.I.A.

◄
Seagal's finest motion-picture moment was Oscar-nominated in the Best Effects and Best Sound categories, and even spawned a sequel, *Under Siege 2: Dark Territory* (1995).

operative William Stranix, but it doesn't matter. A winning combination of Davis's pacey direction, J. F. Lawton's witty script, Jones's insanely impish villain, and Seagal's theatrical antics make *Under Siege* a classic action romp.

An immensely likable action hero, Seagal delivers his lines like a slightly chastened schoolboy as he slaps, stabs, punches, and generally blows his way up to saving the world from

> *"ARE YOU, LIKE, SOME SPECIAL FORCES GUY?"* JORDAN TATE *"NAH. I'M JUST A COOK . . . A LOWLY, LOWLY COOK."* CASEY RYBACK

nuclear war. The all-action hero is ably supported by Playboy "playmate" Jordan Tate (Erika Eleniak), a stripper who had come on board to help celebrate the captain's birthday. As such, the film swings wildly in tone between hard-nosed action flick and slightly comic tomfoolery. In many ways, the film is typical of Steven Seagal's body of work: action-packed, ever so cheesy, and immense fun.

Davis does a good job of representing the cramped conditions aboard ship, all of which helps to add a sense of claustrophobia, meaning we never quite know what is around each corner or how Ryback is ultimately going to foil Stranix's somewhat bizarre master plan. But perhaps the film is best remembered for former Baywatch starlet Erika Eleniak bursting out of a gigantic birthday cake dressed as a naval officer, demonstrating exactly why her character was *Playboy*'s Miss July 1989. **RH**

▶
In *Under Siege* Steven Seagal plays Casey Ryback, the meanest, toughest looking, kick-ass Navy cook ever to inhabit the screen.

A murdered wife.
A one-armed man.
An obsessed detective.
The chase begins.

HARRISON FORD IS **THE FUGITIVE**

THE FUGITIVE 1993 (U.S.)

Director Andrew Davis **Producer** Arnold Kopelson **Screenplay** Jeb Stuart, David Twohy, Roy Huggins **Cinematography** Michael Chapman **Music** James Newton Howard **Cast** Harrison Ford, Tommy Lee Jones, Sela Ward, Julianne Moore, Joe Pantoliano, Tom Woode, Ron Deane, Jeroen Krabbé

Modern-day Hollywood can easily give the impression that it's given up hopelessly on the idea of coming up with anything new and interesting. Thus we see a vogue for producing big-money blockbusters based on remakes of old or foreign language movies or plundering TV series from an earlier age. In most cases the results are unsatisfying and, odd given their ubiquity, sometimes financially disastrous. We get dull and bombast (*Mission Impossible*), fun with ironic nods and winks (*Starsky and Hutch*), or the simply unwatchable (*The Avengers*). One glaring exception is Andrew Davis's *The Fugitive*. Based on the U.S. TV serial that ran during the mid-1960s, it is one of the finest action movies ever made.

The film retains much of the original TV show's premise. Dr. Richard Kimble (Harrison Ford), a respected Chicago surgeon, returns home from work to find his wife in a pool of blood and a mysterious one-armed figure making an escape. With circumstantial evidence pointing to Kimble as the killer, he is tried, convicted of first-degree murder, and sentenced to the death penalty. While being transported to prison, a group of convicts attempt an escape. In the ensuing melee, the driver is

◄

The Fugitive itself spawned an offshoot, with Tommy Lee Jones reprising his role as Samuel Gerard in the rather pedestrian *U.S. Marshals* (1998).

shot, sending the vehicle rolling down a hill, where it comes to rest on a railway line. Moments later a high-speed train hurtles toward the wreckage: with seconds to spare Kimble pulls himself free and flees the scene on foot, leaving behind him the mother of all movie explosions. Kimble knows that the only way he can prove his innocence is by finding the killer himself, and he can only do that by staying on the run. The task of

"I DIDN'T KILL MY WIFE!"
DR. RICHARD KIMBLE "I DON'T CARE!"
MARSHAL SAMUEL GERARD

tracking and capturing the fugitive doctor goes to U.S. Marshal Samuel Gerard (Tommy Lee Jones). The ensuing manhunt, and numerous close calls, is the meat and bones of this gripping movie. Eventually Kimble comes to realize the shocking identity of the killer, leading to a tense public "J'accuse" and a frantic climax in which Gerard must decide who is the guilty party.

Why does *The Fugitive* work when so many other remakes fail so miserably? The answer is almost too obvious: take a gripping yarn; give it a plausible script and the highest production values (the sort that a $44 million budget can provide); hire a director experienced in relentless, edge-of-the-seat pacing (see *Under Siege*); and, of course, take brilliant turns from two of Hollywood's finest actors. *The Fugitive* does, of course, have one big advantage: the original series has not been seen widely since, and so managed to reach new generations. **TB**

► A pivotal leap of faith that took Harrison Ford and *The Fugitive* into the ranks of "Best Of" action-thrillers. The movie also garnered his pursuer, Tommy Lee Jones, an Oscar for Best Supporting Actor.

THE HEROIC TRIO 1993 (HONG KONG)

Director Johnnie To **Producer** Cora Cheng, Ching Siu-Tung, Johnnie To, Brian Yip
Screenplay Sandy Shaw (English version by Jack Maeby) **Cinematography** Tom
Lau, Poon Hang-Sang **Music** William Wu **Cast** Michelle Yeoh, Anita Mui, Maggie
Cheung, Anthony Wong, Yen Shi-Kwan, Damian Lau

Martial arts cinema tends to be a very macho dominated affair,
with women only featured in minor roles; but occasionally a
gutsy girl can break through the ranks and become a star in her
own right. This movie gives us the chance to marvel at the
talents of not just one but three of those who have managed to
do just that. It's no chick flick, though—these girls have made it
by taking the boys on at their own game. So there are still
plenty of gun battles, kung fu, wire work, and explosions to
enjoy—it's your classic Hong Kong movie, but just a lot prettier
to look at. Cynically, you could also say that it was designed to tap
into the rise in popularity of the Asian babe market (especially
given some of the skimpy costumes our heroines Michelle
Yeoh, Anita Mui, and Maggie Cheung get to run around in).

The hugely enjoyable if rather loopy plot has a very comic
book feel about it. Think Charlie's Angels taking on one of
Gotham City's most dastardly bad guys and you might be
halfway there. Babies are going missing, and the villain behind
this evil plot is a vile, sewer-dwelling eunuch who is intent on
finding a baby with royal blood to be the new emperor when
he takes over China. And he shoots poisoned darts from his

◄
**The choreography
was done by the
legendary Ching
Siu-Tung, who is
responsible for the
film's outrageously
fantastical action
scenes and
certainly knows
how to get the best
out of his leads.**

fingers. The police are having trouble sorting this out, so our brave heroines step up to save the day. We have Wonder Woman (Mui), housewife by day, masked, roof-prowling crime fighter by night; the Thief Catcher (Cheung), a leather-clad biker chick and bounty hunter who'll catch bad guys for bucks; and Invisible Woman (Yeoh) who's, well, invisible at times and has to be won over to the side of good, as initially she's in the employ

> *"WE DON'T NEED YOUR SERVICES HERE."* LAU *"SERVICES? COMMANDER, YOU MAKE ME SOUND LIKE A HOOKER."* CHAT

of the evil master. Yeoh (Crouching Tiger) is given plenty of opportunity to show off her kung fu skills, Miu can throw a sword like no one else (you try pining a baby to the wall with a dart and no damage), and Cheung is stupendous as the gun-toting Thief Catcher.

Johnnie To makes the whole thing a visual joy, too. While clearly made on a budget, the cartoonish sets are impressive, and the conceits such as the floating flower petals and butterflies around our heroines are beautifully poetic. He also manages to shoehorn in some dramatic scenes between the onslaught of battles, and succeeds in making them emotive and quite affecting. Special mention should also go to Anthony Wong, who excels as a mute, zombiesque henchman: he wields the film's most hilariously brilliant and brutal weapon—a decapitation bucket. **RP**

► **Part classic kung fu, part comic book fantasy, this one is epic on all levels.**

CLINT EASTWOOD
JOHN MALKOVICH · RENE RUSSO
IN THE LINE OF FIRE
COLUMBIA PICTURES AND CASTLE ROCK ENTERTAINMENT PRESENT
AN APPLE/ROSE PRODUCTION A WOLFGANG PETERSEN FILM CLINT EASTWOOD JOHN MALKOVICH RENE RUSSO "IN THE LINE OF FIRE"
DYLAN McDERMOTT GARY COLE FRED DALTON THOMPSON AND JOHN MAHONEY
PRODUCTION DESIGNER LILLY KILVERT DIRECTOR OF PHOTOGRAPHY
EXECUTIVE PRODUCERS WOLFGANG PETERSEN GAIL KATZ AND DAVID VALDES
CASTLE ROCK
R
COLUMBIA PICTURES

IN THE LINE OF FIRE 1993 (U.S.)

Director Wolfgang Petersen **Producer** Jeff Apple, Gail Katz **Screenplay** Jeff Maguire **Cinematography** John Bailey **Music** Ennio Morricone **Cast** Clint Eastwood, John Malkovich, Rene Russo, Dylan McDermott, Gary Cole, Fred Dalton Thompson, John Mahoney, Gregory Alan Williams, Jim Curley, Sally Hughes

Clint Eastwood and John Malkovich turn in tour-de-force performances as government-trained killers in this well-paced thriller directed by Wolfgang Petersen. Eastwood plays aging Secret Service agent Frank Horrigan, a man haunted by his failure to save President John F. Kennedy from assassination when he worked on the president's protection detail. The film portrays him as a man racked by a sense of guilt who feels that he could have done more to save his leader. He is known throughout the service as a living legend: the only agent still on active duty who was there on that fateful sunny day in Dallas.

Malkovich plays Mitch Leary, a former C.I.A. agent who has suffered a mental breakdown and feels betrayed by the organization he once served. Both characters are tired by the years of service they have given to their country and the dirty tricks they have performed in its name. While the maverick Horrigan has merely become cynical over the years, Leary has become psychotic and obsessed with the idea of exacting his revenge on his former employer by killing the president. Malkovich's character stalks both the president and Horrigan, who he sees as a worthy adversary and perhaps the only person

◄

Petersen's deft direction of cast and crew creates a movie of omnipresent brooding menace, punctuated by acts of random violence performed by the brutal Leary (Malkovich).

able to understand his motivation. He taunts Horrigan for his past failure, goading Horrigan into questioning whether he has what it takes to make a split-second decision and make the ultimate sacrifice of risking his own life for that of a president. The cat-and-mouse game between the two men, Eastwood's careful take on the careworn Horrigan, and Malkovich's brilliantly chilling rendition of the creepy Leary make the

"DO YOU REALLY HAVE THE GUTS TO TAKE A BULLET FOR THE PRESIDENT, FRANK?" MITCH LEARY

psychological tension in the movie run high. Aided by the Oscar-winning film editing skills of Anne V. Coates (*Lawrence of Arabia* (1962), no less) and a score written by the maestro of spine-tingling music Ennio Morricone, Petersen milks that tension to the fullest. So much so that even Horrigan gets jumpy, as the hero is shown to be an ordinary, fallable guy with flaws rather than an omnipotent superhero. Made with the active cooperation of the Secret Service, the movie is also highly realistic in its depiction of the daily routine of an agent.

In the Line of Fire put Petersen on the Hollywood map and a long way from *The Never Ending Story* (1995). His action sequences rely more on stunts rather than special effects, making for a classy actioner that has the audience sitting on the edge of their seats to see if Horrigan will find redemption or find himself standing over the grave of another dead president. **CK**

▶
Secret Service agent Horrigan (Eastwood) in a literally nail-clinging scene.

IRON MONKEY 1993 (HONG KONG)

Director Woo-Ping Yuen **Producer** Hark Tsui (plus Quentin Tarantino, 2001 U.S. version) **Screenplay** Tai-Muk Lau, Cheung Tan, Pik-Yin Tang, Hark Tsui **Cinematography** Arthur Wong **Music** Richard Yeun (James L. Venable, 2001 U.S. version) **Cast** Yu Rang-Guang, Donnie Yen, Tsang Sze-Man, Jean Wang

This film was first released in the early 1990s to great acclaim in Asia, but it took the success of *Crouching Tiger Hidden Dragon* (2000) to get martial arts master Woo-Ping Yuen's highly influential movie a theater release in the United States in 2001. In fact, if it hadn't been for martial arts fan Quentin Tarantino leaning on Miramax, it may still be gathering dust in your local video store. This was the first of his series of "Quentin Tarantino Presents . . ." movies, which has seen the star use his Hollywood status to publicize small or foreign movies. He was right to push for it, as it benefits hugely from being seen on the big screen.

The plot, such as it is, could be viewed as a prequel to Jet Li's *Once Upon a Time in China* (1997). It follows the fortunes of the Chinese folk hero Wong Fei Hung as a young boy (here played by actress Tsang Sze-Man) and his kung fu master father Kei-Ying (Donnie Yen) as they travel the country. Arrested on suspicion of being the Iron Monkey, a Robin Hood-style local hero who steals from the rich to give to the poor, Kei-Ying finds himself in court in front of the evil governor. Even when it transpires that he can't possibly be guilty, Kei-Ying's son is held captive until he brings the real Iron Monkey to book.

◀

A story of greed, corruption, and cowardice versus honesty, selflessness, and heroism, *Iron Monkey* is a perfect example of why Woo-Ping Yuen is a hero of Asian cinema.

This being Hong Kong cinema, however, we can't really pit the two heroes against one another for long, and soon enough (following the daring escape of his son) Kei-Ying and the monkey (Yu Rang-Guang) team up to take on corruption. All this is really just a hook on which to hang a series of amazing action sequences. As you'd expect from Yuen, the martial arts are spectacular; in fact, there are so many memorably brilliant

"WOO-PING SHOWS THE ACTOR HEAD TO TOE. THE WHOLE BODY MOVES, AND THE ACTION [IS] NOT CHOPPED." *JET LI*

shots that you lose count (Yen is a particularly creative and graceful fighter). The performances were, of course, helped by Yuen's insistence that all the actors were also trained martial artists, bringing a legitimacy to the movie that's so often missing from lesser offerings. It all builds to a fantastic fiery climax, which sees our heroes and villains doing battle atop poles while flames rage beneath them.

► **Not surpisingly after the success of this movie perhaps, director Woo-Ping Yuen went to choreograph the action scenes for *Crouching Tiger Hidden Dragon* (2000).**

There's also the obligatory dose of cheesy humor and wisecracks so beloved by Hong Kong audiences, though this in itself was controversial—the film's release date was delayed when producer Hark Tsui insisted that more jokes were added even though director Yuen had declared the project finished. Ironically, when it was released in the United States, nearly all of the humor was edited out as it was thought that U.S. audiences just wouldn't get it. **RP**

TRUTH

NEEDS A

SOLDIER.

HARRISON FORD

CLEAR
AND
PRESENT
DANGER

PARAMOUNT PICTURES PRESENTS A MACE NEUFELD AND ROBERT REHME PRODUCTION HARRISON FORD CLEAR AND PRESENT DANGER
WILLEM DAFOE ANNE ARCHER AND JAMES EARL JONES MUSIC COMPOSED JAMES HORNER MUSIC SUPERVISOR TIM SEXTON COSTUME DESIGNER BERNIE POLLACK
EDITED BY NEIL TRAVIS A.C.E. PRODUCTION DESIGNER TERENCE MARSH DIRECTOR OF PHOTOGRAPHY DONALD M. McALPINE A.C.S. EXECUTIVE PRODUCER RALPH SINGLETON BASED ON THE NOVEL BY TOM CLANCY
SCREENPLAY BY DONALD STEWART AND STEVEN ZAILLIAN AND JOHN MILIUS PRODUCED BY MACE NEUFELD AND ROBERT REHME DIRECTED BY PHILLIP NOYCE

COMING AUGUST 3   SOUNDTRACK ALBUM AVAILABLE ON   READ THE BERKLEY #1
MILAN CDs AND CASSETTES   NEW YORK'S BESTSELLER

CLEAR AND PRESENT DANGER

1994 (U.S.)

Director Phillip Noyce **Producer** Mace Neufeld, Robert Rehme
Screenplay Donald Stewart, Steven Zaillian, John Milius (novel by Tom Clancy)
Cinematography Donald McAlpine **Music** James Horner **Cast** Harrison Ford,
Willem Dafoe, Anne Archer, Miguel Sandoval, Joaquim de Almeida, Henry Czerny

---

Tom Clancy was a successful thirty-seven-year-old insurance
man when his first novel—*The Hunt For Red October*—appeared
in 1984. Overnight he was transformed into one of America's
most popular (and subsequently most prolific) thriller novelists,
establishing as his central character the figure of Jack Ryan,
happily married ex-Marine, stockbroker, scholar, and now top
C.I.A. man. Clancy's yarns (or "techno-thrillers" as they are
sometimes described) concern themselves with the detail of
advanced military technology and covert intelligence
operations employed by U.S. government agents in the
ongoing war against enemies of the state—first the Soviet
Union, later Middle Eastern extremists and terrorists.

Clancy's novels were *made* for cinema adaptation. Garnering
few literary plaudits, his novels are *all* plot and little else. They
are deeply patriotic affairs, where the heroic male protagonist
must exhibit the superior moral authority that ensures the
triumphant destiny of the United States. Unsurprisingly, they
find great favor with those of a neo-con leaning. So, if you're a
fan of tense, breakneck, action-packed movie thrillers, where

◄
**Outstanding,
high-octane,
edge-of-seat
entertainment.**

technology and detail stand center stage, and you can put the patriotic breast-beating to one side, you'll love *Clear and Present Danger* and other Hollywood-Clancy collaborations.

Setting the scene, a coast guard patrol boat stops a suspicious yacht. On board an American businessman and his family have been slain: the murdered man, it transpires, happens to have been a very close friend of the President of the United States. It

"JACK, COMPUTER THEFT IS A SERIOUS CRIME." *ROBERT RITTER* "SO ARE CRIMES AGAINST THE CONSTITUTION." *JACK RYAN*

becomes clear that this was the work of a notorious Colombian drug cartel headed by the ruthless Ernesto Escobedo (a character based on the real-life drug lord Pablo Escobar). Further investigation reveals that the businessman was more closely involved and had been taken out for skimming off cartel profits. Since there is a direct presidential link, the C.I.A. is called in to bring down the gang.

▶
This was Harrison Ford's second outing as Jack Ryan, having starred in the similarly successful *Patriot Games* two years earlier. Ford brings his trademark grizzled gravitas to the role.

With a budget of $65 million to play around with, the makers of *Clear and Present Danger* were clearly confident that the huge popularity of the novel would transfer to the screen. Indeed, sequence upon sequence of the most lavish action—high-speed powerboats in combat, dramatic helicopter attacks, and the spectacular destruction of a drug lord's mansion—leave the viewer breathless and dizzy throughout. A huge hit with audiences across the globe, the film grossed $207 million. **TB**

BRANDON LEE

BELIEVE

IN

ANGELS

THE CROW

BRANDON LEE "THE CROW"
AN EDWARD R. PRESSMAN PRODUCTION IN ASSOCIATION WITH JEFF MOST PRODUCTIONS

ALSO STARRING ERNIE HUDSON MICHAEL WINCOTT MUSIC BY GRAEME REVELL PRODUCTION DESIGNER ALEX McDOWELL EDITORS BOY HOENIG A.C.E. AND SCOTT SMITH COSTUMES DESIGNED BY DARRISE VIDINSKI
EXECUTIVE PRODUCERS CALDECOT CHUBB AND JAMES A. JANOWITZ CO-PRODUCER ROBERT L. ROSEN STORY BY JAMES O'BARR SCREENPLAY BY DAVID J. SCHOW AND JOHN SHIRLEY
PRODUCED BY EDWARD R. PRESSMAN AND JEFF MOST DIRECTED BY ALEX PROYAS

ORIGINAL SOUNDTRACK AVAILABLE ON ATLANTIC RECORDS, AUDIOSCOPE RECORDS Cassettes and Compact Discs

INCLUDING NEW MUSIC BY NINE INCH NAILS, STONE TEMPLE PILOTS, THE CURE, HELMET, ROLLINS BAND, PANTERA, VIOLENT FEMMES AND THE JESUS AND MARY CHAIN

THE CROW 1994 (U.S.)

Director Alex Proyas **Producer** James O'Barr **Screenplay** David J. Schow, John Shirley (from the comic book series by James O'Barr) **Cinematography** Dariusz Wolski **Music** Graeme Revell **Cast** Brandon Lee, Sophia Shinas, Rochelle Davis, Ernie Hudson, Michael Wincott, Bai Ling, David Patrick Kelly, Michael Massee, Angel David

Alex Proyas's *The Crow*, based on the James O'Barr comic book series of the same name and adapted for the screen by renowned horror writers David J. Schow and John Shirley, has become a "goth culture" classic as much for the dark attire and skull-like face paint of its undead hero, Eric Draven, as for the tragic accidental death of its star, Brandon Lee (son of martial arts legend Bruce Lee) during the final stages of the film's production. Killed by an empty shell casing that, inadvertently lodged within the barrel of a prop pistol, was propelled through his chest by the force of an exploding blank, Brandon Lee brought an almost preternatural sense of menace to the role of Eric Draven, leading audiences to speculate upon the career that may have blossomed for Lee had his senseless death been avoided.

Set in a nightmarish version of Detroit that Dante's Virgil would be hesitant to set foot in without an armed escort, *The Crow*'s narrative is an ultraviolent take on two of Western literature's most enduring and often interconnected themes: love and revenge. Murdered along with his fiancée, Shelly, on "Devil's Night," which is also ironically the eve of their Halloween wedding, local rock star Eric Draven is resurrected a year later

◄
A supernatural rock-star revenge action movie that tragically took the life of lead actor Brandon Lee.

by a crow tapping upon his tombstone. This crow leads Draven on a quest to wreak vengeance on those responsible for his and his beloved's death, recovering Shelly's engagement ring from a shady pawn shop owner in the process.

Each encounter with the diabolical men responsible for permanently spoiling his impending nuptials is increasingly brutal, but perhaps the film's most iconic set piece is Draven's

" I HAVE SOMETHING TO GIVE YOU . . . THIRTY HOURS OF PAIN ALL AT ONCE, ALL FOR YOU." ERIC DRAVEN

first act of vengeance, in which he kills knife-wielding Tin Tin with his own blades before stealing Tin Tin's coat, an act that leaves a crow-shaped bloodstain on an alley wall.

As his henchmen begin to perish and rumors that Eric Draven has returned from the dead as The Crow become increasingly credible, Detroit's feared crime lord, Top Dollar (Michael Wincott), and his beautiful stepsister and lover, Myca (Bai Ling), arrange to battle their resurrected nemesis. They kidnap Sarah (Rochelle Davis), an adolescent girl for whom Draven feels great compassion, and wound Draven's crow, rendering Draven mortal. The movie culminates in a pretty gory, acrobatic showdown transpiring, appropriately enough, on a gargoyle-bedecked church—a locale that provides the suitably ghoulish setting for several of the film's most spectacular action sequences. **JMcR**

► **Brandon Lee as Eric Draven, taking revenge for his own and his fiancée's murders.**

FIST OF LEGEND 1994 (HONG KONG)

Director Gordon Chan **Producer** Chui Yin Lam, Jet Li **Screenplay** Gordon Chan, Lan Kay Toa, Kee-To Lam, Kwong Kim Yip **Cinematography** Derek Wan **Music** Joseph Koo **Cast** Jet Li, Shinobu Nakayama, Chin Siu Ho, Yasuaki Kurata, Billy Chow

Having studied martial arts since childhood, Jet Li was considered the cinematic heir apparent to Bruce Lee, and what better way to solidify this reputation than by remaking Lee's classic *Fist of Fury* (a.k.a. *The Chinese Connection*, 1972). Despite being a remake, *Fist of Legend* is an excellent martial arts film on its own and is considered by many the crowning achievement of Li's Hong Kong film career.

Shanghai, China, 1937—the first year of full-scale conflict in the Second Sino-Japanese War—finds the Chinese under occupation of the Japanese imperials. Chinese martial artist Chen Zhen (Li) returns from studying abroad in Japan upon receiving the news that his master was killed in a challenge with a Japanese dojo leader. Zhen quickly seeks his revenge and, in defeating the Japanese master, discovers that his master was poisoned before the fight.

With the Jingwu School in disarray, Zhen struggles to maintain order alongside his forbidden romantic relationship with Japanese student Mitsuko (Shinobu Nakayama), whose own uncle Funakoshi (Yasuaki Kurata) has been hired by the Japanese government to challenge the school.

◄

Fist of Legend is up there with Bruce Lee's *Enter the Dragon* (1973) and Jackie Chan's *Drunken Master* (1978). It was choreographed by Yuen Woo-Ping, who later worked his magic on *The Matrix* (1999).

Having completed an astonishing twenty films in a decade, Jet Li was no stranger to performing action on-screen. *Fist of Legend*, however, finds Li at the top of his game, both in terms of physical ability and on-screen charisma. Li offers a decidedly different take on the Chen Zhen character that Bruce Lee originated. One need only compare the dojo fight scenes in their respective films to see the difference—Lee offers

"THE GOAL OF STUDYING MARTIAL ARTS IS TO MAXIMIZE ONE'S ENERGY."

FUNAKOSHI

screaming rage and uncompromising brutality, whereas Li seems more content with calmly neutralizing and exposing his attacker's approach. Other highlights include the opening with Li taking on a group of Japanese segregationists, and a blindfolded battle with Kurata where both men educate each other in their particular martial art. The final battle between Zhen and General Fujita (Billy Chow) is brutally intense, yet also graceful. The martial arts choreography by veteran stuntman/actor/director Yuen Woo-Ping is some of the finest of the era, realistically portraying hand-to-hand combat with kinetic power and never veering into the realm of unbelievable.

▶

Jet Li's *Fist of Legend* is amazing, featuring some of the most dynamic yet elegant martial arts action of the last two decades.

The film opened the door to Hollywood for both Yuen—who made his Western choreography debut with *The Matrix* (1999)—and Li, who arrived in 1998 and has balanced work in the United States, Europe, and China ever since. **WW**

GAUMONT PRÉSENTE

LÉON

UN FILM DE LUC BESSON

JEAN RENO   GARY OLDMAN   NATALIE PORTMAN ET DANNY AÏELLO

DIRECTEUR DE LA PHOTOGRAPHIE THIERRY ARBOGAST   DIRECTEUR DE PRODUCTION BERNARD GRENET   CHEF MONTEUSE SYLVIE LANDRA   DÉCORATEUR DAN WEIL

UNE PRODUCTION GAUMONT / LES FILMS DU DAUPHIN © 1994

COLUMBIA   Sony Music   MUSIQUE ERIC SERRA

LÉON 1994 (FRANCE)

Director Luc Besson **Producer** Claude Besson, John Garland, Bernard Grenet, Luc Besson, Patrice Ledoux **Screenplay** Luc Besson **Cinematography** Thierry Arbogast **Music** Eric Serra **Cast** Jean Reno, Gary Oldman, Natalie Portman, Danny Aiello, Peter Appel

Perhaps the most prominent director of the so-called "*Cinéma du look*" movement of the late 1980s and early 1990s, Luc Besson built upon the international success of *La Femme Nikita* (1990) with the release of *Léon*, otherwise known as *The Professional*, and his first American movie. The film also further cemented Jean Reno's reputation as a rising star of French cinema and introduced the film world to Natalie Portman, who was only eleven when she was cast as Mathilda, the charismatic waif with a taste for revenge.

Like Nikita, Reno's Léon is a professional killer who, despite a cool and seemingly content exterior, wrestles with the desire to be more than simply an anonymous and disposable human weapon. This chance for transformation and redemption comes in the form of Portman's Mathilda, who returns from running an errand to find that her entire family—including her four-year-old brother, the only person she really loved—has been murdered by a corrupt Drug Enforcement Agent named Norman Stansfield (Gary Oldman). Mathilda, wise and jaded beyond her years, quickly discovers that her neighbor Léon is a hit man (a "cleaner") for a local mafioso, and soon asks him to

◀

Also titled *The Professional*, Besson steers edgily between splatter thriller and whimsical fairy tale-style relationship.

teach her the skills of his trade in exchange for her labor as a housekeeper. Léon reluctantly agrees to train her in the "talents" she will need to avenge her brother's death; in the process, he becomes an awkward father figure, soon realizing that caring for a rebellious twelve-year-old is far more challenging than tending for the lone plant in his apartment. When Mathilda admits to Léon that she is falling in love with him, a proclamation

"AND STOP SAYING 'OKAY' ALL THE TIME. OKAY?" *LÉON* "OKAY." *MATHILDA* "GOOD." *LÉON*

to which Léon never responds, their unorthodox relationship becomes even more discomforting. When Mathilda's attempt to kill Stansfield goes awry, Léon rescues her, killing several D.E.A. officers and evoking Stansfield's ire in the process. Using his notoriously spurious tactics, Stansfield tracks down Léon and Mathilda, setting the stage for a memorable climactic confrontation followed by a tender denouement.

Several versions of *Léon* exist, including a 136-minute "international version" that often gets assigned the descriptor, "Director's Cut." Luc Besson, however, considers the film's original 110-minute release his preferred version. Whichever version you see, Reno and Portman make a great odd couple, and watch out for Gary Oldman's chilling performance as a psychotic rogue officer who can literally sniff out a lie and lives by "the only good witness is a dead witness" code. **JMcR**

▶ **The tender relationship between the assassin (Reno) and his apprentice (Portman) proves one of this motion picture's strongest components.**

KEANU REEVES   DENNIS HOPPER   SANDRA BULLOCK

GET READY FOR RUSH HOUR.

TWENTIETH CENTURY FOX PRESENTS A MARK GORDON PRODUCTION KEANU REEVES DENNIS HOPPER SANDRA BULLOCK "SPEED" JOE MORTON AND JEFF DANIELS MUSIC BY MARK MANCINA EDITOR JOHN WRIGHT, A.C.E. PRODUCTION DESIGNER JACKSON DeGOVIA DIRECTOR OF PHOTOGRAPHY ANDRZEJ BARTKOWIAK EXECUTIVE PRODUCER IAN BRYCE WRITTEN BY GRAHAM YOST PRODUCED BY MARK GORDON DIRECTED BY JAN DeBONT

SPEED 1994 (U.S.)

Director Jan de Bont **Producer** Mike Gordon, Ian V. Bryce, Allison Lyon
Screenplay Graham Yost **Cinematography** Andrzej Bartowiak
Music Mark Mancina **Cast** Keanu Reeves, Sandra Bullock, Dennis Hopper,
Jeff Daniels, Joe Morton, Alan Ruck, Beth Grant, Glenn Plummer

Jan de Bont's 1994 film *Speed* boosted the popularity of
nascent screen presence Sandra Bullock and sent Keanu
Reeves's star stock through the roof. In his big-screen directing
debut, de Bont surprised audiences by shooting frenzied
action sequences localized, for much of the film, in small
interior physical spaces: an elevator, a train, and, most notably,
a bus. The film that many thought would be too much like *Die
Hard*—for which de Bont had served as cinematographer—
achieved huge commercial success, won two Oscars, and
made its way on to the American Film Institute's list of Top 100
Heart-Pounding Movies of all time.

The film's villain, Howard Payne (Dennis Hopper), is a
revenge-driven bomber who rigs and then threatens to
detonate a passenger-laden Los Angeles city bus. The officer
on the case, Jack Traven (Reeves), had foiled another of Payne's
ransom plots, making Payne's latest extortion attempt personal
for both men. The depiction of Traven hindering Payne's
original plan, as well as the scenes in which Traven finds and
boards the speeding bus, are edge-of-your-seat sequences
that comprise only about the first quarter of the film.

◀
Speed picked up
two Oscars for Best
Effects–Sound
Effects Editing, and
Best Sound in 1995.

The film's main action takes place on the wired bus itself, with Traven aware of the following rules: if the speed of the bus falls below 50 miles per hour, or if passengers attempt to exit the bus, the bus will explode—a neat action movie premise.

As Traven tries simultaneously to thwart Payne, calm frantic passengers, and safely navigate L.A. traffic, he is assisted by innocent bystander Annie Porter (Sandra Bullock). Porter, a

"POP QUIZ, HOTSHOT. THERE'S A BOMB ON A BUS . . . WHAT DO YOU DO? WHAT DO YOU DO?" HOWARD PAYNE

regular passenger who steps in when the bus's driver is shot, provides capable, level-headed assistance; she also brings a more-than-believable competence to the role (Bullock actually earned her bus driver's license as a result of this film), as well as some fairly flirtatious banter.

Speed's commercial success was such that it spawned numerous pop culture references and various spoofs. It also led to a sequel, *Speed 2: Cruise Control* in 1997, also directed by de Bont and starring Bullock, this time along with Jason Patric and Willem Dafoe. The sequel, which takes place mainly on a cruise liner, tried to recapture *Speed's* tense circumstances and frenzied pace, but was not nearly as successful as the original. *Speed's* feverish action sequences, astounding special effects, and compelling romantic subplot helps to claim its place among the best of U.S. action films. **AK**

▶
L.A. cop Traven (Reeves) is the nonstop action hero forever trying to catch the bus. The pace never lets up; in fact, you'll believe a bus can fly in this movie.

When he said I do,
he never said
what he did.
Schwarzenegger
True Lies
A JAMES CAMERON FILM
TWENTIETH CENTURY FOX PRESENTS A LIGHTSTORM ENTERTAINMENT PRODUCTION A JAMES CAMERON FILM ARNOLD SCHWARZENEGGER JAMIE LEE CURTIS
TRUE LIES TOM ARNOLD BILL PAXTON ART MALIK TIA CARRERE MUSIC BY BRAD FIEDEL EDITED BY MARK GOLDBLATT, A.C.E. AND CONRAD BUFF AND RICHARD A. HARRIS
PRODUCTION DESIGNER PETER LAMONT DIRECTOR OF PHOTOGRAPHY RUSSELL CARPENTER SPECIAL VISUAL EFFECTS BY DIGITAL DOMAIN EXECUTIVE PRODUCERS RAE SANCHINI ROBERT SHRIVER LAWRENCE KASANOFF
SCREENPLAY BY JAMES CAMERON BASED UPON A SCREENPLAY BY CLAUDE ZIDI, SIMON MICHAEL AND DIDIER KAMINKA PRODUCED BY JAMES CAMERON AND STEPHANIE AUSTIN
SOUNDTRACK AVAILABLE ON LIGHTSTORM/EPIC SOUNDTRAX
DIRECTED BY JAMES CAMERON
R RESTRICTED
UNDER 17 REQUIRES ACCOMPANYING PARENT OR ADULT GUARDIAN
VERSION B
Printed in U.S.A.

TRUE LIES 1994 (U.S.)

Director James Cameron **Producer** James Cameron, Stephanie Austin
Screenplay James Cameron **Cinematography** Russell Carpenter
Music Brad Fiedel **Cast** Arnold Schwarzenegger, Jamie Lee Curtis, Tom Arnold,
Bill Paxton, Art Malik, Tia Carrere, Charlton Heston, Eliza Dushku

True Lies reunites the winning combination of director James
Cameron and actor Arnold Schwarzenegger, who had worked
together on the sci-fi blockbusters *The Terminator* (1984) and
Terminator 2: Judgment Day (1991), and contains as many thrills,
spills, and special effects as its precursors, plus a heavy dose of
comedy; this is an action movie that does not take itself too
seriously and provides all-around entertainment.

Schwarzenegger plays Harry Tasker, who has led a double-
life for fifteen years as an undercover spy posing as a computer
salesman. Not even his wife, Helen, played by Jamie Lee Curtis,
guesses his duplicity; in fact, she is bored by her husband's
apparent geeky love of technology and frustrated by his long
stints working away from home. She yearns for adventure and,
in a Shakespearian twist, finds the spice lacking in her marriage
in the shape of a computer salesman, Simon, played by Bill
Paxton, who pretends he is a spy to win her affection.

When Harry discovers his wife's dalliance, he and fellow agent
Albert Gibson, played by Tom Arnold, use the resources of the
organization they work for, the Omega Force, to spy on Helen
and provide her with the excitement she craves by giving her a

◄

When *True Lies* was
made, it was the
most expensive
production to date,
costing more than
$110 million.
Cameron of course
surpassed himself
and that budget,
and he certainly
has a talent for
spending money
wisely.

fake mission. Problems arise when an Islamic terrorist outfit called the Crimson Jihad, led by the extremist Salim Abu Aziz, played in suitably evil vein by Art Malik, kidnaps the Taskers. A battle against time ensues when Aziz threatens to launch a nuclear missile at the United States and the Taskers attempt to stand in his way.

This is a movie that barely catches its breath as it veers from one action-packed sequence to the next. Schwarzenegger

> ## *"WHENEVER I CAN'T SLEEP, I ASK HIM TO TELL ME ABOUT HIS DAY: SIX SECONDS AND I'M OUT." HELEN TASKER*

puts in the kind of bravado performance that had already made him a star as he slugs it out with baddies on ski slopes and on a horse in a hotel elevator, pilots a Harrier Jump Jet, dodges multiple explosions and machine gunfire, packs firearms ranging from a Beretta 92FS to a Glock 17, and shows he can tango against the clock with sexy terrorist Juno Skinner, played by Tia Carrere.

► **Harry Tasker (Schwarzenegger) on the trail of stolen nuclear weapons in one of the most relentlessly action-packed movies ever to hit the big screen.**

Jamie Lee Curtis shows she too can be a hero when she grabs hold of a MAC-10 pistol, dangles from a helicopter, and does a striptease, often with amusing consequences. There are a host of memorable one-liners and comic turns from Arnold, Paxton, and Curtis, and a wonderful cameo from Charlton Heston as the head of Omega, although it's Curtis and Schwarzenegger who provide the real comic touches when the truth about Mr. Tasker's day job comes to light. **CK**

MARTIN LAWRENCE   WILL SMITH

A DON SIMPSON and JERRY BRUCKHEIMER PRODUCTION

BAD BOYS

WHATCHA GONNA DO?

COLUMBIA PICTURES PRESENTS A DON SIMPSON and JERRY BRUCKHEIMER PRODUCTION STARRING MARTIN LAWRENCE WILL SMITH "BAD BOYS"
TEA LEONI TCHEKY KARYO THERESA RANDLE and JOE PANTOLIANO MUSIC BY MARK MANCINA EDITED BY MICHAEL DILBECK and HAPPY WALTERS
FILM EDITOR CHRISTIAN WAGNER PRODUCTION DESIGNER JOHN VALLONE DIRECTOR OF PHOTOGRAPHY HOWARD ATHERTON, B.S.C. EXECUTIVE PRODUCERS BRUCE S. PUSTIN and LUCAS FOSTER
STORY BY GEORGE GALLO SCREENPLAY BY MICHAEL BARRIE & JIM MULHOLLAND and DOUG RICHARDSON
PRODUCED BY DON SIMPSON and JERRY BRUCKHEIMER DIRECTED BY MICHAEL BAY

COLUMBIA
PICTURES

SOUNDTRACK ON WORK

BAD BOYS 1995 (U.S.)

Director Michael Bay **Producer** Don Simpson, Jerry Bruckheimer **Screenplay** Michael Barrie, Jim Mulholland, Doug Richardson, Thomas Pope (story by George Gallo) **Cinematography** Howard Atherton **Music** Mark Mancina **Cast** Will Smith, Martin Lawrence, Téa Leoni, Tchéky Karyo, Theresa Randle, Joe Pantoliano

The story of *Bad Boys* begins before the actual shooting. It was intended as a vehicle for *Saturday Night Live*'s Jon Lovitz and Dana Carvey (the latter also Mike Myers's dweeb partner in *Wayne's World* in 1992), until producer Don Simpson, Hollywood's *uber* wild child, allegedly scared Carvey off on a two-day drug-fueled, sex-crazed "bonding mission" to Vegas. The coproducers decided to "blacken up" and brought in Will Smith and Martin Lawrence, hot from TV success, but still not major movie stars—and therefore cheap. By the time this high-explosive, pistol-packing action grosser, fizzing with wit, had done the rounds, they were movie stars.

The plot is the simple, staple diet of a thousand police procedure movies: Marcus (Lawrence) is a hen-pecked family man, whereas Mike (Smith) is more of a free spirit. It's a sharp-speaking, comic buddy setup. Partners on the Miami Police Department, they are put in charge of a highly dangerous case: $100 million in heroin, from the biggest drug bust of their careers, has been stolen from police headquarters. They have seventy-two hours to reclaim the heroin before the Internal Affairs Division gets involved, or Miami P.D. is toast.

◀

In the style of *48 Hrs.* and *Lethal Weapon*, there is plenty of foul-mouthed joshing, bloody shoot-outs, and a sequel *Bad Boys II* (2003).

They're soon hot on the trail of French drug overlord Fouchet (Tchéky Karyo). Mike asks Maxine (Karen Alexander), a hooker, to keep an eye open for high rollers. Maxine gets a call from former cop Dominguez (Emmanuel Xuereb), who's high on drugs and wants to spend $2,000, so she asks best friend Julie (Téa Leoni) to tag along. Julie's not a hooker but the guy's so out of it, Maxine claims, that they'll be out of there with the

"WHAT ARE OUR CHANCES?" MARCUS "REMEMBER CLUB HELL?" MIKE "YEAH." MARCUS "WORSE." MIKE

▶
After early shenanigans, the role of Mike was destined for Arsenio Hall until director Michael Bay caught an episode of long-running TV series *The Fresh Prince of Bel Air* and said he wanted its star instead. Smith capitalized on this break big time.

cash in minutes. But at Dominguez's house, it all goes belly up—Fouchet kills Maxine. Julie's seen the murder, so she contacts the police, but she's willing to talk only to Mike. Mike's not around (don't ask!), so Marcus is forced to impersonate him; when Mike returns, he has to be Marcus. The latter has a wife Theresa (Theresa Randle) and three kids, while Mike is Mr. Single Seducer, so this ain't a very close fit. Their pursuit of villain Fouchet slams into overdrive when his henchmen kidnap Julie from under their noses. Cue mayhem—and a hot wisecracking partnership that propelled Smith and Martin into the big time.

Then the tragic coda (and it's not *Bad Boys II*): despite his huge success (or maybe because of it), Simpson, regularly OD'ing on prescription drugs, coke, and S&M games—and that was just before breakfast—was found dead in January 1996. He was the real bad boy. **MH**

DESPERADO 1995 (U.S.)

Director Robert Rodriguez **Producer** Bill Borden, Robert Rodriguez **Screenplay** Robert Rodriguez **Cinematography** Guillermo Navarro **Music** Los Lobos **Cast** Antonio Banderas, Salma Hayek, Joaquin de Almeida, Cheech Marin, Steve Buscemi, Carlos Gomez, Quentin Tarantino, Carlos Gallardo, Danny Trejo

Desperado is a sequel to Robert Rodriguez's first film, *El Mariachi* (1992, a.k.a. *The Musician*), famously made for $7,000 in Mexico, and revisits the original's plot to a point that some have regarded as beyond self-homage. So it may be the same, more or less, but what a thrilling genre riot it is, the peer of the great John Woo actioners.

A man, Buscemi (brilliantly played by Steve Buscemi, not as easy as it sounds), walks into a bar. He tells a story of a stranger, a wandering musician—El mariachi, in other words—who is thirsting for revenge. This troubadour has been shot by the villain, maimed so he can't play guitar, and lost his girl into the bargain: the eponymous first movie's plot. Now the stranger is heading for this town, seeking the baddie—and vengeance.

In his commentary on *El mariachi* (1992), Rodriguez gives a brilliant primer in how to make a great movie for peanuts. He states convincingly that the absence of money is often a great spur to creativity, causing directors to seek new, exciting ways around cinematic conundrums. So what was he planning when he got a Hollywood budget one thousand times larger than his original movie? Well ... do the same thing again, with

◄

This $7 million Hollywood version of the $7,000 low-budget *El mariachi* (both directed by Robert Rodriguez) had, in effect, one thousand times the budget of the original.

better actors and bigger explosions. A cynic might argue that Rodriguez has proved his earlier case in reverse: money is a bulwark against creativity. In any case, Rodriguez shows what happens when you let talent loose—basically, you can have a whale of a time. Antonio Banderas is fantastic as El Mariachi, the beautiful Salma Hayek (fighting off the equally wondrous Jennifer Lopez in casting) sizzles. The day that Rodriguez and

> ## "BLESS ME, FATHER, FOR I HAVE KILLED QUITE A FEW MEN . . ." *EL MARIACHI*
> ## "NO SHIT!" *BUSCEMI (MASQUERADING AS PRIEST)*

Guillermo Navarro shot the love scenes between Banderas and Hayek, the entire crew surprisingly decided they all had pressing reasons to be on set. As for the rest of the cast, Joaquin de Almeida is well shady, Cheech Marin and Buscemi are hilarious, and the music by L.A. band Los Lobos is terrific: even Tarantino plays himself with aplomb.

Desperado is not simply an attempt to cash in on an earlier version (but it is still a looser, big-budget remake nonetheless), nor is it a great artistic statement (for that, see *Once Upon A Time In The West*, 1968—although, of course, Rodriguez did make *Once Upon A Time In Mexico* (2003) but that doesn't count). It's just, quite simply, one of the best no-holes-barred gratuitously violent action movies of the 1990s, its balletic grace the forerunner of the *Matrix* movies. And what's more, it's also one of the funniest. **MH**

► **Banderas resurrected the gun-slinging role established in the "shoestring" *El mariachi* where the budget was so low they resorted to water pistols as well as real (borrowed) guns.**

ALBERT R. BROCCOLI presents PIERCE BROSNAN as IAN FLEMING'S JAMES BOND 007® in "GOLDENEYE"

GOLDENEYE

No limits. No fears. No substitutes.

ALBERT R. BROCCOLI presents PIERCE BROSNAN as IAN FLEMING'S JAMES BOND 007® in "GOLDENEYE" SEAN BEAN IZABELLA SCORUPCO
FAMKE JANSSEN and JOE DON BAKER music Eric Serra editor ANTHONY WAYE and TERRY RAWLINGS director PHIL MEHEUX production PETER LAMONT TOM PEVS
MICHAEL FRANCE screenplay JEFFREY CAINE and BRUCE FEINSTEIN story MICHAEL G. WILSON and BARBARA BROCCOLI directed MARTIN CAMPBELL UNITED
BONO and THE EDGE performed TINA TURNER SOUNDTRACK ON VIRGIN RECORDS

GOLDENEYE 1995 (U.S. • U.K.)

Director Martin Campbell **Producer** Barbara Broccoli **Screenplay** Jeffrey Caine, Bruce Feirstein, story by Michael France (based on Ian Fleming's characters) **Cinematography** Phil Meheux **Music** Eric Serra **Cast** Pierce Brosnan, Sean Bean, Isabella Scorupco, Famke Janssen, Joe Don Baker, Judi Dench, Robbie Coltrane

This was the seventeenth James Bond movie but it saw the introduction of a new, fifth version of the British hero. There was a lot riding on Pierce Brosnan's first outing as 007. Illness and death had ravaged the original production and writing teams, and only "Q" remained of the long-standing cast. In movie land it had been a long wait.

But the hiatus between the last Bond outing, *Licence to Kill* (1989)—after which Timothy Dalton decided he'd had enough— and this movie enabled the creative team to come up with a new, retooled version of Bond that was suitable for the times. They (and new producer Barbara Broccoli, Cubby's daughter) correctly judged that the world had changed irrevocably, since the Soviet Empire's collapse and the Cold War's demise.

Now the chief criminal was, in a twist worthy of this amorphous age, a former colleague of Bond's, the rugged 006, played by Sean Bean. More used to playing rugged heroes himself (most consistently as Sharpe in the long-running, big-budget TV saga), he revels in the chance to play a turncoat. (A case could be made for Bean as a credible Bond himself.) Yet Brosnan was well cast for the role, adept at smooth one-liners

◄

Not just the first outing for Brosnan as Bond, but the first Bond movie ever to be released on DVD. The title refers to Ian Fleming's Jamaican beachfront house—where he wrote all his Bond stories.

in the best Roger Moore tradition, yet also tough in the Dalton and Sean Connery mold. The latter two are the best actors of the four Bonds who lasted more than one picture (and in consequence took the role more seriously than it maybe merited). Indeed, Brosnan, ex-husband of Liverpudlian "Countess" Cassandra Harris from *For Your Eyes Only* (1981), had almost "Bonded" in 1988 but was contractually compelled to

> ## "WHO'S THE COMPETITION?" JAMES BOND
> ## "EX-KGB GUY. GOT A LIMP . . . KNOW HIM?"
> ## JACK WADE "I GAVE HIM THE LIMP." JAMES BOND

endure further episodes as the lead in TV's *Remington Steele*.

The plot is broadly similar to many other Bond movies: Natalya (played by Isabella Scorupco), the survivor of an explosion at a nuclear plant, gets together with 007 to stop bad boy Bean and pals from taking over the world. Meanwhile tough girl Xenia Onotopp (Famke Janssen) creates merry mayhem with her preferred method of execution: squeezing her victims between her thighs during acrobatic lovemaking.

Kiwi director Martin Campbell stuck to stunts, superb music from Eric Serra, better known for his moody electronics in *La Femme Nikita* (1990) and *Léon* (1994), and a theme song sung by Tina Turner with Bono and The Edge (both of U2) on hand, as well as cool locations (take a bow, St. Petersburg). The gamble was successful. *GoldenEye* took $219 million worldwide, reviving the moribund franchise. **MH**

▶
Good old-fashioned physical effects, i.e., stunts were prominent in *GoldenEye*.

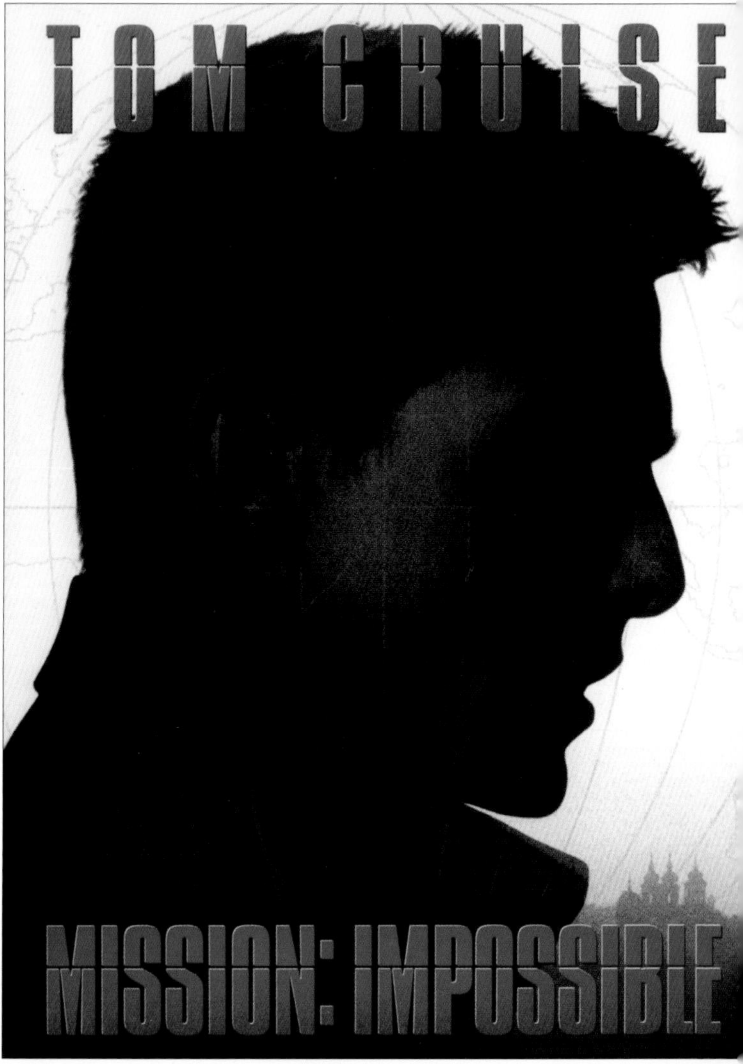
TOM CRUISE
MISSION: IMPOSSIBLE

MISSION: IMPOSSIBLE 1996 (U.S.)

Director Brian De Palma   **Producer** Tom Cruise, Paula Wagner
Screenplay David Koepp, Robert Towne (story by David Koepp, Steven Zaillian)
Cinematography Stephen H. Burum   **Music** Danny Elfman   **Cast** Tom Cruise, Jon
Voight, Emmanuelle Beart, Henry Czerny, Jean Reno, Ving Rhames, Kristin Scott Thomas

The original TV series *Mission: Impossible*, which ran from 1966
to 1973, depicted the adventures of a team of covert American
intelligence operatives. With its gadget-festooned narratives,
the series was very much an expression of a 1960s technocracy,
and in its anxieties about enemy infiltration and subversion it
also had some obvious Cold War resonances.

As directed by Brian De Palma, the big-screen version of
Mission: Impossible was a slick, big-budget package that, just
beneath its glossy surface, offered a surprisingly perverse
interpretation of its source material. Elements familiar to fans of
the TV show were carried over—the complicated missions, the
improbably convincing disguises and face masks, a heavy
reliance on technology, and, of course, Lalo Schifrin's instantly
recognizable TV theme music—but the tone was different, in
parts more playful but also darker. By contrast, the TV version
had bristled in self-confidence while also being generally a
humorless experience.

The film begins in true TV style with Jim Phelps (played by
Jon Voight) leading his team on a counterintelligence mission.
Disaster strikes almost immediately, with most of the team

◄
**The movie's major
achievement is
to hold together
many unwieldy
elements while
maintaining a
coherent and
intelligent tone.
The film's two
sequels were just
as spectacular, if
not more so, but
they lacked the
original's depth.**

killed and agent Ethan Hunt (played by Tom Cruise) accused of being a traitor and forced to go on the run. After some complex plot developments, the villain is revealed to be Jim Phelps himself, whose sordid motivation is financial gain. A possible subtext for this is provided by the end of the Cold War and the dissolution of old loyalties. However, the film seems more preoccupied with developing a quasi father-son relationship

"MY TEAM IS DEAD. THEY KNEW WE WERE COMING, MAN . . . AND THE DISK IS GONE." *ETHAN HUNT*

between Phelps and Hunt. Any sense of a torch being passed from one generation to the next is here troubled by the father figure's treachery, and an oedipal spin is added through having Hunt grow emotionally close to Phelps's young wife.

Operating in counterpoint to what, in effect, is a mix of dour political thriller and psychodrama, is a series of impressive action scenes. The most suspenseful of these involves Hunt and his new team breaking into the C.I.A.'s Langley headquarters. De Palma's work has often shown the influence of Hitchcock, and it's visible here, in the restricted setting and the precisely articulated sense of the space through which Hunt moves. By contrast, the final and most spectacular scene is a special effects-laden extravaganza involving a helicopter flying through a tunnel in pursuit of a high-speed train, with Hunt defeating his enemies with the aid of some exploding bubble gum. **PH**

▶

Hunt's (Cruise's) initial illegal infiltration into his own C.I.A. headquarters seems—in our post "War on Terror" world—laughably easy, but his subsequent descent on wires into a room armed with an amazing array of security devices remains a classic sequence.

THE ROCK 1996 (U.S.)

Director Michael Bay **Producer** Don Simpson, Jerry Bruckheimer **Screenplay** David Weisberg, Douglas S. Cook, Mark Rosner **Cinematography** John Schwartzman **Music** Nick Glennie-Smith, Hans Zimmer **Cast** Sean Connery, Nicolas Cage, Ed Harris, Michael Biehn, William Forsythe, Vanessa Marcil

When a group of tourists take a trip to visit San Francisco's infamous Alcatraz prison, little do they realize that their tour will end with them being the rock's reluctant inmates, held hostage by U.S. Marines led by the disenchanted Brigadier General Francis X. Hummel (Ed Harris). Hummel feels his men have been treated unfairly and their families deserve compensation for work they did on covert special-ops missions, which in some cases led to their death. Tired of being sidelined, Hummel decides the only way to get his government's attention is to capture the tiny island and threaten to launch a chemical weapon at San Francisco. Unsurprisingly, the U.S. government finally sits up and takes notice, sending in a team of Navy SEALs to seize control of the island, liberate the hostages, and disarm the weapon. Given that Alcatraz is supposedly impenetrable, the government calls in the services of the one man who has, unbeknown to the public, ever escaped from its prison, a British spy, John Patrick Mason (Sean Connery). Mason is a man who knows too many secrets, ones that could be damaging to the United States, hence his incarceration. Despite successfully fleeing Alacatraz, he was later captured and imprisoned, and

◀

Quentin Tarantino, Ian La Frenais, Dick Clement, Aaron Sorkin, and Jonathan Hensleigh also had an uncredited hand in the sharp script. It helped turn Cage from nervous nerd into action hero.

he is released to help on the mission. A geeky FBI chemical weapons expert, Dr. Stanley Goodspeed (Nicolas Cage), joins Mason in his quest.

With such a lineup of talented tough-guy role actors, *The Rock* immediately smacks of a pedigree production. But that's not all it has to recommend it. Producers Don Simpson and Jerry Bruckheimer of *Top Gun* (1986) fame assembled the

> ## "ALL I KNOW IS THAT YOU WERE BIG IN VIETNAM. I SAW THE HIGHLIGHTS ON TELEVISION." JOHN PATRICK MASON

perfect crew to make a top-class actioner. Directed by a master of action adventures, Michael Bay, the film is jam-packed with action on land, sea, and air. There are many notable scenes, from a massacre in a shower room when the Marines and SEALs go head-to-head, a bloody standoff when Hummel's men mutiny, and a spectacular climax in which Goodspeed finds himself in the middle of an air strike. John Schwartzman's cinematography is superb, the soundtrack is stirring, and the script flows breezily with fast, intelligent dialogue. Such is the quality of the writing that even Hummel comes off as a sympathetic character who has been ignored, abandoned, and marginalized by the government he has served heroically rather than someone who is merely a demented marine turned mercenary. But the best parts of the movie are the scenes between Mason (Connery) and Goodspeed (Cage). **CK**

► Connery delivers an impressive performance as a devious old hand in the espionage game, making the most of the wry comedy and furious action that the film affords.

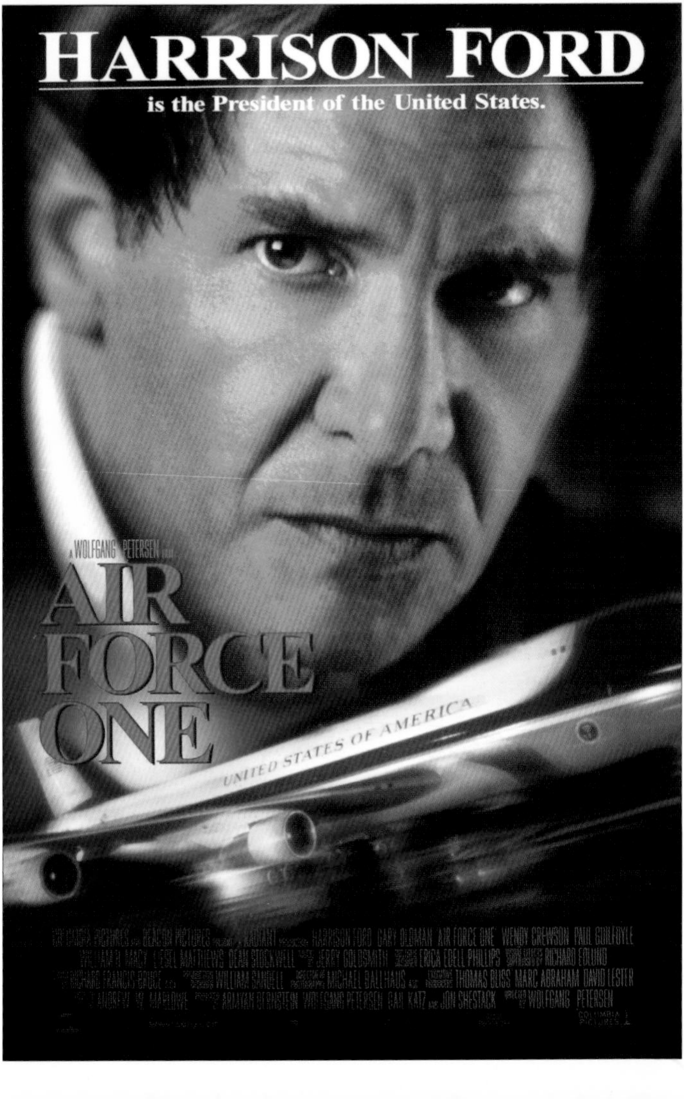
HARRISON FORD
is the President of the United States.
A WOLFGANG PETERSEN FILM
AIR FORCE ONE
UNITED STATES OF AMERICA

AIR FORCE ONE 1997 (U.S.)

Director Wolfgang Petersen **Producer** Marc Abraham, Armyan Bernstein, Wolfgang Petersen **Screenplay** Andrew W. Marlowe **Cinematography** Michael Ballhaus **Music** Jerry Goldsmith **Cast** Harrison Ford, Gary Oldman, Glenn Close, William H. Macy, Dean Stockwell, Jurgen Prochnow

Here's a plot riddled with more holes than Swiss cheese: it includes a group of terrorists who manage to assume the identities of a news crew along with their fingerprints; a fax that no one sees but is acted upon; the solution to disabling the plane lying within the colors of the American flag; and a president who is as handy with a gun as he is with words—and is able to pilot an airplane with little help. Although this all requires an extreme suspension of belief, *Air Force One* is an enjoyable action-thriller, well directed by Wolfgang Petersen on his third major Hollywood feature.

Lacking the moral subtly of his earlier films including *The Boot* (a.k.a. *Das Boot*, 1981) and *Enemy Mine* (1985), *Air Force One* pits an idealized American president, James Marshall (Harrison Ford) against a group of Russian terrorists led by Ivan Korshunov (Gary Oldman). Harrison Ford is perfect as the diplomatic head of state turned action hero, who manages to single-handedly save the day—and Western democracy—when a group of terrorists hijack Air Force One in an attempt to get the deposed leader of Kazakhstan General Alexander Radek (Jurgen Prochnow) freed from jail.

◄

An imagined security threat before the days of 9/11, when bad guys had accents and America could imagine itself as the protector of Western democracy and impenetrable to terrorist threats.

The final high-thrills confrontation between Marshall and Korshunov has the remaining passengers escorted off the plane onto a C-130 Hercules plane using a zipline, while the crosscutting between events on the plane and in the White House gives an extra tense dynamic. While Marshall battles the bad guys on the plane, on the ground Vice President Kathryn Bennett (Glenn Close) is having her own battle with

> ## "REAL PEACE IS NOT JUST THE ABSENCE OF CONFLICT; IT IS THE PRESENCE OF JUSTICE." WOLFGANG PETERSEN

members of the Cabinet who, led by Secretary of Defense Stanton Dean (Dean Stockwell), are seeking to get the President removed from power, and thereby sentence all on Air Force One to death. Eventually, Marshall overcomes his nemesis and escapes to safety. With the events of 9/11 and the subsequent invasion of Iraq, the simplistic politics of *Air Force One* seem strangely prescient as a case in which real life has come to imitate art, *but* without the peace and justice that *Air Force One* presupposes.

► The claustrophobic setting of the airplane leads to inventive and generally exciting scenes, including the final confrontation between Marshall (Ford) and Korshunov (Oldman).

While the nature of film, especially Hollywood action films, necessitates overcoming conflict and restoring order, real life is much messier as current events attest to. Even given the Disneyfication of real-world politics, *Air Force One* is a thrilling ride and one well worth taking. It also functions as a powerful reminder of how much simpler things were before 9/11. **CB**

FACE/OFF 1997 (U.S.)

Director John Woo **Producer** Terence Chang, Michael Douglas, Christopher Godsick **Screenplay** Mike Werb, Michael Colleary **Cinematography** Oliver Wood **Music** John Powell **Cast** Nicholas Cage, John Travolta, Alessandro Nivola, Joan Allen, Dominique Swain, Gina Gershon

From Hong Kong to Hollywood, John Woo's third Hollywood feature film *Face/Off* successfully merges the best of Hong Kong cinema with the best of Hollywood. Big-budget explosions, balletic choreography, and fine performances by John Travolta and Nicholas Cage as archenemies, F.B.I. agent Sean Archer and his nemesis, Castor Troy, a deranged terrorist, makes *Face/Off* essential viewing for the action aficionado.

Face/Off begins with Troy attempting to kill Archer while he is at a playground with his young son, Michael, who dies instead of his father. Fast-forward six years and Archer is still trying to capture the elusive Troy, despite his marriage coming apart and his fractured relationship with his daughter. Acting on information that Troy's brother, Pollux (Alessandro Nivola), has chartered a plane at an L.A. airport, Archer and his team rush to stop Pollux and Troy from escaping. In an explosive action sequence, both Pollux and Troy are captured, with Troy ending up in a coma. Discovering that before his capture, Troy had planted a biological bomb somewhere in Los Angeles, the F.B.I. resorts to desperate measures to find out its location. As Pollux will only talk to his brother, the latest high-tech

◄

Face/Off is Woo's best Hollywood outing to date and is an important film in that it redefined the parameters of the action genre.

surgery is used to swap Archer's face for Troy's, and modify his body and voice so that he is the mirror image of Troy, indistinguishable from the real person. When Troy wakes up unexpectedly from his coma, with his "face off," he is forced to assume the identity of Archer. While Troy/Archer languishes in prison, Archer/Troy locates the bomb, disarms it, and becomes a hero in the process. This forces Troy/Archer to escape from

"I WANT TO TAKE HIS FACE . . . OFF. EYES, NOSE, SKIN, TEETH. IT'S COMING OFF."

SEAN ARCHER

prison and assume the lifestyle and identity of his nemesis, thus becoming the very thing that he has sworn to defeat.

Bringing heroic bloodshed to Hollywood cinema with its highly stylized aesthetics, reflective surfaces, and dynamic action sequences including multiple Mexican standoffs, Woo introduces a new type of action cinema to Hollywood that is as emotional as it is exciting. In one spectacular scene, a young boy stands in the middle of an apartment listening to "Somewhere Over the Rainbow" as death and destruction rain around him: radiant light illuminating the presence of good in the midst of so much evil. *Face/Off* is a high-octane thriller that is reminiscent of Woo's Hong Kong films—including *A Better Tomorrow* (*Ying hung boon sik*) from 1986—in the mirroring of hero and villain, explosive action sequences, and the philosophical meditation on the nature of identity. **CB**

▶
Travolta doing what he does best when he isn't dancing. Woo's Hollywood offering also had hints of his previous work *The Killer* (*Dip huet seung hung*) released in 1989.

CON AIR 1997 (U.S.)

Director Simon West **Producer** Jerry Bruckheimer **Screenplay** Scott Rosenberg
Cinematography David Tattersall **Music** Mark Mancina, Trevor Rabin
Cast Nicolas Cage, John Cusack, John Malkovich, Ving Rhames, Nick Chinlund,
Steve Buscemi, Colm Meaney, Rachel Ticotin, Dave Chappelle, Mykelti Williamson

Jerry Bruckheimer has been a producer synonymous with the action film since the mid-1980s, when he made films such as *Beverly Hills Cop* (1984) and *Top Gun* (1986). The year before *Con Air*, Bruckheimer produced *The Rock* (1995), with Nicolas Cage in the role of a scientist turned reluctant action hero. For *Con Air*, Cage took a more traditional action lead, and Bruckheimer placed directing duties with first-timer Simon West, who had made the transition from making commercials. Cage's Cameron Poe is a little reminiscent of Bruce Willis in the *Die Hard* films, even down to the dirty white vest that he wears throughout much of *Con Air*. He is a nonchalant yet honorable family man who happens to be in the wrong place at the wrong time. There is also a touch of Rambo to Poe, as both received an honorable discharge from an elite unit of the American army. However, unlike the overly muscular action heroes of the 1980s, Poe is not a warmonger and survives more through a combination of guile and a desire to see his family again.

    Imprisoned after accidentally killing a drunken man, and while defending himself and his wife, Poe is paroled after eight years inside as a model inmate. For his release, he is transported

◄
The premise is ludicrous and Cage's hair seriously bad, but the movie works because it sends itself up while delivering high-octane action, testosterone, and plenty of expletives.

in a special airplane along with a collection of highly dangerous prisoners who are being transferred to a new, super-maximum prison. Once in flight, the prisoners, led by Cyrus "The Virus" Grissom (John Malkovich), take over the plane with seemingly only Poe standing in the way of their escape plan. *Con Air* is a prison film, even though it is largely devoid of any prison scenes. Like many prison films, this is a distinctly male-centric

"THEY SOMEHOW MANAGED TO GET EVERY CREEP AND FREAK IN THE UNIVERSE ONTO THIS PLANE." *CAMERON POE*

action arena, but here the filmmakers have cranked up the motley cargo of villains to an almost comic book level, and intensified the situation by focusing much of the action within the confines of the airplane.

Part of this film's appeal is the plane's motley crew of prisoners played by a strong cast that includes Ving Rhames, Danny Trejo, and a creepy Steve Buscemi (as the serial killer "The Marietta Mangler"). The plane is central to the film's action sequences, with its rough landing at an airfield an excuse for a mass performance of masculinity as the prisoners physically pull the aircraft out of a hole together. With the plane airborne again it flies toward Las Vegas, where it is forced to land on the Vegas Strip. Crashing through all the glitz and show of Vegas, the hurtling plane's destruction of this gambling wonderland is a spectacle set against a fitting backdrop of excess. **IC**

► Lots of six-packs, ripped T-shirts, bristling muscles, and shoot-'em-up stunts all rolled into action man Cage. Malkovich provides the nasty, while Cusack does the cute.

BRUCE WILLIS
JERRY BRUCKHEIMER
ARMAGEDDON
FOR LOVE. FOR HONOR. FOR MANKIND.
A
MICHAEL BAY
FILM
TOUCHSTONE PICTURES PRESENTS A JERRY BRUCKHEIMER PRODUCTION IN ASSOCIATION WITH VALHALLA MOTION PICTURES A MICHAEL BAY FILM
BRUCE WILLIS "ARMAGEDDON" BILLY BOB THORNTON LIV TYLER BEN AFFLECK WILL PATTON PETER STORMARE KEITH DAVID AND STEVE BUSCEMI MUSIC BY TREVOR RABIN
COSTUME DESIGNER MICHAEL KAPLAN FILM EDITORS MARK GOLDBLATT, A.C.E. CHRIS LEBENZON GLEN SCANTLEBURY PRODUCTION DESIGNER MICHAEL WHITE DIRECTOR OF PHOTOGRAPHY JOHN SCHWARTZMAN EXECUTIVE PRODUCERS JONATHAN HENSLEIGH
JIM VAN WYCK CHAD OMAN STORY BY ROBERT ROY POOL AND JONATHAN HENSLEIGH ADAPTATION BY TONY GILROY AND SHANE SALERNO SCREENPLAY BY JONATHAN HENSLEIGH AND J.J. ABRAMS
PRODUCED BY JERRY BRUCKHEIMER GALE ANNE HURD MICHAEL BAY DIRECTED BY MICHAEL BAY

ARMAGEDDON 1998 (U.S.)

Director Michael Bay **Producer** Michael Bay, Jerry Bruckheimer, Gale Anne Hurd **Screenplay** Jonathan Hensleigh, J. J. Abrams **Cinematography** John Schwartzman **Music** Trevor Rabin **Cast** Bruce Willis, Billy Bob Thornton, Liv Tyler, Ben Affleck, Will Patton, Peter Stormare, Keith David, Steve Buscemi

Harry Stamper (Bruce Willis), the world's best deep-core oil driller, has to lead his drilling crew into space to blow up a massive asteroid that is set to hit Earth and destroy all life. The first hour of *Armageddon* follows the interaction between sensible but panic-stricken N.A.S.A. men and oddball oilmen.

It's largely played for laughs, although a sequence of astronaut training intended to spoof *The Right Stuff* (1983) is too long and not funny enough ("Talk about the wrong stuff," one observer remarks, just in case you miss the reference). Interspersed are apocalyptic sequences of destruction as meteorites break off the asteroid and fall to Earth. There are great comic turns by Steve Buscemi as the womanizing genius Rockhound, and Peter Stormare as a drunk, unshaven, Russian cosmonaut. Billy Bob Thornton's character Dan Truman, the head of N.A.S.A., provides a contrast to the noisy antics of the drillers, so calm and steady that it is easy to accept his suspect pseudoscience. The movie is less satisfying, however, in the romance between the bland Liv Tyler and Stamper's pretty-boy protégé A. J. (Ben Affleck), an affair so wishy-washy you wonder how they can even remember each other when separated for a few days.

◀
Don't expect subtle when you watch a Michael Bay movie. The director behind big-budget blockbusters including *Pearl Harbor* (2001) doesn't do subtle.

The action takes off once the crew gets into space. Critical moments follow thick and fast, as they accidentally blow up a space station, crash a shuttle, and break the drill they're using to burrow into the asteroid. Back on Earth, the clock is ticking, and in case that's not sufficiently panic-inducing, there's a ticking nuclear bomb to be fought over and then defused. There's noise and shouting, some ghastly one-liners, and lots and lots

> ## "THE UNITED STATES GOVERNMENT JUST ASKED US TO SAVE THE WORLD. ANYONE WANT TO SAY NO?" HARRY STAMPER

of explosions. Once the bomb is in place, it turns out that the detonation mechanism has been damaged, so someone has to stay behind to detonate it. After a bit of an "I'm nobler than you" struggle, naturally Stamper is the one to sacrifice himself to save the world. And, in a movie that's determined to play every trump, there's one last moment of panic, as Stamper falls and struggles to press the button in time for the bomb to work.

► Willis and others save the world, if not themselves, from this disaster movie. "It's what we call a global killer. Nothing will survive—not even bacteria," says Thornton, no doubt about the fate of the planet, if not the fate of the film.

This is a movie written around its special effects. Silly, shallow, and jingoistic it may be (the scenes of people around the world awaiting the impending disaster raise eyebrows), but the effects are impressive, look authentic, and are tied together with simple, effective storytelling. As he did with *The Rock* (1996), Bay does noisy, flashy, slick action with a minimum of plot and characterization. And he does it with commercial success, even if critics would prefer some more depth. **CW**

WESLEY SNIPES
BLADE
STEPHEN DORFF

Against an army of Immortals,
one warrior must draw first blood.

New Line Cinema Presents an Amen Ra Films Production in association with Peter Frankfurt a Stephen Norrington Picture Wesley Snipes Stephen Dorff "Blade" Kris Kristofferson N'Bushe Wright
Donal Logue Co-Producers Andrew J. Horne and Jon Divens Costume Designer Sanja Milkovic Hays Music by Mark Isham Edited by Paul Rubell A.C.E. Production Designer Kirk M. Petruccelli
Director of Photography Theo Van De Sande, A.S.C. Executive Producers Stan Lee Avi Arad Joseph Calamari Lynn Harris Produced by Peter Frankfurt Wesley Snipes Robert Engelman
Blade and Dracon Front Characters Created for Marvel Comics by Marv Wolfman & Gene Colan Written by David S. Goyer Directed by Stephen Norrington

   SOUNDTRACK AVAILABLE ON TVT COMPACT DISCS AND CASSETTES   www.lycos.com/blade   DOLBY SURROUND   COLOR

BLADE 1998 (U.S.)

Director Stephen Norrington **Producer** Robert Engelman, Peter Frankfurt, Wesley Snipes **Screenplay** David S. Goyer **Cinematography** Theo van de Sande **Music** Mark Isham **Cast** Wesley Snipes, Stephen Dorff, Kris Kristofferson, N'Bushe Wright, Donal Logue, Udo Kier

Since the dawn of cinema, vampires have haunted movie screens as the epitome of things that go bump in the night. Combining excessive gore and mile-a-minute action, *Blade* gives the vampire genre a much-needed blood transfusion and prepares it for the new millennium.

Wesley Snipes stars as Blade, a vampire killer who is a combination of Bruce Lee and Van Helsing. With the help of gunsmith Whistler (Kris Kristofferson), Blade wages a high-tech war against a legion of vampires who have their fangs in everything from politics to finances. Dissidence emerges within the vampires in the form of Deacon Frost (Stephen Dorff), a renegade bloodsucker attempting to translate an ancient text to resurrect the vampire god La Magra. To complicate matters even further, Blade himself is half-man, half-vampire and must fight the urge to feed.

Based on a Marvel comic book series, *Blade* resuscitated the vampire genre with the ultramodern action on display. From the opening bloodbath rave to the finale in a vampire temple, the film flows with a vibrant kinetic energy. Director Stephen Norrington fills the screen with visceral action that makes the

◄

LL Cool J was apparently the first choice for Blade, but Wesley Snipes made the half-man, half-vampire very much his own.

power, speed, and magnetism of the new-age vampires come to life. Innovative flashes include Blade's state-of-the-art weaponry that causes vampires to disintegrate into ash within seconds and shoot-outs that anticipate the "bullet time" effect seen in *The Matrix* (1999). The film also offers new bits involving vampire hierarchy ("pure bloods" are elitists who are born vampires) and the accepted lore ("Crosses don't do squat").

"THE WORLD BELONGS TO US, NOT THE HUMANS . . . THESE PEOPLE ARE OUR FOOD, NOT OUR ALLIES." DEACON FROST

In addition, *Blade* is one of a handful of U.S. films in the late 1990s to infuse the electric Hong Kong style of action emphasizing flowing martial arts and two-fisted shoot-outs. Nearly every ten minutes there is a fight on-screen, with the battles being bloody and brutal. Wesley Snipes, a real-life practitioner of martial arts, gets to display a variety of skills from sword fighting to hand-to-hand combat. Snipes was already an action star by the time *Blade* debuted, but the grim antihero character allowed him the biggest lack of restrictions within the genre. Utilizing a cool, calm, and stoic stance, Snipes's performance is pitch perfect, and Blade emerged as the signature role of his career. The film was a box office success and Snipes returned to the character in *Blade II* (2002)—directed by Guillermo del Toro and a rare case of a sequel being as good as the original—and *Blade: Trinity* (2004). **WW**

►

Blade (Snipes) and Frost (Dorff) cross swords many a time in this blood-splattering, viscerally violent action movie.

LUC BESSON PRÉSENTE UNE PRODUCTION ARP

SAMY NACERI - FREDERIC DIEFENTHAL - TAXI - UN FILM DE GERARD PIRÈS

MARION COTILLARD - MANUELA GOURARY - EMMA SJOBERG - BERNARD FARCY SCÉNARIO LUC BESSON MUSIQUE IAM

PHOTO JEAN-PIERRE SAUVAIRE DÉCORS JEAN-JACQUES GERNOLLE SON VINCENT TULLI MIXAGE VINCENT ARNARDI DIRECTEUR DE PRODUCTION BERNARD GRENET

PRODUCTEURS LUC BESSON ET LAURENT PETIN PRODUIT PAR ARP PRODUCTION · STUDIO CANAL+ · TF1 FILMS PRODUCTION · STUDIO IMAGE 4

TAXI 1998 (FRANCE)

Director Gérard Pirès **Producer** Luc Besson, Laurent Pétin, Michèle Pétin
Screenplay Luc Besson **Cinematography** Jean-Pierre Sauvaire **Music** Akhenaton
IAM **Cast** Samy Naceri, Frédéric Diefenthal, Marion Cotillard, Emma Sjöberg,
Manuela Gourary, Bernard Farcy

Ever since cars began rolling off assembly lines, filmmakers
have been obsessed with showcasing the speed and power of
the automobile. From the early Keystone Kops shorts to
modern-day classics like *The French Connection* (1971), the car
chase has been an integral cornerstone of the movie-going
experience. Helping continue the trend into the new millennium
is Luc Besson's *Taxi* series.

Streetwise taxi driver Daniel Morales (Samy Naceri) is forced
to do the unthinkable: he must help the police after driving-
deficient cop Émilien Coutant-Kerbalec (Frédéric Diefenthal)
catches him speeding and threatens to take away his newly
acquired license. The assignment: this odd couple must catch
the Mercedes Gang, a German group of taunting criminals that
have been robbing the banks of Marseilles.

As is the norm in the car chase subgenre, the plot is minimal
and merely an excuse to show lots of cars smashing into each
other. As big-budget Hollywood grew increasingly idle and let
computers do their stunt work for them, the French filmmakers
went back to the basics for their intricate vehicle stunts. An
early highlight presents clumsy Émilien making one wrong

◄
**The high-speed
maneuvers though
Marseilles are
simply stunning—
and made more
so by crosscutting
with driver close-
ups and one-liner
wisecracks.**

move during a stakeout, resulting in a massive pileup of cars on the street that equals the vehicular mayhem of *The Blues Brothers* (1980). The film's finale showcases Morales in his highly customized gleaming white Peugeot taxi racing the Mercedes-driving criminals through the streets and highways of Marseilles. Director Gérard Pirès keeps the fluid camera at street level, seemingly placing the audience in the passenger seat during

"DO YOUR INTERROGATIONS ALWAYS END UP LIKE THIS, OR ARE YOU JUST TRYING TO IMPRESS ME?" DANIEL MORALES

the high-octane chases as the cars screech through Marseilles avenues, elevated carriageways, and side streets. Most importantly, the production understands the beauty of cinematic car chase history and utilizes real cars for all of the scenes.

Besson's first foray into producing an action movie proved a success, as *Taxi* became the third highest grossing French film in his homeland that year. A trilogy of equally successful crash-and-bang sequels followed with Gérard Krawczyk at the helm. Besson also coproduced an ill-conceived U.S. remake in 2004 with Jimmy Fallon and Queen Latifah as the cop and taxi driver, respectively (which, oddly enough, resorted to computer-enhanced chases). Besson continued delivering fast and furious auto action with Hollywood budgets in Europe over the ensuing decade, producing several Jet Li vehicles, the *District 13* films, and the highly successful *The Transporter* series. **WW**

► Helping to balance out the accelerated action is some genuinely funny odd couple comedy from leads Naceri and Diefenthal that is reminiscent of *48 Hrs.* (1982).

RONIN 1998 (U.S. • U.K.)

Director John Frankenheimer **Producer** Frank Mancuso, Jr. **Screenplay** David Mamet **Cinematography** Robert Fraisse **Music** Elia Cmiral **Cast** Robert De Niro, Jean Reno, Natascha McElhone, Stellan Skarsgård, Katarina Witt, Michael Lonsdale, Sean Bean, Jonathan Pryce, Skipp Sudduth

The truly spectacular car chases in *Ronin* make it worth watching for them alone. The final car chase through the streets, tunnels, and pavements of Paris is so nerve-tinglingly realistic it is almost too frightening to watch. It is true to say that they really do not make films like this any more. Director John Frankenheimer used thousands of extras and hundreds of stuntmen to shoot the sequences live using no special effects—and it shows. There are no cartoonlike explosions as would be expected from modern-day actioners; this is a sequence that thrills because of speed, skids, superb driving, crashes, breathtaking timing, and general mayhem.

The film's title sums up what it is about. Ronin are samurai without masters who opt to become mercenaries or bandits. The ronin of the movie are a ragtag bunch of five former spymasters and Special Forces military men made redundant by the end of the Cold War. They arrive in Paris, where they are met by an Irish revolutionary Deidre, played by Natascha McElhone. She wants them to steal a mysterious silver suitcase being transported by an armed convoy through France, the contents of which she does not reveal. The men accept.

◄
Frankenheimer creates a refreshingly different action movie that harks back to the classic feel of movies like *The French Connection* **(1971).**

Given that the team consists of big-screen hard men Robert De Niro as Sam, Jean Reno as Vincent, Stellan Skarsgård as Gregor, Sean Bean as Spence, and Skipp Sudduth as Larr, it is not long before the action kicks off. Soon the team not only has to contend with stealing the suitcase, as they discover that one of them is a fraud. Nor are they the only ones who want the suitcase, and they find themselves up against rivals in the form

"WHENEVER THERE IS ANY DOUBT, THERE IS NO DOUBT. THAT'S THE FIRST THING THEY TEACH YOU." SAM

of ruthless Russian mobsters. And as might be expected from a samurai no longer beholden to an honorable tradition, one of the ronin turns traitor and decides to steal the suitcase for himself. The chemistry between De Niro and Reno is magical as they strike up an on-screen camaraderie as hitmen that can only occur when one great actor plays opposite another.

Ronin is, in fact, not your average Hollywood fare. It was shot on location in France with an international cast of the aforementioned actors from the United States, Britain, France, Sweden, and Germany; David Mamet's skill is evident in the labyrinthine plot of crosses, double crosses, and triple crosses, and streetwise dialogue verging on the cryptic; Robert Fraisse's moody color palette helps create a sense of unwashed grime; and Elia Cmiral's edgy score based on techno rhythms was innovative for the time. **CK**

► **The performances all around are top notch—De Niro as a fast-talking, wise-cracking, tough know-it-all, and Reno as the less talkative but equally professional take on a Gallic assassin.**

CROUCHING TIGER HIDDEN DRAGON
2000 (TAIWAN • HONG KONG • U.S. • CHINA)

Director Ang Lee **Producer** Bill Kong, Hsu Li Kong, Ang Lee
Screenplay Wang Hui Ling, James Schamus, Tsai Kuo Jung
Cinematography Peter Pau **Music** Tan Dun **Cast** Chow Yun Fat,
Michelle Yeow, Chang Chen, Zhang Ziyi, Cheng Pei-pei

The first action scene of *Crouching Tiger Hidden Dragon*, a chase across rooftops in which the actors leap unencumbered by gravity, is shockingly unnatural to an audience unused to the traditions of martial arts movies. Before long, though, you become accustomed to this fantastic dance-like action. The action sequences were arranged by Yuen Woo-Ping, the choreographer responsible for the groundbreaking action in *The Matrix* (1999). The martial arts become more than fighting. They are about developing an inner strength that makes all things possible, even walking on water. And it is not all abstract dance; the clashing weapons and thudding kicks and punches are real enough, as are those fabulous moves where someone is suddenly thrown to the floor or disarmed in the blink of an eye.

The plot involves the conflict between restrained obedience to social codes and passionate romance. Yu Shu Lien (Michelle Yeoh) and Li Mu Bai (Chow Yun Fat) are martial arts masters on the trail of a stolen sword, the Green Destiny. Shu Lien and Mu Bai repress their personal desires, including their unspoken love for one another, and express themselves only when they fight.

◄

Unlike most *Wuxia* movies, here the men play the contemplative supporting roles, while the female characters have the dominant roles and are involved in most of the exhuberant action scenes.

The Green Destiny has been taken by Jen (Zhang Ziyi), a rich aristocrat by day and skilled martial arts villain by night. Young and passionate, Jen longs to break free from the constraints of her existence and the prospect of an arranged marriage to live the life of a warrior. She has been secretly trained by her governess, Jade Fox (Cheng Pei-pei), longtime enemy of Shu Lien and Mu Bai. There's a love story, too, told slightly confusingly

"WE HAVE ALWAYS SEEN IT AS SENSE AND SENSIBILITY WITH MARTIAL ARTS."

JAMES SCHAMUS

in flashback, to explain Jen's desire for freedom. Though Jen starts out the villain, once her identity is uncovered, she becomes the hero, refusing to be bound by convention and eventually throwing off all the bonds that bind her: family, teachers, even love. The epic plot carries us through stunning Chinese landscapes—deserts, mountains, forests—and cities bustling with colorful street vendors and acrobats.

► **Zhang Ziyi as the physically skilled villain-hero, who's balletic martial arts through the bamboo branches is both poetic and awe-inspiring.**

Before this film, Taiwanese director Ang Lee had been previously known for making movies about family relationships, such as The Ice Storm (1997) and Sense and Sensibility (1995), rather than action movies. Lee grew up watching the martial arts movies known as *wuxia*, which have always been a major part of Chinese cinema. Lee has taken the genre and stretched it to fit his own style, making it not just an energetic action film, but also a powerful emotional drama. **CW**

GLADIATOR 2000 (U.K. • U.S.)

Director Ridley Scott **Producer** David Franzoni, Branko Lustig, Douglas Wick
Screenplay David Franzoni, John Logan, William Nicholson **Cinematography** John
Mathieson **Music** Lisa Gerrard, Hans Zimmer **Cast** Russell Crowe, Joaquin Phoenix,
Connie Nielsen, Oliver Reed, Richard Harris, Derek Jacobi

"At my signal, unleash hell," says Maximus (Russell Crowe), a general in the service of Emperor Marcus Aurelius (Richard Harris). At his back stands an army of professional soldiers. Against him is a troop of Germanic tribesman armed with axes and shielded by animal hides. There's a moment of anticipation, the whinny of horses, the clank of metal, and a host of arrows infiltrate a primeval forest. The sky darkens and Maximus defeats his enemy, crazed with blood wrath but ready for a peaceful return to the arms of his wife and son.

In this epic adventure, moral simplicity meets capital intrigues. Violence meets violence. Limbs are hewed and skulls crushed, and our hero remains true to a code of loyalty and goodness that echoes marriage, for Maximus is surely wedded to both his wife and to the idea that is "Rome."

When Commodus (Joaquin Phoenix), the emperor's son, kills Aurelius to gain the throne, Maximus refuses to serve him and is forced into gladiatorial combat. Under harsh conditions, he gives up the will to live. But the talents that aided Maximus in his military career prove unusually helpful in the Colosseum where the one-time general-turned-slave becomes more

◄
**A swords and
sandals Hollywood
epic—the likes of
which hadn't been
produced in
decades—
Gladiator is a
hero's journey
without apology.**

popular than Commodus. It's easy to read this story point as elevating the prototypically American ideal of honest honorable, action (i.e., Maximus) over dishonest, dishonorable statecraft (i.e., Commodus). What makes *Gladiator* so satisfying, though, is its ark of revenge.

Maximus is a wronged man. He's taken from the pinnacle of power and made a slave. He's trained by freed gladiator

"WHATEVER COMES OUT OF THESE GATES . . . DO YOU UNDERSTAND? IF WE STAY TOGETHER WE SURVIVE." MARCUS AURELIUS

Proximo (Oliver Reed) and hatches a plot to kill Commodus. He befriends fellow gladiator Juba (Djimon Hounsou) and the pair make an alliance to survive brutal combat that is their tribute to Roman vice. What stays in memory long after the movie is over is the series of trials Maximus endures. Scored by Hans Zimmer and leavened by a sharp script by David Franzoni, John Logan, and William Nicholson, Maximus stabs and parries, trains and leads, and is always the most capable fighting man in any contest.

▶
Watch Maximus fight a tiger! Watch him fight a giant! Watch him take on charioteers! And, best of all, watch him win.

Gladiator's slick surface is due to Ridley Scott's direction which remains focused on the achievement of revenge. To that end, Crowe's performance presents a hero with an eye for both herb gardens and entrails. At once reserved and bloodthirsty, give the man a short sword and see him transformed from reluctant soldier into avenging angel. **GC-Q**

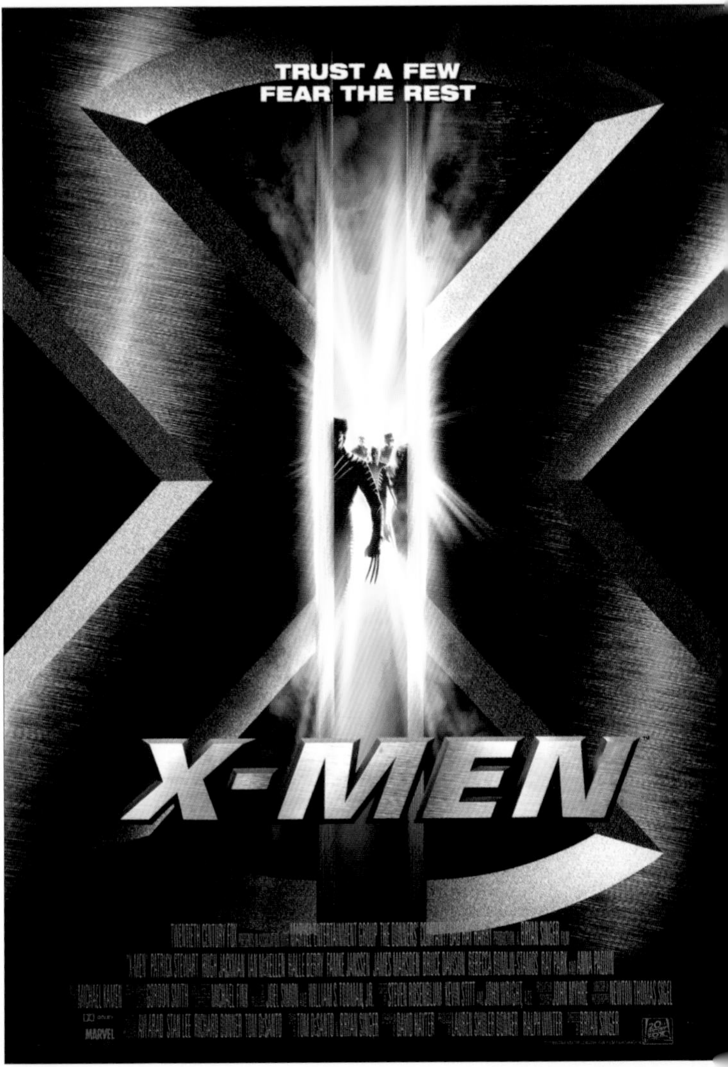
TRUST A FEW
FEAR THE REST
X-MEN
MARVEL

X-MEN 2000 (U.S.)

Director Bryan Singer **Producer** Lauren Shuler Donner, Ralph Winter, Joel Simon **Screenplay** David Hayter, Tom DeSanto, Bryan Singer **Cinematography** Newton Thomas Sigel **Music** Michael Kamen **Cast** Patrick Stewart, Ian McKellen, Hugh Jackman, Famke Janssen, Halle Berry, James Marsden, Anna Paquin

Action film fans would be hard-pressed not to admire *X-Men*, the first film in what is now recognized as the *X-Men* film franchise. Bryan Singer's 2000 feature consisted of solid acting, a compelling story line, and of course, stunning action sequences. The great ensemble cast is anchored by the performances of two acting legends: Patrick Stewart and Ian McKellen, both former members of England's famed Royal Shakespeare Company.

Based on characters from Marvel's highly successful *X-Men* comic book series, the film centers on a group of humans with special powers as a result of a leap forward in evolution. These so-called "mutants" constitute a growing segment of the world's population, but they are still marginalized and feared by nonmutant humans. Former friends and colleagues Professor Xavier (Stewart) and Magneto (McKellen) now head the two clashing factions of mutants: Professor Xavier's X-Men, who are committed to protecting both mutant and nonmutant humans alike, and Magneto's Brotherhood of Mutants, who aim to eliminate the nonmutant humans who have hounded and oppressed them. Magnifying the conflict is the looming threat

◀
The huge success of this initial *X-Men* film paved the way for a thriving Hollywood franchise including *X2* (2003), *X-Men: The Last Stand* (2006), and *X-Men Origins: Wolverine* (2009).

of a "Mutant Registration Act," which if passed will force mutants to register their names and abilities with the government.

Much of the action of this film is focused on the experience of two characters recently brought into Professor Xavier's fold: the seemingly indestructible Wolverine (Hugh Jackman) and the power-poaching Rogue (Anna Paquin). As the jaded man and the troubled girl attempt to make Professor Xavier's unique

"MUTATION: IT IS THE KEY TO OUR EVOLUTION."

PROFESSOR CHARLES XAVIER

school their home, they are pulled into a battle between the two factions. The X-Men, including Storm (Halle Berry), Dr. Jean Gray (Famke Janssen), Cyclops (James Marsden), and Professor Xavier himself, must battle the Brotherhood of Mutants in order to rescue Rogue, save the nonmutant humans, and convince Wolverine to put his powers to use for their cause.

One could argue that the feared and marginalized mutants function as a metaphor for real-life communities of marginalized citizens, including those of a non-majority race, religion, or sexual orientation, a theme explored further in the first *X-Men* sequel, *X2*. In fact, an opening sequence of young Erich Lensherr (later Magneto) as a boy watching his family forced into a World War II concentration camp, remains with the viewer and renders the "villain" a multifaceted and often sympathetic character. **AK**

► Halle Berry as Storm creating her eponymous powers as one of the X-Men.

THE FAST AND THE FURIOUS
2001 (GERMANY • U.S.)

Director Rob Cohen **Producer** Neal H. Moritz, Doug Claybourne, John Pogue
Screenplay Gary Scott Thompson, Eric Bergquist, David Ayer (story), Gary Scott
Thompson **Cinematography** Ericsson Core **Music** BT **Cast** Paul Walker, Vin Diesel,
Michelle Rodriguez, Jordana Brewster, Rick Yune, Chad Lindberg, Ja Rule

An adrenaline rush from the truck hijacking start to the mano-
a-mano climax, *The Fast and the Furious* is a superstructure built
upon a magazine article by Ken Li about the street-racing gangs
of L.A., called *Racer X*, which appeared in 1999. Producer Neal
Moritz, who appears with his black Ferrari in the buildup to race
day, sneering "more than you can afford, pal" to Brian's polite
enquiry about the retail value ("smoke him," advises Dom—
and they do), snapped up the story rights and twinned it with
the title rights to the 1955 movie of the same name, directed by
king of the drive-ins, Roger Corman. There was also a 1939 movie
Fast and Furious, starring Franchot Tone and Ann Sothern.

The plot is standard old-school B-Movie fare, albeit driven
home with utter conviction from all concerned. Implausibly
good-looking L.A.P.D. cop Brian O'Conner (Paul Walker) goes
undercover to discover whether tough garage boy Dom
Toretto (Vin Diesel) is the hijacker responsible. Despite
skepticism from Dom and his gang members (with good
reason), Brian gradually infiltrates the petrol-head band.
Needless to say, Brian falls for Dom's luscious sister, Mia

◀
**Amazing good
looks for male
and female leads
provided the eye
candy, while the
race stunts and
revved-up cars
provided the
testosterone.**

(Jordana Brewster), giving him even extra motivation to prove to his bosses that Johnny Tran's bad crew are the real villains.

Director Rob Cohen has superb form for superior action movies—*Dragonheart* (1996) and *XXX* (2002), also with Diesel—and unleashes the entire arsenal at his command: thundering soundtrack, squealing tyres, high-voltage cars in vivid colors flashing down city streets, empty canyon roads,

"WE SHOULD GO OUT SOMETIME." BRIAN O'CONNER *"THAT'S SWEET, BUT I DON'T DATE MY BROTHER'S FRIENDS."* MIA TORETTO

and the vast desert, surrounded and sometimes driven by hot girls looking hotter by the second (it's my pleasure, Rodriguez). Indeed, it's a great contest between Michelle Rodriguez and Jordana Brewster for the unwritten leading lady rights, a fight to the finish as close as that between Walker and Diesel for male lead at that time. (Obviously, in films featuring cars, someone called Diesel was going to win over a Walker in the long run.)

▶

With *The Fast and The Furious*, you'll not get too many surprises, but enjoy plenty of authentic thrills and spills, using many real street racers along the way.

Walker apparently edged out Christian Bale and Mark Wahlberg for the role. And when you factor in that the part of Mia was written for Eliza Dushku (who turned it down) and Jessica Biel, Kirsten Dunst, Sarah Michelle Gellar, Bijou Phillips, and Natalie Portman (in alphabetical order, not gorgeousness rating) all auditioned for it, you realize casting sessions must have been a hell of a lot of fun as well. **MH**

LARA CROFT
TOMB
RAIDER

PARAMOUNT PICTURES AND MUTUAL FILM COMPANY PRESENT A LAWRENCE GORDON PRODUCTION IN ASSOCIATION WITH EIDOS INTERACTIVE LIMITED
A SIMON WEST FILM ANGELINA JOLIE "LARA CROFT : TOMB RAIDER" JON VOIGHT IAIN GLEN NOAH TAYLOR DANIEL CRAIG MUSIC GRAEME REVELL COSTUME PETER AFTERMAN
EDITED TOMB PICKETT, KLEIN ROBERT DUFFY DALLAS & PART II CO SEAN SCANLON PRODUCED KIM H. PETROSKI DESIGNED PETER MENZIES, JR. EDITED BY EIDOS INTERACTIVE GINA BERSON
PRODUCED JEREMY HEALL, SWS CO PRODUCERS LAWRENCE GORDON LLOYD LEVIN COLIN WILSON BY MIKE WERB & MICHAEL COLLEARY SCREENPLAY SARA B SCRIPER ANO DEAN SCANTLEBURY
DIRECTED SIMON WEST PRODUCED PATRICK MASSETT & JOHN ZINMAN SCREENPLAY BY SIMON WEST
www.tombraidermovie.com

IN THEATRES JUNE 15

TOMB RAIDER 2001 (U.S.)

Director Simon West **Producer** Lawrence Gordon, Lloyd Levin, Colin Wilson
Screenplay Patrick Massett, John Zinman **Cinematography** Peter Menzies, Jr.
Music Graeme Revell **Cast** Angelia Jolie, Jon Voigt, Iain Glen, Noah Taylor,
Daniel Craig, Chris Barrie, Richard Johnson, Julian Rhind-Tutt, Leslie Phillips

It shouldn't have been all that hard to turn the best-selling computer game *Tomb Raider* into an entertaining movie. After all, most of it's there already: a strong central character, exotic settings, and exciting action sequences. All you need is a plot and a few fleshed-out characters. What a shame both these elements seem to have been forgotten.

Angelina Jolie is the perfect embodiment of tomb raider Lara Croft, stalking around showing off her unfeasibly large breasts and tiny waist as she bashes villains and swipes treasures. She's feisty, athletic, intelligent, and gorgeous. Having said that, the cardboard cutout villains and sidekicks around Lara make her look *almost* three-dimensional.

The plot, such as it is, involves a race to find two interlocking pieces of an ancient artifact called the Triangle of Light, which can control time. A group of villains called the Illuminati, who look like a group of sinister old-school gentlemen bankers, are after the Triangle for some nefarious and unexplained purpose. Lara Croft (Jolie) has been charged by her dead father to destroy the Triangle before the Illuminati can get their hands on it. The dull, plodding scenes that provide all this information

◀
Marksmanship is just one of the attributes Angelina Jolie transfers with ease from the computer game to the live action offering.

hold up the movie's momentum and are full of glaring holes and inconsistencies. Why can Lara save Alex West (Daniel Craig) from death but not bring back her father (Jon Voigt)? Who is the mysterious little girl spirit guide who helps her find her way? What is the significance of the fact that Lara's father was a member of the Illuminati? And who needs plot and character in an action movie anyway?

"TIME TO SAVE THE UNIVERSE AGAIN, IS IT?" HILLARY "ABSOLUTLEY." LARA CROFT

The action sequences here are superb: noisy and flashy and beautifully choreographed, with more than a hint of Indiana Jones about them. We have screeching vehicles, big gun, and hand-to-hand fighting set among world landmarks or mysterious, mystical locations. Jolie is stunning, particularly as she swings around in white silk pajamas from a bungee cord in the great hall of her ancestral mansion fighting off black-clad baddies. The movie's game origins are the model for much of the action: a direct hit makes villains fall and stone monsters crumble; Lara has to work out how to jump and duck at just the right moment to reach the "sun" at the center of the mechanical solar system in Siberia. Jolie bounces back unscathed from each encounter, just like a game character, with a couple of strands of hair escaping from her tight plait and once with a wound that is instantly healed by a magic potion. **CW**

► Gorgeous to stare at (and Craig, too), but just like a computer game, there's no sense of suspense or peril. Even if Lara died, she'd just pop right back up again. Lara Croft may be in a movie, but she's still just a computer game avatar.

SPIDER-MAN

COLUMBIA PICTURES PRESENTS A MARVEL ENTERPRISES/LAURA ZISKIN PRODUCTION "SPIDER-MAN" STARRING TOBEY MAGUIRE WILLEM DAFOE KIRSTEN DUNST JAMES FRANCO
CLIFF ROBERTSON ROSEMARY HARRIS MUSIC BY DANNY ELFMAN COSTUME DESIGNER JAMES ACHESON VISUAL EFFECTS JOHN DYKSTRA, A.S.C. VISUAL EFFECTS BY SONY PICTURES IMAGEWORKS INC. EDITED BY BOB MURAWSKI·ARTHUR COBURN, A.C.E.
PRODUCTION DESIGNER NEIL SPISAK DIRECTOR OF PHOTOGRAPHY DON BURGESS, A.S.C. EXECUTIVE PRODUCER AVI ARAD·STAN LEE BASED ON THE MARVEL COMIC BOOK BY STAN LEE and STEVE DITKO SCREENPLAY BY DAVID KOEPP PRODUCED BY LAURA ZISKIN·IAN BRYCE DIRECTED BY SAM RAIMI

2 MAY

sony.com/Spider-Man

SPIDER-MAN 2002 (U.S.)

Director Sam Raimi **Producer** Laura Ziskin **Screenplay** David Koepp
Cinematography Don Burgess **Music** Danny Efman **Cast** Tobey Maguire, Willem
Dafoe, Kirsten Dunst, James Franco, Cliff Robertson, Rosemary Harris, J. K. Simmons,
Joe Manganiello, Gerry Becker, Bill Nun, Jack Betts, Stanley Anderson

When a "genetically engineered" spider bites him, Peter Parker
(Tobey Maguire) develops spider skills: super strength, agility,
the ability to climb walls and spin webs, and heightened senses.
At first, Peter tries to use his new abilities for himself to impress
the girl next door, Mary Jane (Kirsten Dunst). But after his uncle
(Cliff Robertson) is killed in an accident Peter blames himself for,
he decides to use his powers to fight crime under a secret
identity: Spider-Man. Soon he's faced with a terrifying
opponent, as the cackling Green Goblin (Willem Dafoe) attacks
New York and endangers Peter's loved ones.

The appeal of *Spider-Man* lies in the contrast between nerdy
teen and superhero. Maguire is perfect for the role, conveying
just the right combination of adolescent uncertainty and inner
strength. We follow Peter's comic ineptitude as he discovers his
spider abilities, from his realization that he can see without
glasses, to his glee at his new six-pack and his clumsy first
attempts at web spinning.

The supporting characters live up to Maguire's lead. Dunst is
sexy and vulnerable as Mary Jane, battling against the men in
her life while unaware that Peter is there for her. Dafoe takes the

◀

Spider-Man
**works on the big
screen because
it has strongly
developed,
emotionally
involving
characters and
taut intelligent
plotting.**

hamminess to just the right degree in his Jekyll and Hyde roles as the intense scientist and the insane Green Goblin. Newspaper editor Jameson (J. K. Simmons) is straight out of a comic strip complete with flattop haircut and barking misanthropy.

Raimi's deft direction brings out the movie's comic book origins, from the initial stylized credits to the dive through strands of Peter's D.N.A. as the spider bites him, and the bright

"I WILL NEVER FORGET THESE WORDS. 'WITH GREAT POWER COMES GREAT RESPONSIBILITY'." PETER PARKER

flat color of the movie, with its emphasis on reds and blues. The slo-mo scene when Peter fights the school bully owes something to *The Matrix*, but a lot to the frames of a comic book that can show detail and point of view so precisely. Particularly exhilarating are the scenes when a point-of-view shot carries you, the audience, amid the towering buildings just like Spider-Man. There are genuine chills among the teen-movie comedy and popcorn action. There's an unsettling scene when Osborn sees his face in the mirror and realizes with horror that he is the Goblin. In the final showdown between Spider-Man and the Goblin, Peter's face shows through Spider-Man's mask, and we see him as frail and human compared to the armor-plated Goblin. Ultimately, *Spider-Man* is warm, funny, and charming, as well as stylish and tense— pretty rare for an action flick. **CW**

▶
Some of the C.G.I. is clumsy, but the scenes of *Spider-Man* swinging down the canyon-like streets of New York on his spider threads are glorious.

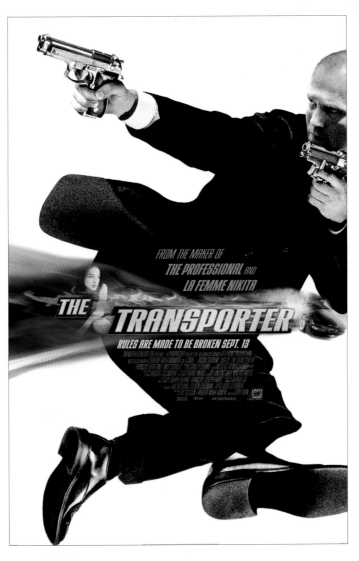

THE TRANSPORTER 2002 (FRANCE • U.S.)

Director Corey Yuen **Producer** Luc Besson, Steve Chasman **Screenplay** Luc Besson, Robert Mark Kamen **Cinematography** Pierre Morel **Music** Stanley Clarke **Cast** Jason Statham, Qi Shu, Matt Schulze, François Berleand, Ric Young, Doug Rand, Didier Saint Melin, Vincent Nemeth

The Transporter (known as *Le Transporteur* in France) is a lean, mean action-thriller, which, like *The Fast and the Furious* (2001) has spawned a series by virtue of its runaway success. Between them, they've set the template for early twenty-first-century speed and explosion junkies to feast upon.

Frank (Jason Statham, performing nearly all his own stunts in macho fashion) drives around the South of France a lot, and usually he's gunning the motor very fast. His clients are a shady bunch and he doesn't ask them too many, if any, questions. As a result, they like him and refer him to even badder Riviera dudes. There's a whole mess of revving, chasing, and shooting, most of it in swooning locations (see 007 films for prototype). And there's a girl, naturally—the toothsomely sexy Qi Shu as Lai. And sure, her dad turns out to be the baddest baddie of them all. It might be thin on plot, and clearly director Corey Yuen, or "artistic director" Louis Leterrier are hardly going to win awards for this stuff, but it's the vehicle that's the thing.

Admittedly, Statham and Qi Shu carry the main thrust of the thinly sketched plot development with skill. The romance between rule-bound, strong, silent getaway driver and chatty

◄

The U.S. poster for the movie credits Corey Yuen as director and Louis Leterrier as artistic director. However, the European release for the film lists Louis Leterrier as director and Corey Yuen as action director in the opening credits.

young beauty is surprisingly affecting. As a result of his previous year's heroics in surprise hit *The Fast and the Furious*, Matt Schulze plays Wall Street, the villain who isn't Chinese. Clearly his presence is what great action-thrillers need. Meanwhile, François Berleand plays the local police inspector with just the right amount of Gallic worldweariness, while bad Dad Ric Young is thoroughly evil. Statham is an interesting

"IF I'M LUCKY, SHE'LL SEE THE LIGHT." MR. KWAI "YEAH, AND IF SHE'S LUCKY, MAYBE YOU'LL GET HIT BY A TRUCK." FRANK MARTIN

new type of action hero. As the once mighty quadrumvirate of Gibson, Willis, Stallone, and Schwarzenegger fade into direction, politics, or worse, tough Englishmen Statham (and Daniel Craig from the last two Bond movies) reflect new strong, silent types, not much given to witty word play, apart from the exceptionally laconic variety. Statham had come a long way from *Lock, Stock and Two Smoking Barrels* (1998) and *Snatch* (2000).

But even though the acting is, both individually and collectively, perfectly good, no one is really pretending it's the main draw for the movie. The only raison d'être for *Le Transporteur*, in fact, is the shoot-'em-up, smash-'em-up, energy-packed, testosterone-fueled, nonstop action. Believe you me, it's quite enough to carry anyone with a taste for volcanic thrills through ninety minutes. **MH**

► **Jason Statham as Frank Martin performs most of his own spectacular stunts.**

THE 4TH FILM BY QUENTIN TARANTINO
KILL BILL
VOLUME 1
WRITTEN AND DIRECTED BY QUENTIN TARANTINO
CRANE

KILL BILL 2003/2004 (U.S.)

Director Quentin Tarantino (animated sequence by Mamoru Oshii)
Producer Lawrence Bender **Screenplay** Quentin Tarantino **Cinematography**
Robert Richardson **Music** RZA **Cast** Uma Thurman, Lucy Liu, Daryl Hannah, David
Carradine, Vivica A. Fox, Michael Madsen, Julie Dreyfus, Chiaki Kuriyama, Sonny Chiba

Quentin Tarantino burst on to the scene with the instant cult
classic, heist-gone-wrong flick *Reservoir Dogs* (1992). It
introduced many of the aesthetics that would become his
stock-in-trade: violent criminals; nonlinear plot; memorable,
witty, (and profane) dialogue; and a ton of pop culture
references. Tarantino would embark on an impressive run,
producing two further benchmark masterpieces, *Pulp Fiction*
(1994) and *Jackie Brown* (1997).

Then followed *Kill Bill*, an epic revenge drama in which
Tarantino—himself a serious aficionado on world cinema—
creates a personalized homage to some of his favorite cult film
genres: Hong Kong martial arts; Chinese *wuxia*/Japanese
"chanbara" (oriental swashbucklers); Italian horror and "spaghetti"
Westerns, and U.S. blaxploitation films of the early 1970s.
Conceived at first as a single film in ten "chapters," *Kill Bill* came
in at four hours in length and was thus halved and given
separate cinema releases six months apart.

The premise for *Kill Bill* is based broadly on *Lady Snowblood*, a
1973 Japanese film with a small cult following in the West, in
which a woman seeks revenge on those who have wronged

◄
Cult film nerds
have littered the
Internet with so
many cross-
referencing
websites of other
movies that you
could be forgiven
for thinking that
Kill Bill is little more
than a compilation
of Tarantino's
favorite clips.

her, crossing them off a list one by one as she kills them. The central character here is an assassin (Uma Thurman), known simply as "The Bride." Pregnant, she quits intending to lead a normal life. But at her wedding rehearsal, her ex-boss (and ex-lover) Bill turns up with a team of assassins, the Deadly Vipers, and everyone in the chapel is brutally massacred. Before Bill shoots her in the side of the head leaving her for dead, she tries

"THOSE OF YOU LUCKY ENOUGH TO HAVE YOUR LIVES, TAKE THEM WITH YOU." *THE BRIDE*

to explain that he is the father of the baby. She wakes up in a hospital ward to find she has been in a coma for four years, then escapes and seeks vengeance.

In each scene of choreographed violence, Tarantino invariably references a scene from another movie. In one fight sequence Uma Thurman dons a yellow tracksuit—a tribute to martial arts icon Bruce Lee; a snowbound fight sequence is taken directly from *Sex & Fury*, a 1973 revenge/soft-core porn flick from Japan. Yet, for all its allusion, *Kill Bill* doesn't require an in-depth knowledge of post-1960s trash cinema. It does, however, demand an appreciation of the same aesthetic. For this is a simulacrum universe with its own internal logic, the natural laws of the manga and comic book worlds taking complete control, where gravity doesn't seem to apply and life is cheap. In other words, this is pure, thrilling action fantasy. **TB**

▶

In a series of sumptuous scenes, The Bride (Uma Thurman) tracks down one after another from her list of assassins and gets extremely physical—all fights are to the death, geysers of blood gush from severed limbs, and nobody dies easily.

THE JOURNEY ENDS

LORD OF THE RINGS: THE RETURN OF THE KING 2003 (U.S. • N.Z. • GERMANY)

Director Peter Jackson **Producer** Peter Jackson, Barrie M. Osborne, Fran Walsh **Screenplay** Fran Walsh, Philippa Boyens, Peter Jackson **Cinematography** Andrew Lesnie **Music** Howard Shore **Cast** Elijah Wood, Sean Bean, Billy Boyd, Sean Astin, Cate Blanchett, Ian McKellan, Viggo Mortensen, David Wenham

The basic narrative of J. R. R. Tolkien's three novels about the fantasy world of Middle Earth—and filmmaker Peter Jackson's resulting movie trilogy—traces the influence of a powerful ring, which is also the source of absolute evil. Ultimately, though, the fate of the world rests in the hands of the most unexpected creature, a hobbit—a little person with hairy feet, an affection for food and drink, and very little interest in adventure, save for one Frodo Baggins (Elijah Wood).

As Frodo undertakes the destruction of the ring of power, since that is the only way to remove certain doom from the world, he collects a ragtag group, including an elf, a dwarf, three hobbit friends, and two men. The fellowship sets out for the birthplace of the ring, Mordor, and they are immediately set upon by the minions of their nemesis, and the other party chiefly interested in possession of the ring, Sauron.

Describing the story in this way, while accurate, does nothing to convey the grandeur of Jackson's finished film. There is a New Zealand-derived world strangely similar to our

◄

Often read as a nuclear age allegory, Tolkien preferred a literal description of a place where humans live alongside friendly and unfriendly creatures, including elves, dwarves, orcs, and various other folkloric species.

own but distinctly separate, too. Middle Earth is a place of natural fecundity, monstrous destruction, instantaneous violence, and soul-lifting friendship.

Freeing the camera from having to shoot live actors with all the limitations live actors present, such as limited flexibility and endurance, Jackson swoops through scenery, unhindered by the usual practical considerations. This technical ability is an

"IT IS ONLY THE DAMP OF THE FIRST SPRING RAIN . . . I DO NOT BELIEVE THIS DARKNESS WILL ENDURE." FARAMIR

extraordinary formal achievement. Time attenuates for minute details. Heroism is fetishized as high virtue. Evil is personified in monsters, and the trials of war become a testing ground for moral certitude, even as swordplay and horseback chases enable scene after scene to awe audiences in a state much like the sublime.

Frodo's journey is a travelogue for what's possible inside the graphical user interfaces of high-end computer animators. But Jackson's creative team also manages to make this story about the survival of civilization into an adventure so captivating that only the most jaded viewer can resist satisfaction. What we are left with are some of the most well-executed action sequences of orc-killing, hobbit-hunting, and arrow-shooting vigor that it's hard to believe there was ever any doubt as to the viability of shooting Tolkien's whole trilogy simultaneously. **GC-Q**

▶
Faramir (David Wenham), the Captain of Gondor, in one of the many epic battle scenes where live action and C.G.I. mix seamlessly.

ONG-BAK 2003 (THAILAND)

Director Prachya Pinkaew **Producer** Somsak Techaratanaprasert, Prachya Pinkaew **Screenplay** Prachya Pinkaew, Panna Rittikrai, Suphachai Sittiaumponpan **Cinematography** Nattawut Kittikhun **Music** Richard Wells (U.K. version) **Cast** Tony Jaa, Petchtai Wongkamlao, Suchao Pongwilai,

"No computer graphics! No stunt doubles! No wires!" With that declaration, Thailand's *Ong-Bak* burst onto the international action scene and took many moviegoers by surprise. Catching audiences off guard like the powerful strikes it highlights, the film made an immediate action star out of lead Tony Jaa.

The plot of *Ong-Bak* is incredibly simple: following the theft of the Ong-Bak statue's head, young Ting (Jaa) is sent from his tiny village to the big city to find it. Naturally, the metropolis proves to be a formidable land for this country boy and he reluctantly teams up with Humlae (Petchtai Wongkamlao), a former country kid turned street-wise hustler. By chance, Ting is forced into a series of fights, and one spectator taking a beating on Ting's wins is Komtuan (Suchao Pongwilai), a wheelchair-bound crime lord who stole the Ong-Bak artifact.

A bare-bones plot if ever there was one, *Ong-Bak*'s main goal is to highlight Muay Thai—a martial art from Thailand known for brutal knee and elbow strikes—and the incredible skills of star Tony Jaa. By the time *Ong-Bak* went into production, stunt coordinator Panna Rittikrai was already an old pro, having carved out a twenty-year career starring, directing, and

◀

The start of a kick-boxing franchise that made Tony Jaa an instant action film hero and saw the follow-ups *Ong Bak 2* (2008) and *Ong Bak 3* (2010).

choreographing cheap yet brutal action films inspired by films from Hong Kong. Jaa (born Panom Yeerum) spent ten years training under mentor Rittikrai, occasionally displaying his acrobatic skills in bits and pieces.

Ong-Bak is Jaa's show and serves as his coming out party. Director Pinkaew deftly moves from fight to fight, highlighting Jaa's amazing flips, dizzying kicks, and crushing elbows that hit

" . . . EXCITEMENT THAT OFTEN HASN'T BEEN SEEN SINCE THE EARLY DAYS OF JACKIE CHAN'S CAREER." THE TIMES

► **Tony Jaa (as Ting) and *Ong-Bak's* filmmakers reminded the international action community of the entertainment value and inherent artistry of displaying real martial arts on film.**

full force on willing stuntmen. Intricate moves are often shown twice, repeating in slow motion to show audiences what they might have missed. Highlights include a chase through the alleys that shows Jaa slide under a moving truck while doing the splits; fights with numerous challengers in a bar culminating with Jaa kneeing an opponent as they both blast through a second-story glass window; and a final fifteen minutes featuring fights with twenty rivals and enough uncompromising action for three films (includes a jaw-dropping bit where Jaa kicks a foe with his legs on fire).

As Hollywood embraced computer-enhanced stunts in films like *The Matrix* (1999), *Ong-Bak* brought back the primal realism kept alive by Bruce Lee in the 1970s, Jackie Chan in the 1980s, and Jet Li in the 1990s that was fast disappearing from modern action films. **WW**

LUC BESSON PRESENTE

B13
BANLIEUE 13
BIENVENUE EN **ENFER** !

DISTRICT 13 2004 (FRANCE)

Director Pierre Morel **Producer** Luc Besson **Screenplay** Luc Besson, Bibi Naceri
Cinematography Manuel Teran **Music** Bastide Donny, Damien Roques
Cast David Belle, Cyril Raffaelli, Bibi Naceri, Dany Verissimo, Tony D'Amario,
François Chatot, Nicolas Woirion, Patrick Olivier, Ludovic Berthillot

French director Luc Besson had already made a name for himself in the action field with *La Femme Nikita* (1990) and *Léon* (a.k.a. *The Professional*, 1994) before he started producing action films. An avowed fan of the hard-hitting style seen in Hong Kong, Besson incorporated that approach into his homegrown productions, resulting in action flicks with a French flair like *Banlieue 13* (2004, its original French title).

Paris, France, 2010—due to increasing civil unrest, lawmakers have isolated the ghettos with walls, allowing criminals to thrive. Trouble arises when District 13 gangster Taha (Bibi Naceri) steals an armored car that contains a prototype neutron missile. When the bomb is inadvertently activated, the French government turns to supercop Damien (Cyril Raffaelli), who has only twenty-four hours to defuse the device. Damien teams with Leito (David Belle), a principled District 13 resident with a grudge against Taha, who has Leito's sister Lola (Dany Verissimo) hostage. What neither man knows is that rogue members of the government sent the bomb into the ghetto on purpose and, complicating matters, Taha has aimed the missile toward central Paris. Looking to French youth culture, the filmmakers

◄

Known as *Banlieue 13* on its French release, the success of the movie spurred Raffaelli and Belle to return for the Besson-produced follow-up *District 13: Ultimatum* (2009).

set their action film apart by incorporating the methods of parkour (used also to great effect in 2006 in *Casino Royale*). In order to ensure faithfulness to the discipline, parkour cofounder David Belle was cast as one of the film's leads. Alongside Belle is circus-trained martial artist Cyril Raffaelli, a regular supporting player and stunt choreographer in Luc Besson's action productions. Together the protagonists perform a wide variety

"WE MAKE AN ABSOLUTELY FANTASTIC TEAM, YOU KNOW?"

CAPT. DAMIEN TOMASO

of insane and amazing stunts—darting through the tiniest of openings and leaping from rooftop to rooftop, all without the aid of wires or computer enhancement.

The film also offers social commentary of the current state of France. Damien and Leito are on opposite sides of the wall but realize they have the same morals and, by the end, can work together against a common enemy (in both gangsters and corrupt politicians). When law-abiding Damien admonishes Leito for his people burning cars, Leito responds that there is no other way for his people to get the attention of politicians, an exchange eerily prophetic of the 2005 civil unrest and riots in France. Director Morel's excellent eye for action found even greater worldwide success when he reteamed with producer Luc Besson for *Taken* (2008) with Liam Neeson and *From Paris with Love* (2010) with John Travolta. **WW**

▶
The use of parkour—a unique acrobatic style of navigating urban settings through running, jumping, and climbing fixed buildings and objects—adds great authenticity to the action.

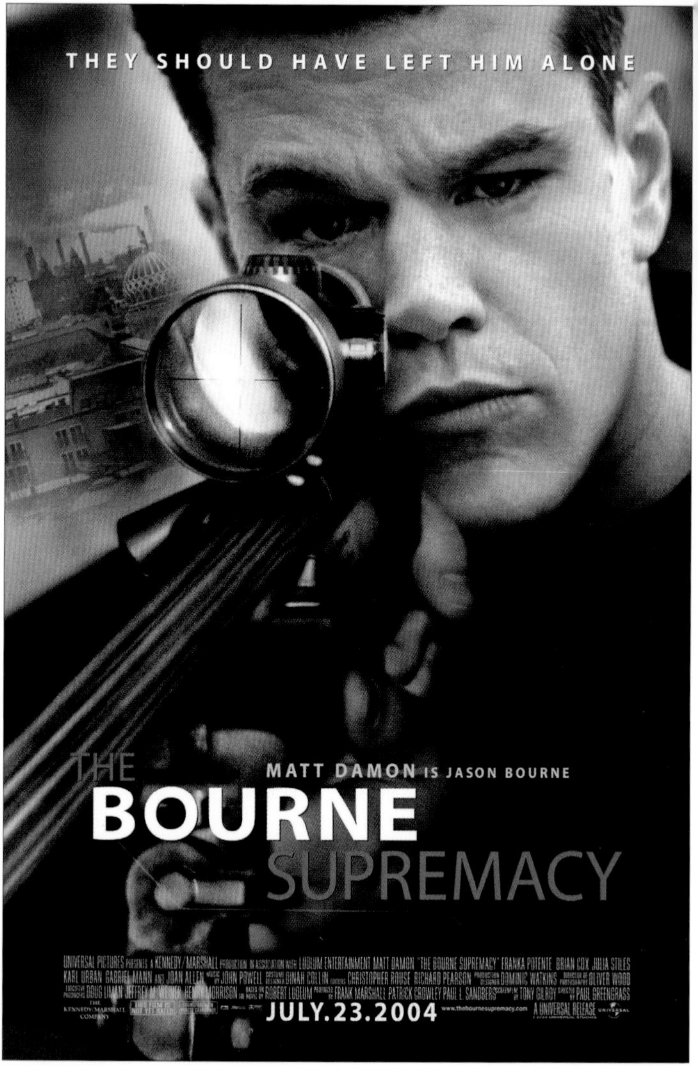
THEY SHOULD HAVE LEFT HIM ALONE
MATT DAMON IS JASON BOURNE
THE
BOURNE
SUPREMACY
UNIVERSAL PICTURES PRESENTS A KENNEDY/MARSHALL PRODUCTION IN ASSOCIATION WITH LUDLUM ENTERTAINMENT MATT DAMON "THE BOURNE SUPREMACY" FRANKA POTENTE BRIAN COX JULIA STILES
KARL URBAN GABRIEL MANN AND JOAN ALLEN MUSIC BY JOHN POWELL COSTUME DESIGNER DINAH COLLIN EDITORS CHRISTOPHER ROUSE RICHARD PEARSON PRODUCTION DESIGNER DOMINIC WATKINS DIRECTOR OF PHOTOGRAPHY OLIVER WOOD
EXECUTIVE PRODUCERS DOUG LIMAN BASED ON THE NOVEL BY ROBERT LUDLUM PRODUCED BY FRANK MARSHALL PATRICK CROWLEY PAUL L. SANDBERG SCREENPLAY BY TONY GILROY DIRECTED BY PAUL GREENGRASS
THE KENNEDY/MARSHALL COMPANY
JULY.23.2004
www.thebournesupremacy.com
A UNIVERSAL RELEASE
UNIVERSAL

THE BOURNE SUPREMACY 2004 (U.S.)

Director Paul Greengrass **Producer** Patrick Crowley, Frank Marshall, Paul L. Sandberg, Doug Liman **Screenplay** Tony Gilroy, Brian Helgeland (original novel by Robert Ludlum) **Cinematography** Oliver Wood **Music** John Powell
Cast Matt Damon, Joan Allen, Brian Cox, Julia Stiles, Franka Potente, Karl Urban

Matt Damon first brought Jason Bourne to the screen in 2002 with *The Bourne Identity*. Based on the popular Robert Ludlum novel, it told the tale of a former C.I.A. agent struck down by psychogenic amnesia who spends the movie trying to figure out who he really is and what he's done in the past, and wondering why complete strangers keep trying to kill him.

Two years later a new episode of the adventure kicks off. Living anonymously in Goa, Bourne begins to recover some parts of his memory but finds himself continually troubled by fragmented flashbacks of an assassination he seems to have carried out. He is also—hardly surprising, under the circumstances—hyperalert to anything even slightly out of the ordinary, and so, when an out-of-place stranger keeps appearing in his vicinity, Bourne senses that his past is once again in pursuit.

The Bourne Supremacy contains all the obvious thriller ingredients we'd expect with pile-driving action sequences hammering our senses thick and fast, and with Bourne leaping across the globe from India to Italy to Germany to Russia; . . . think of a Bond movie with the silly stuff taken out. Realism

◄
The poster reveals Bourne as he is: a hunted man and the world's most evasive moving target. But can he find the skill to outmaneuver the collective gun sights of the C.I.A.?

throughout these scenes is enhanced a notch through the use of a handheld cinematic style, which is, depending on your point of view, exhilarating, a little pretentious, or simply annoying.

Action aside, one reason that *The Bourne Supremacy* works so well is because, once again, Matt Damon gives our hero plausibility—we do genuinely believe his past is an unimaginable puzzle. Bourne has all the attributes of a movie

" YOU'RE GONNA TELL ME THE TRUTH OR I SWEAR TO GOD I'M GONNA KILL YA." *JASON BOURNE*

secret agent—he's clever, endlessly inventive, and a highly skilled professional killer—but he doesn't know for certain why he has these skills and so uses them without resorting to flashy heroism. We also care about him. Why is somebody going to such lengths to wipe him out? Is it an old foe? Is it the C.I.A.? Bourne certainly doesn't know, but the viewer is always kept a few steps ahead of him. As gripping a mystery as it is, our overriding concern is that he should survive this continuous assault, as he faces one lethal trap after another, leaping off bridges, crashing cars—including a spectacular Destruction Derby in the streets of Berlin—and still somehow managing to evade capture. *The Bourne Supremacy* grossed almost $300 million at the box office. It was also surprisingly well regarded by the kind of critics who traditionally take a hard line on Hollywood action blockbusters. **TB**

▶
Karl Urban as Kirill, a Russian assassin on the trail of Jason Bourne (Damon) and Marie (Franka Potente).

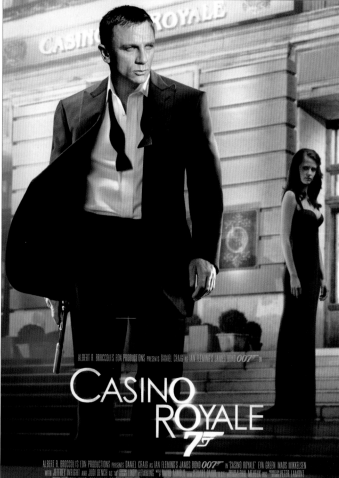

ALBERT R. BROCCOLI'S EON PRODUCTIONS PRESENTS DANIEL CRAIG AS IAN FLEMING'S JAMES BOND 007 IN

CASINO
ROYALE
007

ALBERT R. BROCCOLI'S EON PRODUCTIONS PRESENTS DANIEL CRAIG AS IAN FLEMING'S JAMES BOND 007 IN "CASINO ROYALE" EVA GREEN MADS MIKKELSEN
WITH JEFFREY WRIGHT AND JUDI DENCH AS "M" COSTUME LINDY HEMMING MUSIC DAVID ARNOLD EDITOR STUART BAIRD PRODUCTION PETER LAMONT
EXECUTIVE ANTHONY WAYE CALLUM McDOUGALL SCREENPLAY NEAL PURVIS & ROBERT WADE AND PAUL HAGGIS PRODUCED MICHAEL G. WILSON AND BARBARA BROCCOLI
DIRECTED MARTIN CAMPBELL

FEATURING "YOU KNOW MY NAME" PERFORMED BY CHRIS CORNELL

CasinoRoyaleMovie.com

COLUMBIA
PICTURES

NOVEMBER 17

CASINO ROYALE

2006 (U.K. • CZECH REPUBLIC • GERMANY • U.S.)

Director Martin Campbell **Producer** Michael G. Wilson, Barbara Broccoli
Screenplay Neal Purvis, Robert Wade, Paul Haggis **Cinematography**
Phil Meheux **Music** David Arnold **Cast** Daniel Craig, Eva Green, Mads Mikkelsen,
Judi Dench, Jeffrey Wright, Giancarlo Giannini, Isaach de Bankole, Jesper Christiansen

By 2006, the James Bond franchise had been off-screen for four
years and was close to being rendered irrelevant by the Bourne
franchise, which took the espionage genre to a higher level in
terms of both technology and action. After 2002's *Die Another
Day*, one of the most ridiculous films in the franchise, critically
reviled and disliked by fans, it was decided that Pierce Brosnan
was out and the search was on for a new Bond. The choice was
thirty-eight-year-old Daniel Craig, who had some respectable
films to his credit—most notably *Road to Perdition* (2002) and
Layer Cake (2004)—and was, gasp!, the first blond Bond. But it
was a change that was needed to shake up the stale series.
Additionally, many aging, moribund franchises—Batman, for
instance, with Christopher Nolan's *Batman Begins* (2005)—
recently had successful "reboots." *Casino Royale* turned out to
be the best 007 entry in many years.

   Craig's Bond has just been promoted to 00-status, and M
(Judi Dench, held over from the Brosnan era) is already
regretting it after the arrogant, hot-headed, gaffe-prone agent
kills an unarmed target (Sebastien Foucan) after a hair-raising

◄
**Craig returned
for his second
outing in 2008's
lesser-but-still-
worthwhile
Quantum of Solace,
a direct sequel—a
first for the Bond
franchise series.**

parkour chase through a Madagascar construction site. She regards him with utter disdain ("Utter one more syllable and I'll have you killed," she hisses). Conducting an investigation on his own time involving an attempted terrorist attack at Miami International Airport, he finds the trail leads to Le Chiffre (Mads Mikkelsen), a banker-to-the-terrorists who's just lost the money belonging to his customers. Needing to regain $100 million, Le

"SO YOU WANT ME TO BE HALF-MONK, HALF-HITMAN." JAMES BOND "ANY THUG CAN KILL . . ." M

Chiffre organizes a high-stakes game of Texas Hold 'Em at the Casino Royale in Montenegro. Accompanying Bond is Treasury liasion Vesper Lynd (Eva Green).

Even though the centerpiece of the film is a long card game, there are some jaw-dropping action sequences throughout— the airport scene in Miami, and Bond's fight with two terrorists in a hotel stairwell—and it's a meaner, harder, bloodier Bond film than we've seen before (the film had to be toned down to get a PG-13 rating in the United States). The challenge the Bond franchise faced was making itself viable in the world of Jason Bourne. Gone was the glib playfulness of Pierce Brosnan's Bond, as Craig is cold, merciless, and all business, and he learns the hard way what happens when you let emotions get in the way. Craig is an outstanding—if impulsive—Bond in his debut outing, and he's ably aided by a strong heroine. **MT**

▶
Daniel Craig not only made the first blond Bond, he also made him the most visceral of his motion-picture incarnations.

300 2006 (U.S.)

Director Zack Snyder **Producer** Mark Conton, Bernie Goldman, Gianni Nunnari, Jeffrey Silver **Screenplay** Zack Snyder, Kurt Johnstad **Cinematography** Larry Fong **Music** Tyler Bates **Cast** Gerard Butler, Lena Headey, Dominic West, David Wenham, Vincent Regan, Michael Fassbinder, Tom Wisdom

A close adaptation of the 1998 graphic novels by Frank Miller, *300* impresses with a visual style that mixes animation and live action through extensive use of digital effects and bluescreen technology. Set in 480 B.C., this action-war film is a fantasy of one of history's most heroic last stands. At the narrow pass of Thermopylae, King Leonidas of Sparta (Gerard Butler) with his army of 300 Spartans, bravely fight the immense Persian army of King Xerxes that numbers more than 120,000. Director Zack Snyder had previously breathed new life into the living dead subgenre with *Dawn of the Dead* (2004), an action-horror film that features running zombies. A filmmaker who appears to favor slow-motion shots where others would employ multiple edits, Snyder was keen to be as faithful as possible to the original *300* comics and in many instances he has directly imitated the original graphics.

Miller, a cult artist of comics and graphic novels, had drawn the groundbreaking *Batman: The Dark Knight Returns*, and later *Sin City* (filmed in 2005 and codirected by Miller). His dark, dystopian environments of criminals, corruption, tough men, and brutality are inspired by hard-boiled detective stories and

◄

Not exactly the lively sword and sandals epic of *The 300 Spartans* (1962), but rather a C.G.I. enhanced visceral thriller where *Sin City* meets *Saving Private Ryan* (1998).

film noir. There is also a political dimension in Miller's work, and he has spoken openly on Muslim society and the War on Terrorism. Some critics of *300* the film have argued that it is racist, with the movie perceived as a gung ho reaction to an assault from the Middle East, and with American rhetoric detected in character monologues. Other critics have challenged the film for the liberties it takes and the many

"SPARTANS! READY YOUR BREAKFAST AND EAT HEARTY . . . FOR TONIGHT, WE DINE IN HELL!" DILIOS

inaccuracies it presents in capturing a historic battle. The film is essentially, though, a graphic novel fantasy and it unleashes a healthy horde of invaders, a series of wild imaginings as to the nature of the Persian army that includes the exotic, such as war rhinos and elephants and ninja assassins, and the outright unreal as seen in the humongous troll. The Spartans' camaraderie, machismo, and adrenalin-boosting chants are reminiscent of popular images of American special forces units. It also connects with the Italian peplum and "sword and sandal" films of the 1960s that featured adventure, classical history, legends, and multiple musclemen. Each new wave of the Persian army presents a new challenge to the honed fighting skills of the Spartans, and while the bulk of this film is a series of battle scenes, the variety of foes and the scope of the fantasy prevents any repetition. **IC**

► **Drama and tension are enhanced by the absurd odds that emerge against the Spartans winning, the narrowness of the space being defended, and the sheer drop of the cliff along which they fight.**

MATT DAMON

THE
BOURNE ULTIMATUM

THIS SUMMER BOURNE COMES HOME

THE BOURNE ULTIMATUM 2007 (U.S.)

Director Paul Greengrass **Producer** Frank Marshall, Patrick Crowley **Screenplay** Tony Gilroy, Scott Z. Burns, George Nolfi **Cinematography** Oliver Wood **Music** John Powell **Cast** Matt Damon, Joan Allen, David Strathairn, Julia Stiles, Albert Finney, Paddy Considine, Edgar Ramirez, Joan Allen, Corey Johnson, Daniel Brühl

Paul Greengrass's Oscar-winning *The Bourne Ultimatum* (2007) is the third film based on Robert Ludlum's best-selling Jason Bourne novels. Expanding upon the story line established in the two preceding films, *The Bourne Ultimatum* finds the eponymous hero alternately escaping from and pursuing government operatives who hope to silence the rogue agent.

As the film opens, the exceptionally skilled former assassin, Jason Bourne, is still seeking answers to his true identity. Unable to recall details about either his childhood or most of his adult life, and still aching from the loss of his girlfriend Marie, Bourne is once again forced to outrun and outsmart some of the best operatives from around the globe. Like the first two films in the series, *The Bourne Ultimatum* features fast-paced action sequences that leave audiences breathless. Excellent performances from Joan Allen and Julia Stiles, who also appeared in the previous installment *The Bourne Supremacy* (2004), help to elevate this film from mere action flick status.

Indeed, *The Bourne Ultimatum* is at heart a mystery of the most vital kind, as Jason Bourne continues to seek out who he was, what he became, and who helped to change him.

◄

The well-regarded third installment of the Bourne franchise won three Academy Awards in 2008: for Best Achievement in Editing, Best Achievement in Sound, and Best Achievement in Sound Editing.

In the process, Bourne comes in contact with a newspaper reporter who may have found a key to solving the mystery. In a series of brilliantly conceived action sequences, Bourne walks the line between prey and predator, both escaping traps set for him by various enemies and relentlessly pursuing the truth from those who continue to hide it from him. Journeying tirelessly from Paris to London to Madrid to

"DO YOU EVEN KNOW WHY YOU'RE SUPPOSED TO KILL ME?"

JASON BOURNE

Tangier, Bourne finally ends up at the Deep Cover C.I.A. Bureau in New York City in an attempt to confront his past.

Preceded by *The Bourne Identity* (2002) and *The Bourne Supremacy*, *The Bourne Ultimatum* once again features Matt Damon in the title role. Damon's performances have brought intensity and integrity to the role of Jason Bourne and helped propel the series' success. While the Bourne movies are superior action films with incredible chase sequences, amazing fight scenes, and spectacular explosions, they include performances by award-winning actors, such as Damon and Allen. Other notable actors who have graced the series include Brian Cox, Franka Potente, David Strathairn, Albert Finney, and Clive Owen. Although there was talk about a fourth Bourne film, to date there is nothing definite in the works, and *The Bourne Ultimatum* might literally be the ultimate contribution to the series. **AK**

►
Matt Damon as Jason Bourne stealing an off-road bike and providing his own chase stunt sequence.

HOT FUZZ 2007 (U.K.)

Director Edgar Wright **Producer** Tim Bevan, Eric Fellner, Nira Park **Screenplay** Simon Pegg, Edgar Wright **Cinematography** Jess Hall **Music** David Arnold **Cast** Simon Pegg, Nick Frost, Timothy Dalton, Jim Broadbent, Paddy Considine, Rafe Spall, Billie Whitelaw, Bill Bailey, Bill Nighy, Edward Woodward, David Threlfall

Hot Fuzz is a rare creature, a comedy-action film that succeeds in being both funny and thrilling. It offers a striking combination of American action conventions and distinctly British characters and settings, with much of its narrative turning on the improbability of action scenarios in an idyllic village.

The creative team behind *Hot Fuzz*—notably its director Edgar Wright and its star and cowriter Simon Pegg—had already done something similar with the zombie film *Shaun of the Dead* (2004), which referenced both American and European horror films while retaining a recognizably British sensibility. *Hot Fuzz* develops this in a more sustained and self-conscious manner by having its main characters discuss some of the American action dramas, which they later seek to emulate.

The film tells the story of a straight, dedicated police officer, Nicholas Angel (played by Simon Pegg), who is unwillingly assigned to the village of Sandford. There, he investigates a series of brutal murders disguised none too convincingly as accidents and eventually discovers that the local neighborhood watch association is killing off anyone who threatens a peaceful rural village lifestyle.

◄

In *Hot Fuzz*, fantasy and reality meld into a seamless bloody mess, as British "bobbies" Nick (Pegg) and Danny (Frost) get to live out being *"Bad Boys ... Die Hards ... Lethal Weapons."*

However, it draws considerable humor from the disparity between the likes of *Bad Boys* (1995) and *Point Break* (1991) and the slower, less trigger-happy routines of British village life. Even as it does this, the film also connects itself to a tradition of rural horror, with an urban outsider (embodied by Angel) realizing that some of the locals are dangerous and savage in the manner of, say, rural dwellers in the American *The Hills Have Eyes* (1977)

"HAVE YOU EVER FIRED TWO GUNS WHILE JUMPING THROUGH THE AIR?"

DANNY BUTTERMAN *"NO."* NICHOLAS ANGEL

or the British *The Wicker Man* (1973), the latter underlined by the casting in *Hot Fuzz* of *Wicker Man* star Edward Woodward.

Hot Fuzz offers a heady brew then, and with all its inside jokes and allusions could easily have become a self-indulgent mess. However, at the film's core is a touching relationship between Angel and naive local police officer Danny (played by Nick Frost), which gives a focus to all the other elements that the filmmakers enthusiastically throw at us. This relationship, and the broader narrative, culminates in a spectacular extended shoot-out in the village main street. Here, the pleasure of all the violence and destruction on show is in part the conventional pleasure of the action movie as the good guys take on the villains, but it also connects with the delight of Nick and particularly Danny as they finally get to play out a whole set of action movie conventions. **PH**

▶ As two British policemen, Simon Pegg and Nick Frost get to act out their favorite U.S. rogue cop movies: they are clearly not sending up the genre; indeed they display a deep knowledge of, and affection for, this type of cinema.

CHRISTIAN BALE
MICHAEL CAINE
HEATH LEDGER
GARY OLDMAN
AARON ECKHART
MAGGIE GYLLENHAAL
AND MORGAN FREEMAN
THE DARK KNIGHT
JULY 18
WWW.THEDARKKNIGHT.COM

THE DARK KNIGHT 2008 (U.S. • U.K.)

Director Christopher Nolan **Producer** Charles Roven, Emma Thomas, Christopher Nolan **Screenplay** Jonathan Nolan, Christopher Nolan **Cinematography** Wally Pfister **Music** Hans Zimmer, James Newton Howard **Cast** Christian Bale, Michael Caine, Heath Ledger, Gary Oldman, Aaron Eckhart, Maggie Gyllenhaal

The Dark Knight, Christopher Nolan's follow-up to *Batman Begins* (2005), is not just your run-of-the-mill summer comic book hero blockbuster. It's not even a comic book blockbuster with a bit of added depth; this is comic book blockbuster trying to be a grittily realistic and thought-provoking thriller.

Batman/Bruce Wayne (Christian Bale) teams up with Lt. Jim Gordon (Gary Oldman) and District Attorney Harvey Dent (Aaron Eckhart) in a mission to destroy organized crime in Gotham City once and for all. But the creepy, unhinged Joker (Heath Ledger) is out to unite all the criminals in Gotham to disgrace and kill Batman. (So far, so comic book.) Batman is tired of his double life and he, along with many of the citizens of Gotham, is beginning to think that his one-man mission to fight crime makes him more lawless vigilante than hero. He sees the clean-cut, all-American Dent as his heir, a truly good man who can take up his mission, but do it legally, taking the fight into the open. "Gotham needs a hero with a face," Batman says. But the Joker's chaotic, murderous spree destroys Batman's hopes and unleashes an unexpected revenge-crazed vigilante on Gotham. There's plenty of soul-searching, but the movie keeps

◀
Heath Ledger's superscary Joker— part *Clockwork Orange*, part *Sid and Nancy*— pervades the whole film and fittingly the film's poster.

up a tremendous pace with exhilarating action sequences that really pull out all the stops. The fights are grittily real, although the worst of the violence is implied rather than actually seen, but even implying shoving a pencil into someone's skull or slitting open their mouth with a knife is enough to make this a movie to keep younger children away from. Batman isn't a superhero, so all his powers are supplied by his own brawn or

"HE'S A SILENT GUARDIAN, A WATCHFUL PROTECTOR, A DARK KNIGHT."

JAMES GORDON

by technology—for instance, the reconstruction of a fingerprint from a used bullet, and the skyhook hanging from a plane to sweep Batman and his captive from the roof of a building.

There are flaws along the way in this best-of-the-bunch Batman outing. The movie is overlong and not half as clever as it thinks it is. Some of the action sequences are very confused, and the message it's trying to convey is not at all clear. But don't think about it too much. Sit back, hold on tight, and *The Dark Knight* will leave you with some fabulous images stuck in your mind: Batman's vertiginous dive to save Rachel (Maggie Gyllenhaal) as she falls from a skyscraper; Lucius Fox (Morgan Freeman) surrounded by walls of flickering screens, doubting the morality of all this surveillance; and, of course, the crazily gleeful dance of Ledger's extraordinary Joker dressed in a nurse's uniform walking away from an exploding hospital. **CW**

► There's some fabulous technology going on in this movie, including the "Batpod," a motorbike with giant wheels that springs from the wreck of Batman's car.

IRON MAN 2008 (U.S.)

Director Jon Favreau **Producer** Avi Arad, Kevin Feige **Screenplay** Mark Fergus, Hawk Ostby, Art Marcum, Matt Holloway, John August, Stan Lee, Larry Lieber, Don Heck, Jack Kirby **Cinematography** Matthew Libatique **Music** Ramin Djawadi **Cast** Robert Downey, Jr., Terrence Howard, Jeff Bridges, Gwyneth Paltrow, Leslie Bibb

Robert Downey, Jr.'s debut as a superhero was one that film critics and audiences alike awaited with bated breath. The actor was past forty when he accepted the role, in what was a bold casting move by director Jon Favreau, and the former Brat Pack star's career had not then recovered from the years in a wilderness brought on by time spent in rehab for substance abuse. The blockbuster proved to be a comeback movie for Downey, and his own dark days helped add a sense of gravitas to that of the character he plays: a billionaire industrialist, Tony Stark.

Stark is a modern-day Leonardo da Vinci, a genius who uses his skills to develop weapons for the company he inherited from his father, Stark Industries. But he is also a gambler, drinker, and womanizer with no innate special powers. So the middle-aged Stark does not seem ideal superhero material, yet his charm and ironic wit make the character appealing. What makes him a superhero is the suit he creates using his incredible engineering skills and his mission to help people.

The film tells the story of Stark's personal odyssey to become Iron Man. Based on the Marvel Comics character of the same name, the film updates the official canon by showing Stark first

◄

This is an action movie that is also a classic tale of redemption of a dissolute man who becomes good; therein lies its appeal.

creating his exoskeletal suit while held captive by terrorists in Afghanistan, and then using it to make his escape. The experience changes the rich playboy both physically and emotionally. Injured while he was captured, he survives thanks to a device that keeps shrapnel from his heart. His gratitude in surviving leads him to decide his company must cease making weapons and that he will use his talents and considerable

"IF I WERE IRON MAN, I'D HAVE THIS GIRLFRIEND WHO KNEW MY TRUE IDENTITY. SHE'D BE A WRECK." TONY STARK

fortune to do good. He soon finds the opportunity when he discovers that his devious business partner Obadiah Stane (Jeff Bridges) has been selling Stark Industries' technology not just to the U.S. government but also to its enemies.

Setting the film in the twenty-first century adds relevance and gives it a depth unexpected for a comic book adaptation. Downey in particular plays well against Gwyneth Paltrow as his doe-eyed love interest, Pepper Potts, while Bridges turns it on as the power-crazed maniac. Favreau's direction reveals he has a sure hand for plot, character, and action in equal measure, so much so he was commissioned to make a sequel. He uses special effects wisely to create action sequences where Iron Man streaks across the skies in his gold and hot-red suit in a dogfight with fighter jets, and packs the footage with mind-boggling technical gadgetry put at Stark's disposal. **CK**

► **Downey excels as Stark: he delivers one-liners with deadpan aplomb and packs a credible punch.**

LIAM NEESON

"I DON'T KNOW
WHO YOU ARE
BUT IF YOU DON'T LET MY
DAUGHTER GO
I WILL FIND YOU
I WILL KILL YOU"

TAKEN

TWENTIETH CENTURY FOX PRESENTS A EUROPACORP M6 FILMS AND GRIVE PRODUCTIONS CO-PRODUCTION WITH THE PARTICIPATION OF CANAL + M6 AND TPS STAR
A FILM BY PIERRE MOREL LIAM NEESON "TAKEN" MAGGIE GRACE LELAND ORSER JON GRIES DAVID WARSHOFSKY KATIE CASSIDY HOLLY VALANCE
AND FAMKE JANSSEN CASTING NATHALIE CHERON A.R.D.A. MUSIC OLIVIER BERIOT EDITOR MARTIN BOISSAU ALEXANDRE WIDMER FRANÇOIS-JOSEPH HORS
MUSIC NATHANAEL MEGHALY SOUND DIDIER HOARAU EDITOR FREDERIC THORAVAL PRODUCTION HUGUES TISSANDIER DIRECTOR OF PHOTOGRAPHY MICHEL ABRAMOWICZ A.F.C.
EXECUTIVE PRODUCER FRANK LEBRETON WRITTEN BY LUC BESSON AND ROBERT MARK KAMEN DIRECTED BY PIERRE MOREL

www.takenmovie.com

TAKEN 2008 (FRANCE)

Director Pierre Morel **Producer** Luc Besson **Screenplay** Luc Besson, Robert Mark Kamen **Cinematography** Michel Abramowicz **Music** Nathaniel Michely
Cast Liam Neeson, Maggie Grace, Famke Janssen, Leland Orser, Jon Gries, David Warshofsky, Xander Berkeley, Katie Cassidy, Holly Valance, Olivier Rabourdin

It's hard to tell if much was expected of *Taken* when it belatedly appeared in U.S. theaters in early 2009, sporting a 2007 copyright. It appeared to be another model off the Luc Besson action assembly line, following in the footsteps of hits such as *The Transporter* (2002) and its sequels. But there was something about *Taken* that was different.

Bryan Mills (Liam Neeson) is a divorced, retired ex-C.I.A. agent who walked away from his job to be a consistent presence in the life of seventeen-year-old daughter Kimmy (Maggie Grace). Unlike his ex-wife Lenore (Famke Janssen), he's leery about letting Kimmy go on a trip to Paris. But he caves in, and sure enough, she and a friend are abducted almost right off the plane by Albanian sex traffickers. Springing into action, Mills goes on a rampage across Paris—stealing cars, breaking necks, torturing, electrocuting, slamming heads in car doors, even shooting a corrupt cop's innocent wife in the shoulder ("It's just a flesh wound!" he barks) to get the information he needs to find his daughter.

Neeson elevates *Taken* beyond the standard shoot-'em-up, pile-'em-high action flick. It's a relentless, ferocious

◄
The body count tallies to just over twenty-five as Mills (Neeson) uses his less than savory C.I.A. skills to trace his "taken" daughter.

performance that lets you look past the clunky exposition (one of Mills's C.I.A. buddies asks, "Does Kimmy appreciate the fact that you've given up your life in order to be closer to her?"), plot contrivances, and the fact that Grace is about a decade too old for her role. Neeson sells this thing from beginning to end, and the implausible plot turns serve their purpose: to get him from one intense action sequence to the next.

> ### "YOU DON'T HAVE TO WORRY . . ." KIMMY MILLS "THAT'S LIKE TELLING WATER NOT TO BE WET, SWEETIE." BRYAN MILLS

Far from simply cracking skulls and blowing away Albanian scum, Neeson shows you the kind of man Mills is in a way that a typical action star wouldn't. As he tells the villains: "If you let my daughter go now, that'll be the end of it. I will not look for you. I will not pursue you. But if you don't, I will look for you, I will find you, and I will kill you."

Mills doesn't fit into Kimmy and Lenore's world with Lenore's rich new husband (Xander Berkeley), and he's only welcome into it once that world is shattered and only he can fix it, using the very skills that have made him an outsider in the first place. As revenge thrillers go, *Taken* hardly breaks new ground, but it was a long time since one was elevated so much by such a commanding lead performance. Without Neeson, *Taken* would've simply been an entertaining action outing. But with him, it's an absolute classic of its kind. **MT**

▶
To add to his considerable on-screen credibility, Neeson had combative and weapons-handling training from a former Special Air Service (S.A.S.) soldier.

AVATAR

AVATAR 2009 (U.S.)

Director James Cameron **Producer** James Cameron, Jon Landau, Brooke Breton, Josh McLaglen **Screenplay** James Cameron **Cinematography** Mauro Fiore **Music** James Horner **Cast** Sam Worthington, Zoe Saldana, Sigourney Weaver, Stephen Lang, Joel Moore, Giovanni Ribisi

Within weeks of its Christmas 2009 release, *Avatar* had become the most successful film of all time in terms of box office receipts. The appeal of the film is manifold. Like director James Cameron's earlier blockbuster *Titanic* (1997), *Avatar* is a family film, with a romance played against an impending calamitous event. The scenes where the military is working with the immoral corporation recall elements of Cameron's *Aliens* (1986). *Avatar*'s spectacle is its technological achievements in creating an immersible future world of floating mountains, exotic creatures, and an entire ecosystem of fantastic forests that glow in rich neon colors at night. Screenings were available in 3D, which added to the spectacle and illusion.

The story is set on the planet Pandora, where a highly valuable mineral called unobtanium has been discovered. Mining enterprises from Earth backed by military might are fixed on extracting the resource at all costs. This includes destroying the natural habitat and homeland of the planet's indigenous population, the Na'vi, who live around a colossal tree that happens to be growing on top of the biggest mineral deposit. The Na'vi are tall, blue-skinned aliens who are very

◄
The sci-fi adventure with an ecomessage that warns of man's destructive behavior was previously present in Cameron's *Abyss* **(1989).**

much attuned to the spirit and power of their environment, and it is through an avatar—a hybrid of human and Na'vi, which has been genetically bred by human scientists—that a disabled marine veteran, Jake (Sam Worthington), is able to enter their world and understand their culture. As an avatar, he has great freedom and agility that allows him to explore the wonders of Pandora, climb the floating Hallelujah Mountains, and ride a

"OUR GREAT MOTHER EYWA DOES NOT TAKE SIDES, JAKE; ONLY PROTECTS THE BALANCE OF LIFE." NEYTIRI

mountain Banshee, a dragonlike flying creature. The man-operated giant exoskeleton robots used by the military also enhance the human form, and it is in the film's climax that one of these, operated by the vicious Colonel Quaritch (Stephen Lang), duels with Jake's borrowed alien body. Leading up to this clash, the film's long last act is a dramatic battle involving Pandora's indigenous people and creatures together defending their land against the overpowering strength of the military, with its gunships, guns, and rockets. Pandora is a multilayered world and this battle, involving a defense of bows and arrows, flying Banshees, and herds of the thundering elephant-like Hammerhead Titanothere, occurs in the air and on land. As an action film, *Avatar* shows that its energy is not just found in moments of conflict but also through harmony with the natural environment and a discovery of the power of the land. **IC**

► Jake Sully's (Sam Worthington) avatar allows the wheelchair-bound marine vet to inhabit a fantastic alien environment.

INDEX

INDEX

CONTRIBUTORS

(AK) Dr Amy Kushner is an English lecturer at the University of Wisconsin-Parkside, U.S. She has contributed to all of the books in the 101 series and is the co-author of *But They Didn't Read Me My Rights: Myths, Lies, and Oddities about our Legal System.*

(CB) Colette Balmain is an independent scholar and author of *Introduction to Japanese Horror Film.* She is currently writing her second book on Korean horror and is the editor for *World Cinema Directory: Korea.*

(CK) Carol King is a freelance writer based in London and Sicily. She writes about cinema, art and travel. She is the author of a biography of British actor and director Peter Glenville.

(CW) Claire Watts is a freelance writer and editor based in southern Scotland.

(FL) Frank Lafond teaches film studies in Lille, France. He has published a book on Jacques Tourneur and edited volumes on George Romero and George Franju.

(GC-Q) Garrett Chaffin-Quiray lives in San Diego County where he teaches media history. He is also a working writer and has been published in various newspapers, journals, and books, including *Senses of Cinema, Kinoeye, Film Quarterly,* and *The San Francisco Chronicle.*

(IC) Dr Ian Conrich is the author or editor of twelve books including *The Cinema of John Carpenter: The Technique of Terror* (2005) , *Film's Musical Moments* (2006) , *Contemporary New Zealand Cinema: From New Wave to Blockbuster* (2008), and *Horror Zone: The Cultural Experience of Contemporary Horror Cinema* (2009).

(JM) Jay McRoy is Associate Professor of English and Cinema Studies at the University of Wisconsin-Parkside, U.S., and author of *Nightmare Japan.*

(LH) Leon Hunt is a Senior Lecturer in Screen Media at Brunel University. He is the author of *British Low Culture: From Safari Suits to Sexploitation, Kung Fu Cult Masters: From Bruce Lee to Crouching Tiger,* and *BFI TV Classics: The League of Gentlemen,* and the co-editor of *East Asian Cinemas: Exploring Transnational Connections on Film.*

(MH) Mike Hobbs is married, lives in London, and has three children. In his spare time he is a screenwriter, novelist, consultant to the LSE, ghostwriter, and business writer, who has had 15 books published to date.

(MT) Mark Tinta is a freelance film writer based in Ohio, and dives into Criterion box sets and Uwe Boll film fests with equal enthusiasm.

(PH) Peter Hutchings is Professor of Film Studies at Northumbria University. His books include *Terence Fisher, The Horror Film* and *The Historical Dictionary of Horror Cinema.*

(RH) Russ Hunter writes on film and is currently co-editing (with Alexia Kannas) *The Cinema of Dario Argento.*

(RP) Rachel Price is a journalist who has written extensively about TV and movies for a wide range of publications including books, magazines and newspapers (*The Daily Telegraph, The Guardian*) . She is also the former Movies Editor of *Sky Magazine* and the Deputy Editor of *Blockbuster Magazine.*

(TB) Terry Burrows has written over 60 books and contributed to numerous periodicals on a diverse range of subjects, including cinema, television, music, business and technology. He is also a widely recorded musician who has taught at universities.

(WW) William Sean Wilson is a film writer currently residing in Williamsburg, Virginia. He graduated from The College of William & Mary with a degree in Literary and Cultural Studies with an emphasis in film.

PICTURE CREDITS

Many of the images in this book are from the archives of The Kobal Collection, which owes its existence to the vision, courage, talent and energy of the men and women who created the movie industry and whose legacies live on through the films they made, the studios they built, and the publicity photographs they took. Kobal collects, preserves, organizes, and makes these photographs available. Quintessence wishes to thank all the film distribution and production companies and apologizes in advance for any omissions or neglect, and will be pleased to make any necessary changes in future editions.

The following images are from The Kobal Collection:
2 Edison 6 Paragon/Golden Harvest 8 Edison 12 Pathé 15 Pathé 16 Hal Roach/Pathé Exchange 20 United Artists 23 United Artists 24 Warner Bros./First National 27 Warner Bros./First National 28 Paramount 43 MGM 44 FilmSonor/CICC/VERA-FONO Roma 47 FilmSonor/ CICC/VERA-FONO Roma 59 DANJAQ/EON/UA 60 DANJAQ/EON/UA 63 DANJAQ/EON/UA 64 Shaw Brothers 67 Shaw Brothers 68 20th Century Fox 72 DANJAQ/EON/UA 80 Warner Bros. 83 Warner Bros. 84 DANJAQ/EON/UA 87 EON/DANJAQ/SONY 88 Warner Bros. 92 Shaw Brothers 94 Columbia Tri-Star 95 Shaw Brothers 96 Solar/First Artists/National General 100 20TH Century Fox 103 20th Century Fox 104 A.I.P. 107 A.I.P. 108 Concord/Warner Bros. 111 Concord/Warner Bros. 112 AIP 115 AIP 116 United Artists 120 United Artists 124 20th Century Fox/Warners 127 20th Century Fox/Warners 128 New World 132 United Artists 139 Miracle FilmS 140 Harbor/Shaw Brothers 144 DANJAQ/EON/UA 147 DANJAQ/EON/UA 148 20th Century Fox/EMI 152 Seasonal Film Corp. 155 Seasonal Film Corp. 156 Shaw Bros. 160 Warner Bros./DC Comics 164 United Artists 167 DANJAQ/EON/UA 168 United Artists 171 United Artists 172 LucasFilm Ltd/Paramount 175 LucasFilm LTD/Paramount 176 Paramount 180 Carolco 188 20th Century Fox 195 Paragon/Golden Harvest 196 Paramount 200 Warner Bros. 204 Cannon 208 20th Century Fox 211 20th Century Fox 212 Warner Bros./DC Comics 217 Eastern Productions 220 Gaumont/Cecchi Gori/Tiger 224 Paramount 228 20th Century Fox 231 20th Century Fox/Richard Foreman 232 Carolco 236 Paramount 239 Paramount 240 Warner Bros./Regency 244 Warner Bros. 256 Golden Harvest/Media Asia/Film Workshop 259 Golden Harvest/Media Asia/Film Workshop 260 Paramount 264 Pressman/Most 268 Eastern Productions 272 Gaumont/Films Du Dauphin 276 20th Century Fox 279 20th Century Fox/Richard Foreman 280 Lightstorm/20th Century Fox 284 Columbia 288 Columbia 292 DANJAQ/EON/UA 296 Paramount 300 Hollywood Pictures 304 Columbia Tri-Star 308 Paramount/Touchstone 312 Touchstone/Jerry Bruckheimer Inc 316 Touchstone 320 New Line 323 New Line 324 ARP/TF1 FilmS 327 ARP/TF1 FilmS 332 Columbia/SONY 336 Dreamworks/Universal 344 Original Films 348 Lawrence Gordon/Mutual Film/Paramount 351 Lawrence Gordon/Mutual Film/Paramount/Alex Bailey 356 20th Century Fox 360 A Band Apart/Miramax 364 New Line Cinema 368 Baa-Ram-Ewe 372 Europa Corp./Magnolia Pictures 375 Europa Corp./ Magnolia Pictures 380 DANJAQ/EON/UA 384 Warner Bros./Legendary Pictures 388 Universal 391 Universal/Jasin Boland 392 Focus Features 396 Warner Bros./DC Comics 404 Europa Corp 408 20th Century-Fox Film Corporation 411 20th Century-Fox Film Corporation

Other images:
11 Everett Collection/Rex Features 19 Allstar/Cinetext/Pathé 31 SNAP/Rex Features 32 SNAP/Rex Features 35 Allstar/Cinetext/Warner Bros. 36 SNAP/Rex Features 39 Allstar/Cinetext/20th Century Fox 40 Allstar/MGM 51 Allstar/Cinetext/MGM 52 Everett Collection/Rex Features 55 Allstar/Cinetext/United Artists 56 Allstar/United Artists 71 20th Century Fox/Everett/Rex Features 75 Allstar/Cinetext/United Artists 76 Allstar/Cinetext/Universal 79 Everett Collection/Rex Features 91 Allstar/Warner Bros. 99 Allstar/Warner Bros. 119 Allstar/Cinetext/ United Artists 123 Allstar/Cinetext/United Artists 131 Everett Collection/Rex Features 135 Allstar/Cinetext/United Artists 136 Allstar/ Overseas FilmGroup 143 Allstar/New World Pictures 151 Allstar/Cinetext/20th Century Fox 163 Allstar/Cinetext/Warner Bros. 179 Allstar/ Cinetext/Paramount 183 Allstar/Cinetext/Thorn EMI 191 Allstar/Cinetext/20th Century Fox 199 Allstar/Cinetext/Paramount 203 Allstar/ Warner Bros. 207 Allstar/Cinetext/Cannon Group 215 Allstar/Warner Bros. 223 Allstar/Cinetext/Samuel Goldwyn 227 Allstar/Paramount Pictures 235 Allstar/Cinetext/Tristar 243 Allstar/Cinetext/Warner Bros. 247 Allstar/Cinetext/Warner Bros. 255 Allstar/Cinetext/Columbia 263 Allstar/Cinetext/Paramount 267 Allstar/Cinetext/Buena Vista 275 SNAP/Rex Features 283 Allstar/Cinetext/20th Century Fox 287 Allstar/ Cinetext/Columbia 291 Allstar/Columbia 295 Allstar/Cinetext/Paramount 299 Everett Collection/Rex Features 303 Allstar/Buena Vista 307 Allstar/Cinetext/Columbia 311 Allstar/Cinetext/Paramount 315 Buena Vista/Everett/Rex Features 319 Allstar/Touchstone 328 Allstar/ United Artists 331 Allstar/Cinetext/United Artists 335 Allstar/Cinetext/Sony 339 Allstar/Cinetext/Dreamworks 340 Allstar/20th Century Fox 343 Allstar/Cinetext/20th Century Fox 347 Allstar/Universal Pictures 352 Columbia Pictures/Everett/Rex Features 355 Columbia Pictures/ Everett/Rex Features 359 Allstar/20th Century Fox 363 Allstar/Cinetext/Miramax 367 Allstar/New Line 371 Allstar/Magnolia Pictures 376 Allstar/Universal 379 Allstar/Universal 383 Allstar/United Artists 387 Allstar/Warner Bros. 395 Allstar/Working Title 399 Allstar/Warner Bros. 400 Paramount/Everett/Rex Feature 403 Paramount/Everett/Rex Features 407 20th Century Fox/Everett/Rex Features

ACKNOWLEDGMENTS

Quintessence would like to thank the following people for their help in the preparation of this book: Dave Kent, Angela Levin, and Phil Moad at the Kobal Collection, Stephen Atkinson at Rex Features and Paul McFegan at Allstar Picture Library.

General Editor Steven Jay Schneider would like to thank all of the contributors, along with everyone at Quintessence.

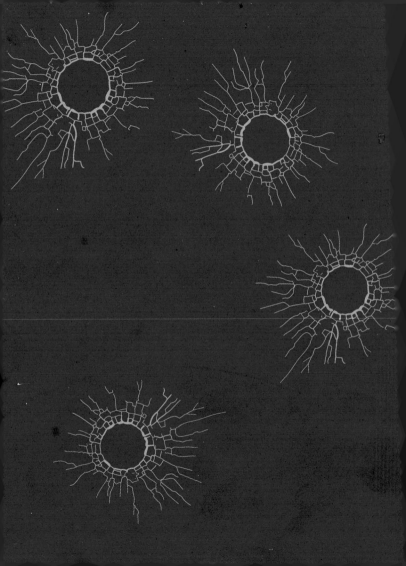